The Internet Initiative

Libraries Providing Internet Services and How They Plan, Pay, and Manage

edited by
Edward J. Valauskas
and Nancy R. John

American Library Association
Chicago and London
1995

...ct editor: Arthur Plotnik

Cover design: Tessing Design

Text design and composition: Bill Vaccaro

This book was created electronically using Adobe PageMaker version 5.0a on an Apple macintosh Quadra 700 accelerated with a Power Macintosh Card and an Apple PowerBook 540c. Art was produced using Adobe Photoshop version 3.0.1. Photographs were scanned on an Apple OneScanner using Ofoto version 2.0 scanning software. Working film was produced with the PostScript language on a Linotronic 530 imagesetter. Body text was set in 11 pt. Minion, an Adobe multiple master typeface. The Adobe Minion and Myriad multiple master typeface families were used throughout the book for display text. Dingbats were set in Zeal.

Printed on 50-pound Thor paper, a pH-neutral stock, and bound in 10-point Carolina C1S by Malloy Lithographing, Inc.

ISBN 0–8389–0668–0

Printed in the United States of America

99 98 97 96 95   5 4 3 2 1

table of contents

section one
visibility
scoring points in the community

---

iii

section four

synergy
building on high-tech capabilities

section five

connection
linking to school and community education

section six

opportunity
a postscript

v

acknowledgments

The editors thank all of the contributors, whose initiative and initiatives made this book possible; Carol Henderson, of the Washington Office of the American Library Association, for expressing the need which led to this book; Art Plotnik for his editorial skill and prodding; Bill Vaccaro for his artistic effort in layout and page design; and finally our spouses for their continued patience under the most trying conditions.

p r e f a c e

Do librarians have a role on the Internet? Or will their perceived loyalty to the printed word and books consign them to the information boonies? Indirectly these questions are looming in the legislatures and corporate boardrooms of America. At the same time, librarians around the country are affirming their role in Internet access with a resounding YES and with pioneering programs to stake their claims in cyberspace.

It's not that the library profession is abandoning books or librarianship. On the contrary; the precepts of information management and information delivery, the profession's strong support of the right of citizens to know, and the skills and interests of library professionals are helping to shape the nation's electronic future.

For some librarians, the time-tested techniques of identifying and organizing collections are paying off as network navigators and signposts spring up under their watchful development. The value we librarians place on communication and collaboration shows through in the efforts of others to start up users groups and support programs.

Other librarians are working to give their parent organizations a presence on the Internet, developing resources rich in information that are also attractive and easy to use. Others are working with policy-makers to expand the public's access to government information. Still others are using technology to extend hours of library access and create new types of access.

It is these hard-working librarians and their replicable ideas that inspired us to compile this showcase. Yes, these practical reports will help other libraries deliver Internet services to their publics, but, more importantly, these good works are keeping alive the dream of a free republic and knowledgeable citizenry in an increasingly complex political and social environment. While corporate giants and politicians discuss how to cut up the electronic pie, legions of America's librarians are serving that pie to the nation's information hungry. We hope that by hearing from those who have done it, you'll be inspired to connect your patrons to the power of the Internet in new and impressive ways.

Nancy R. John
Edward J. Valauskas

introduction

he Internet has been described as

a giant collage[1];

a vast maw of online resources and services[2];

a highway of ideas;

a collective brain;

the world's most important computer bulletin board[3];

an enormous computer network[4];

a well-worn pathway.[5]

It's also been said that "the network is the computer."[6]

We can also assert that the network is the library. A collection of ideas, a library functions as a catalyst for serendipity and creativity much like the Internet. It is no wonder that librarians were among the earliest users of the

---

1. J. A. Savage and Gary H. Anthes, "Internet Privatization Adrift," *Computerworld* 24, no. 48 (Nov. 26, 1990):1

2. Daniel P. Dern, "You Need an Excuse? Four Good Reasons to Bother with the Internet," *MacWEEK* 6, no. 31 (Feb. 24, 1992):21.

3. "It is a highway of ideas, a collective brain for the nation's scientists, and perhaps the world's most important computer bulletin board." From David Coursey, "Riding the Internet," *Infoworld* 13, no. 5 (Feb. 4, 1991):48.

4. A network of all networks, this phrase has been a very frequent description of the Internet, nearly as common as calling it the "information superhighway." See Robert E. Calem, "The Network of All Networks," *New York Times* (Dec. 6, 1993): sec. 3, p. 12.

5. Jon Van, "Research Paves New Links for High-tech Highway," *Chicago Tribune* (Nov. 22, 1993): sec. 4, p. 3.

6. According to the CEO of Sun Microsystems, Scott McNealy, and repeated recently in Randy Johnson and Harris Kern, "The Network Is the Data Center," *Advanced Systems* 8, no. 4 (April 1995):74.

Internet in its precursors, the most vocal advocates for expanded access, and frequent trainers and educators of the public on the practicalities of digital life.

There is no question that the Internet alters an institution and its people. The Internet expands the walls of a collection without building a new facility. It gives patrons access to information that was unavailable under usual non-virtual circumstances. But the Internet is not just collections development and resource building. It is not just new computers and additional software. It's not just a tongue-twisting array of acronyms and abbreviations. The Internet sets off a whole series of waves through a community, its institutions, and its population. The stories in this book provide case-by-case examples of the positive effects of the Internet.

Connecting

What are the social impacts of the Internet on a community, on an organization? Can access to the Internet alter communications in a whole region or even a state? In Bethel, Alaska, hundreds of miles from the nearest city, on the edge of the Bering Sea, there are no roads or interstates. Yet for every one of Bethel's five thousand citizens, there's a wealth of information only a local phone call away. Thanks to the Statewide Library Electronic Doorway or SLED, the Internet and its resources are accessible in Bethel and many other roadless communities. As Susan Elliott and Steve Smith indicate in their chapter, SLED profoundly alters the ways in which ordinary Alaskans are informed.

In rural communities in upstate New York, libraries find it difficult to provide information as quickly as patrons need it. Access to the Internet forever changed this relationship between information and the library user. Denise Garofalo points out in her chapter that many library patrons expected everything to be on the Internet. Education became the key in helping patrons find the right information as quickly as possible without being overwhelmed by the sheer volume of digital detail. Even within the limits of equipment and telephone connections, the Internet became a positive and rewarding experience for both library patrons and staff.

In Maryland, thanks to the state library division's Sailor Project, citizens around the state have a basic level of Internet service, scaled to their needs. It allows them to use information once only available to those with sophisticated equipment and dedicated staff, with a minimal investment of time and money. According to Rivkah Sass in her chapter, the Sailor Project also allows Marylanders to more actively participate in their communities, by being informed and connected as never before.

Seven public libraries in Oakland and Wayne counties, Michigan created an Internet network bringing together citizens, government agencies, and businesses. Gerald Furi, Christine Hage, and Stephen Kershner describe the impact of this network, used thousands of times each month, on their communities. With it, library patrons find answers to once impossible queries, complete homework assignments in record time, and check on family members halfway around the world.

The Triangle Free-Net in North Carolina gives its users an opportunity to exchange their latest recipes, send electronic mail, or locate community databases, all with a personal computer and modem. Local experts on a variety of topics are available for consultation. Librarians scout for new information and point users to it. A new community, born of the Free-Net, permits communication and interactivity on a scale unimaginable before the network. Judy Hallman notes the importance of the Free-Net to re-affirm the community and its dependence on reliable information at any time anywhere.

In Virginia Beach, Virginia, interest in the Internet led to the formation of an Internet users group. Citizens flock to meetings at the public library, according to Carolyn Caywood in her chapter, to learn more about Internet tools, new servers and sites to visit, or watch demonstrations. In the course of these meetings, the citizens learn more about their library and become more vocal supporters of it. Issues facing Internet users and providers are the same issues librarians have wrestled with and will continue to battle over: access, expression, and responsibility.

In Colorado Springs, Colorado, citizens already know that their library is at the forefront of making technologies work to the best possible advantage. Yet even for this community, Internet access via the library opened new opportunities for personal advancement and community promotion. Pointers to Internet Gopher servers around the nation help patrons find facts fast, act as a stimulus to further queries, and reflect accurately the kinds of information available in this library-without-boundaries. David Clark's chapter on the Pikes Peak Library District's MAGGnet tells the story.

How does the administrative climate of an institution change with the Internet? For example, changing sources for information have seriously altered the roles of documents librarians and depositories. No longer is the U.S. Government Printing Office the sole source for documents and reports. Some agencies print their works independently of the Government Printing Office; others find relief in making data available on CD-ROMs, magnetic tapes, or the Internet. Doreen Hansen examines how these efforts of federal bureaucracies have changed the ways depositories deliver government information to their patrons.

x

In Texas, the State Library was faced with an equal-access challenge, as more and more state information was available electronically but not in paper. As Mike Clark and Lisa deGruyter demonstrate, the Internet made it possible for the State Library not only to continue to fulfill its mandate, but to do so efficiently and to as many citizens as possible. This Electronic Library means that some researchers need not travel to Austin to search for documents in the State Archives to locate obscure and out-of-print reports. Other state agencies see the success of the State Library and emulate it in providing better access to information once buried away in files or entombed only in paper.

Finances

Do the financial demands of Internet access force libraries to look to new sources for assistance? Or can it spur a turnaround in local support? In Montana, the largest public library saw its staff cut in half, its bookmobiles disappear from the highways, and its funds for collections development vanish. A group of public spirited citizens met to save the library. Their efforts were spearheaded by a publicity campaign, which earned the library a levy increase and private support. The Internet in Yellowstone County is now available to the public as The Wendy's Connection, thanks to a donation of nearly $147,000 from Wendy's of Montana. Bill Cochran explains how the Internet has excited a community where some 17,000 residents take advantage of this new electronic opportunity. Internet connections to schools and local government will make the library an information hub. All of this came at an investment by Wendy's of $1.23 per person in Billings and Yellowstone County. Indeed, the Internet makes for interesting and new financial arrangements between libraries, their governing bodies, the public, and the private sector.

In private corporations, where the bottom line rules, libraries are increasingly called upon to justify their roles and explain their utility. The Internet has been used by many special libraries as an information source. For some libraries, the Internet is the best way to prove the economic value of the special library to the corporation. Apple Computer Librarian Monica Ertel found just that to be true. In training sessions, software demonstrations, and resource development, the library staff proved its value to the organization in establishing an Internet persona for Apple, in helping staff throughout the organization understand the Internet, and in connecting disparate groups.

Education

How can libraries use the Internet as an educational resource for users? Sharyl G. Smith, in her chapter on UtahLINK, explains how this network overcomes long distances and with minimal educational expenditures provides quality resources to all constituencies, from the state Capitol to the most isolated hamlets. Utah Governor Mike Leavitt endorsed the Network's Internet as an opportunity to revolutionize education.

Terry Metz, at Carleton College, Minnesota, describes how students are involved in the day-to-day availability of the Internet in the library. Student employees, recruited from a number of different departments, coach other students and faculty in using the Internet, track postings on mailing lists, act as intelligent agents searching for new Internet resources, and experiment with new Internet software. This work enlarges the kinds of services the library can offer, while at the same time giving students a new educational opportunity outside the traditional curriculum. The enthusiasm of students for these digital assignments and the favorable response of the Carleton community to these efforts proves the value of this educational application of the Internet.

Specialized interests challenge librarians to find appropriate information in a timely way for students and faculty. The Internet is a way around this resource bind, expanding educational opportunities and making new and different kinds of information available immediately. In a before-and-after report, Mary Pettengill relates the difficulties a small departmental library at the University of Texas had meeting the needs of its clientele prior to Internet. After Internet's arrival, the library was transformed into an information provider not only for its own community, but for a worldwide research interest in petroleum engineering. Owing to well-invented Internet resources, over half of the traffic to Pettengill's specialized server comes from outside the University. Thanks to the Internet, there are abundant educational opportunities for both Texas students and faculty and the research community at large.

There are some who would argue that the Internet is a step away from real literacy, a move to a society filled with electronic zombies addicted to the latest game. Thomas Eland, coordinator, Minnesota/South Dakota Adult Literacy Resource Center, would argue that the network is a catalyst for helping those who need help the most. Thanks to new sites and servers, information on literacy is as convenient as the nearest library or the closest computer and modem. Information once unavailable in many libraries on literacy is now accessible via state and regional networks.

Politics

What are the political or power opportunities when libraries get involved with public-access Internet? In a technologically sophisticated academic institution like Stanford University, the Internet is valued as a publishing and public relations resource, a tool to promote and to influence. In Stanford's Graduate School of Business, the Jackson Library and its access to information on the Internet meant a greater participation in the creation of electronic solutions for students, faculty and staff. Robert Mayer and Suzanne Sweeney show how the Jackson Library moved quickly to take advantage of its role as information provider in this new Internet environment. Efforts with vendors will mean more integrated resources on every desktop, only a connection away from any patron in the school.

In corporations the use of the Internet is a signal of technological savvy, digital awareness, and customer connectivity. For Syntex, an international pharmaceutical concern, the Internet provided the means for the library to educate the organization about electronic resources, train staff in the use of Internet-connected computers, and develop internal digital resources for the research community. Pamela Jajko and her colleagues report on the library's collaboration with the Information Systems Department for Internet activities that won respect for both groups.

At a high-tech organization like Hewlett-Packard, the Internet provides a valuable connection with customers. The Hewlett-Packard home page sees some 10,000 queries from customers every month, so its value both as a source of information and as a publicity vehicle cannot be underestimated. The Hewlett-Packard Laboratories Research Library was a key player in developing this connection with an internal home page that provides information to engineers and scientists. As Eugenie Prime and her co-authors point out, the Internet allowed the library to link to other groups within the organization in ways hardly possible in the past, elevating the library and the importance of information as never before.

Perspectives

As the reports in this book illustrate, providing access to the Internet can profoundly change the way a community works. It can bring a community together by allowing its members to be better informed and to communicate more easily with each other. In turn the Internet alters the bureaucracies of a community, a region, a state, by making them more responsive to a more inquisitive and attentive community.

Internet access is still far from being inexpensive. The Internet forces a new kind of economics based on the value of information access to all. Different groups, organizations, and individuals link together in new ways to provide the financial backing needed to make the Internet work. These economics intro-

xiii

duce a new kind of politics, one made of compromise and partnerships bringing together many interests under one electronic umbrella.

Much discussion has been devoted to the real and assumed educational benefits of Internet access, not only for children but adults, too. Access to information in depth on a rich variety of topics is only one part of the educational experience. Learning how to discriminate between different sources, understanding how to evaluate digital information, is a large and sometimes unrecognized part of education on the Internet. The skills of librarians in evaluating and processing information and in acting as intelligent agents are more valuable than ever before in this new medium. Seeing how others applied their skills will, we hope, inspire you as you connect your own patrons to the wonder (and sometimes headache) that is Internet.

Nancy R. John
Edward J. Valauskas

section one

visibility

scoring points in the community

Access wasn't the bottleneck; the lack of helpful information was.

visibility

Carolyn Caywood

Setting Up an Internet Users Group in the Public Library

n Virginia Beach, Virginia, as Internet access has become widely available, community members needed to share information on how to best use that access. At the suggestion of a commercial access provider, the Virginia Beach Public Library helped organize a users group, the Hampton Roads Internet Association (HRIA). Now in its second year, HRIA enables the community to learn more about the Internet. Through open meetings at the Library, HRIA provides a forum to share information and skills among those with Internet access. This cooperative venture has benefitted the Library and the access providers, as well as users and the general public.

Carolyn Caywood is head of the Bayside Area Library, part of the Virginia Beach Public Library System. Carolyn worked for the Cleveland (Ohio) Public Library in youth services, and came to Virginia Beach in 1979. For the last four years she has also been a columnist for *School Library Journal*, and, in addition to HRIA, helped found Virginians Against Censorship. Mail will reach her at Bayside Area Library, 936 Independence Blvd., Virginia Beach, VA 23455. Phone (804) 460-7519, fax (804) 464-6741, e-mail carolyn@infi.net

I wanted an Internet account worse than I've wanted anything since childhood. My husband had one through his employer and he would occasionally bring me files, like a list of book titles from the alt.cyberpunk newsgroup. I knew there was information out there that I could use. I suppose I wanted to have an e-mail address on my business card to feel a part of the next technological frontier. When I attended the 1992 Computers, Freedom and Privacy (CFP) Conference, I felt like I was the only person on Earth without an Internet account and a laptop. So, when some local citizens decided to start a business offering Internet access called Wyvern Technologies (now InfiNet, L.C.), I jumped on it and became a charter member. It quickly became obvious that there was much more to the Internet than I had guessed. After a few months, I began to find discussion groups for librarians, late in 1992 when public librarians were just beginning to appear on the Net.

A beginning

Since the CFP Conference had made me aware of issues about the Internet that paralleled library concerns about censorship, I recruited Shari Steele from the Electronic Frontier Foundation to speak during Banned Books Week in 1993. The program wasn't particularly well attended. It may have been a year too early, but it received good news coverage. I started hearing from people in the community who wanted to know more about the Internet.

Meanwhile, Wyvern Technologies was growing like Jack's beanstalk. It was difficult for the provider, with a staff of three, to both handle Internet technicalities and help new Internet users. I agreed with the need for help for Internet newbies. In order to learn about Gopher, I had attended a meeting of a Unix user group and I found myself very much in deep water. The access provider, seeing the advantage of the recent Internet session at the Library, proposed that we form a users group to provide the help that was getting harder and harder to provide on an individual basis.

For the Internet provider, the Library could provide a physical meeting place and publicity, without tying it too closely to their company. I saw an opportunity for the Virginia Beach Public Library to be a presence among all these new technological literati, who might otherwise conclude that physical libraries were obsolete. Also, it offered a way for Library staff to become proficient in using the Internet. The Library was already working hard to provide print information about the Internet, now that books were beginning to appear and access was spreading outside the academic and government communities. I wasn't aware, at that time, that some library systems were trying to become Internet access providers themselves. That route wasn't feasible or necessary in our community where, in addition to a local commercial access provider, many employers provide access. Access wasn't the bottleneck; the lack of helpful information was.

In October 1993 we announced an organizational meeting at the Bayside Area Library for an Internet user group. There was indeed a way to string phone cord down the hall to the meeting room, in order to have a live demonstration. At least 80 people crammed into a room suitable only for 40. The conditions were dreadful, but the enthusiasm was palpable. I made haste to book the Central Library's auditorium for the next year, and we finished up 1993 with monthly meetings at the local university.

Organizing HRIA

Parallel to the informational meetings, I scheduled organizational planning meetings, open to anyone. Those who came to hammer out bylaws (see Appendix 1) and formalize the structure became the nucleus of a board for the organization. They included access providers, folks who hoped to go into business selling Internet services, people with accounts, and just those wanting to know more about the Internet. We drew on other local computer groups as models, publicized through them, and borrowed their members' experience. In fact, we were offered the opportunity to join a local association of user groups. Because it was MS DOS-oriented, we didn't join. We wanted to appeal to Mac and Unix users as well. We kept the structure simple and postponed such complexities as filing for nonprofit status. Oddly, the name for the organization caused the longest discussion. Users group didn't seem to fit, but other suggestions were either stuffy or too cute. Despite meeting in Virginia Beach we wanted the whole metropolitan area to feel welcome, so we settled on the Hampton Roads Internet Association.

If I had it to do again, I would begin by identifying existing computer organizations and take greater advantage of what already existed. We were lucky that they found us. It's embarrassing to look back on how little I knew at the time about organizations that were, often as not, meeting in libraries. I'd also look for ways to structure the group to invite ordinary members to feel comfortable giving presentations. We did a survey early on about what people knew and what they needed from HRIA. That survey revealed that most of those attending felt they had little to share but much to learn. That pushed us away from member presentations. We will soon be doing another survey which may show that the balance has changed. Then members can be asked to do more, as they are in other user groups.

By March 1993 we had adopted bylaws and were ready to formally sign up members, accept dues, and elect officers. Members still didn't know each other very well. We may have been lucky that of those elected, at least half actually served. More people joined and some started attending board meetings so we recruited committee chairs. The board has actually become a loose gathering of those who care enough to help with the drudge work of running a club. This includes those who have a commercial interest in the Internet, though we had excluded them from being elected as officers. That suggestion, from a provider, prevented the organization from becoming too closely affiliated with any one vendor.

We have been heavily dependent on the providers, such as Wyvern Technologies, Pinnacle, Exchange, and Internet Presence and Publishing, to furnish equipment and programs. Most of the membership lack overhead monitors to project the computer screen's image up in a large room. And most of the members are shy about demonstrating their expertise. The size of the meetings and the auditorium itself are inhibiting. About 70 folks usually attend each meeting. By April 1994 I was getting concerned that all the programs were being put on by commercial providers. I decided to use a plain-vanilla Library Internet account to illustrate what to look for in selecting Internet access. I made enough mistakes to reassure anyone, but we still lack members willing to put together a program.

The commercial providers (there are more than four now) are always happy to show off what their systems can do while explaining how different Net tools work. Presentations have covered Usenet, Gopher, file transfer, talk, Internet Relay Chat (IRC), World Wide Web, GIFs, government use of the Net, and appropriate Net behavior. We have a literature table outside the auditorium where people can look at new magazines, pick up book lists, learn about classes, and find out about access providers. After the presentations, members share information about everything from the location of good sites to legislative activity that would affect the Internet. We're still experimenting with program formats. We've added a half-hour question and answer session for beginners before the regular two-hour meeting.

While most of the programs have consisted of demonstrations, a couple of presenters have chosen just to lead discussions. In December 1994, recent police raids on a couple of bulletin board systems in Florida had one access provider very concerned. He asked HRIA members to help him understand just what people expected of their Internet access provider. I was amazed at the expression of fierce independence that came out of the group and the number of people who drew analogies with the need to keep libraries uncensored.

6

Something about experiencing the Internet seems to attract or build a strong awareness of the First Amendment and freedom of speech.

Experiments

Meanwhile, we've been looking at moving member communications online. One access provider put files about HRIA on its Gopher and set up some Usenet style newsgroups, but got little traffic. Another provider volunteered to set up a mailing list using *majordomo,* and that was immediately popular. In fact, the list launched another discussion about who should be allowed to subscribe and how it should be used. Currently it is intended for announcements of interest to members. Those with large files to share are encouraged to merely announce their availability. Each organizational step seems to provide a learning experience as well. Since Serial Line Internet Protocol (SLIP) and Point-to-Point Protocol (PPP) accounts have become readily available, the same provider who hosted the mailing list offered to host a World Wide Web home page for HRIA as well. You can examine it at the URL **http://www.hria.org/hria/** and find links to other Internet user groups around the world.

Finding and connecting with an online list of user groups led to my biggest embarrassment. I had been preparing meeting flyers with a bibliography on the back since I booked the meetings. Somehow, a paper flyer was released with the dates off by one week. I only discovered the error when I shared the meeting schedule with the online list of users groups (for a sample of the electronic announcement, see Appendix 2).

Figure 1: The HRIA home page (**http://www.hria.org/hria/**)offers information about the Association as well as pointers to other useful servers.

Tracking down and correcting the incorrect dates on the paper flyer has led us to rely even more on electronic communication, though we still use print to inform the newly curious. Once again, this has created a challenge for the organization. Some of the members are ready to move to conducting organizational business entirely online. That solution presents a problem if HRIA is to continue to serve as a point of introduction for those who are not yet connected to the Internet.

In addition, when we were writing the bylaws, the issue of creating SIGs or special interest groups came up. At that time, we didn't feel ready, but it may soon be time to revisit that idea in order to avoid boring the experienced Internet users or bewildering the newcomers.

HRIA and the library

These issues are important since one of my goals in starting this organization was to create an opportunity for new people to discover the Internet. From the start, I had informal permission to devote my time and Library resources in getting HRIA underway. As I saw what other public libraries were doing to bring the Internet to their customers, I wanted to make a formal connection between the Library and HRIA so the Library would be acknowledged as a leader in supporting public participation in the information infrastructure. I suggested to the Library administration, and to HRIA, that the Library become a co-sponsor of the organization. This would permit meetings to be advertised through Library channels and provide an impetus for upgrading presentation equipment. But mostly, I saw it as enhancing the Library's reputation for increasing access to information. HRIA voted to accept that co-sponsorship about a year after the first meeting. The discussion that preceded the vote reaffirmed the members' desire to be independent. They were primarily concerned that co-sponsorship not mean that the Library would dictate program content or organizational direction. So, it is up to the members to decide how much to provide support for newcomers.

Recognizing the role of members in shaping the direction of HRIA is not easy for me since I have a parent's interest in the organization. I suppose that's true of any founder of a member-driven organization. But the same philosophy that lets a librarian recommend a book but check out whatever the customer chooses stands in good stead here. I am very pleased for the most part with what HRIA has become. Community knowledge of the Internet is far more widespread as a result of its efforts. People have gained valuable skills, gotten help over the rough spots, and learned to value the Library's commitment to access to information through attendance at HRIA's meetings. The Library has

8

a knowledgeable and supportive group to consult as we explore what the library of the next century must become. I am particularly pleased that we have done this, not in competition with the private sector, but in cooperation with it. Everyone has benefited from that cooperation, and whatever HRIA evolves into, I am proud to have had a hand in it.

Conclusion

I think that creating an Internet user group is an excellent approach for libraries in communities where Internet access is readily available. Working with commercial providers has given me an appreciation of the technical problems they face and perhaps even more the legal and social ambiguities on the electronic frontier. Fortunately, a user group can discuss those issues without giving librarians sleepless nights. Eventually, we will have to address the needs of those who can't afford the equipment for their own access, but I hope HRIA may be able to help us with that too. Already the association is discussing setting up a volunteer program to work with people with disabilities who could use the Internet to enhance their lives both socially and economically.

I expect to continue relying on HRIA for customer feedback as the Library incorporates new technology. They may well serve in that capacity for the whole municipal government. The need for such feedback should be even more evident in communities where the library or some other agency of local government is responsible for citizen access to the Internet. I have always believed that the library is the one government service that works best by encouraging individuals to take charge of meeting their own needs. The Internet is similar in its reliance on individual initiative. The combination of the two invites citizen participation, and user groups can focus that participation to achieve the best interests of everyone involved.

Appendix 1

By-Laws of the Hampton Roads Internet Association

ARTICLE I

This organization shall be known as Hampton Roads Internet Association.

ARTICLE II

The objectives of this organization shall be to promote the use of the Internet and to foster a better understanding of the Internet and its uses.

ARTICLE III

Membership is open to all who are interested in the Internet. Members shall pay annual dues of $10.

ARTICLE IV

The conduct of this organization shall be governed by the By-Laws.

ARTICLE V

Meetings shall be held monthly.

ARTICLE VI

There shall be members to serve as officers and committee chairpersons of the Hampton Roads Internet Association. Members currently involved in commercial Internet access provision shall not serve as officers, in order to avoid any appearance of conflict of interest. Officers shall be elected and guided by procedures outlined in the By-Laws. They shall be known collectively as the Executive Board. The officers are elected yearly and shall consist of:

President — presides at meetings
Vice-President — presides in absence of president
Secretary — maintains official records
Treasurer — maintains Association funds.

Officers are elected by majority vote of the members present at the March meeting. Voting is based on one vote for each member present.

10

Appendix 2

A typical HRIA announcement, illustrating how HRIA works.

```
Date: Tue, 21 Feb 1995 20:07:34 -0500
To: hria@hria.org (All Members)
From: mjdowdn@infi.net (M J Dowden)
Subject: Important UPDATE re: Thurs meeting
Sender: owner-hria@www.ip.net


UPDATE RE: NEXT MEETING - Thursday, February 23, 1995

Virginia Beach Central Library Auditorium
4100 VA Beach Blvd, Virginia Beach (next to Loehmanns
Plaza)

- Beginners are urged to come at 6:30 PM for a
questions and answer session.

- Scheduled program at 7:00 PM is Real Estate on the
World Wide Web (WWW)

This presentation is open to the public, you do not
have to be an Internet user to attend.

CHANGES TO THE AGENDA:

6:30 PM - Beginners will meet in the auditorium, not
the "storytime" room as previously planned. It looks
like we will have more new members than will fit into
that room.

SECOND CALL FOR VOLUNTEERS

 The HRIA is experiencing very rapid growth. We are in
need of members who are willing to lend a hand in the
management of the association. A major commitment of
time and effort is NOT necessary. What is needed is a
substantial number of persons who can each make a small
contribution of time and expertise. Your assistance can
mean a great deal to those who look to this association
as a source of information and as a place to benefit
```

11

from the collective experience of its membership. If
you would like to play a role in the HRIA's expansion
and help it better serve its membership, please contact
Ann Harney <aharney@pinn.net>.

 Persons interested in serving on the Board of
Directors are invited to attend the Board meeting,
which will be held at 5:00 PM (the same day) in the
Bangkok Gardens restaurant. That is in the shopping
center just east of the library.

FOR FURTHER INFORMATION:

1) You can look at our World Wide Web page using
Mosaic, Lynx, or other "browser," the WWW address (URL)
is: http://www.hria.org/hria/

2) Send an e-mail message to: majordomo@hria.org
with just the word: info
in the body of message. There will be a different
message each month.

3) Contact a member of the HRIA Board for further
information. The Board is:

Ann Harney <aharney@pinn.net>
Sylvia Solhaug <samhill@infi.net>
Fred M Fariss <count@infi.net>
M J Dowden <mjdowdn@infi.net>
Carolyn Caywood <carolyn@infi.net>
Stephen Zedalis <tintype@infi.net>

See you at the meeting.

In its first year, the library's Internet connection drew in five percent of the county's population by dial-up access alone.

v i s i b i l i t y

Bill Cochran

Wendy's Connects Billings, Montana

he Wendy's Connection is an innovative public-private partnership to support public Internet access. Wendy's of Montana, Inc. is providing nearly $150,000 in a multi-year grant to enable Parmly Billings Library to offer an extensive menu of electronic information services to the 118,830 residents of Billings and Yellowstone County. Resources made available by the project include access to the Internet, indexing and full text for articles in hundreds of general interest and business serials, and community information databases. This chapter reviews the origins and implementation of the Wendy's Connection, discusses Internet account services made possible by the project, and describes plans to expand access into community high schools.

Bill Cochran is Director of Parmly Billings Library, the public library in Billings, Montana. He formerly served the State Library of Iowa as Assistant State Librarian, Director of Library Development, and LSCA Coordinator, and also worked in public libraries in several Iowa communities. He was a delegate to the 1991 White House Conference on Library and Information Services, at which he was elected to the Conference Recommendations Committee, and he serves on the Montana Telecommunications Advisory Council. He may be reached at Parmly Billings Library, 510 North Broadway, Billings, MT 59101. Phone (406) 657-8292, fax (406) 657-8293, e-mail cochran@billings.lib.mt.us

The Wendy's Connection is the unlikely product of financial hard times experienced by Parmly Billings Library, the largest public library in Montana, serving the 118,830 residents of Billings and Yellowstone County. The library struggled for years with a flat budget primarily caused by city charter and state statutory limitations on property taxes. Beginning in the mid-1970's, the library gradually lost hours, cut its staff nearly in half, pulled its three bookmobiles off the road, and still watched its materials budget all but disappear.

By the spring of 1993, and facing additional cuts, the library's board of trustees called for volunteers to serve on a Citizens' Task Force on the Future of the Library. This task force would determine the community's needs for library services for a five- to ten-year period, identify funding to meet those needs, and conduct an informational campaign to secure the required monies. Extensive publicity resulted in a 75-member task force which ultimately recommended a library levy increase. The levy increase passed by a three-to-one margin in April 1994. It restored services previously cut and provided relative financial stability for the library for the near future.

Wendy's Connection

After seeing a task force public service spot on television in early August 1993, Sam McDonald, Jr., chairman of the board and CEO of Billings-based Wendy's of Montana, Inc., contacted library director Bill Cochran and asked how he could help. Cochran proposed to McDonald the project that became known as the Wendy's Connection. The project would give the community hands-on experience with the Internet and other electronic information resources. McDonald agreed and committed $145,980 to the project over a three-year period, to end June 30, 1996.

Following McDonald's initial contact, Library Systems Administrator Thurman Smith, Assistant City Attorney Bonnie Sutherland, and a number of other library and vendor staff worked at an increasingly feverish pace to develop the technological, financial, and legal details of the project so that it could be implemented as rapidly as possible. Planning was difficult because of a lack of models to provide guidance on this sort of new public-private venture.

Architecture

The Wendy's Connection was designed to provide access to the Internet, to indexes and full text of magazine articles, and to community information databases. Access would be possible via the library's automated system, a Dynix public-access catalog operated on an IBM RS6000 minicomputer. The system supports 18 public access terminals, including a VERT/VISTA terminal that

14

magnifies and/or audibly reads what appears on its screen for visually-impaired users. It also supports a number of staff terminals throughout the facility. The single dial-up line then available to home and office personal computer users with modems was expanded to four lines on a rotary as a part of the project. The following year five more lines were added.

The library selected WLN, Inc., headquartered in Lacey, Washington, to be the Internet provider for the project. Just weeks earlier, Seattle (Washington) Public Library, utilizing WLN's services, had become one of the country's first public libraries on the Internet. The project contract called for WLN to provide an Internet connection via a 56 kbps line from Lacey to Billings; to install and maintain the router that connects to the Dynix gateway; to set up and maintain accounts; and, to conduct initial training for all staff and to provide additional training materials as needed. The library contracted with WLN for essentially a turnkey Internet service, including the router connecting to the Dynix gateway.

Information Access Corporation's (IAC) *Magazine Index Plus* and *Magazine Text ASAP* were selected as the initial serials databases to be included in the project, later supplemented by the addition of IAC's *Business Index*. The library became WLN's first reference database services client, obtaining access to the IAC databases from WLN's RS6000 in Lacey via the Internet connection. The project also included acquisition of Dynix's Community Resources module, permitting the development of local databases.

With prices set and contracts signed, we held a press conference to announce the project at the library on September 28, 1993. Attended by some seventy-five people, the press conference generated extensive print and television coverage, including an editorial in *The Billings Gazette*, which called the project "a ticket to the future." Approximately the same number of people

Figure 1: Wendy's of Montana CEO Sam McDonald, Jr. (right) hands the initial Wendy's Connection check to Parmly Billings Library Director Bill Cochran at a September 1993 press conference. (Photo courtesy Parmly Billings Library)

15

attended an "electronic ribbon-cutting" on December 30, when the Wendy's Connection was unveiled and made available to the public.

Soon after the ribbon-cutting, the library sent a brief press release to area media announcing a meeting to discuss the organization of an Internet users group. A gratifying crowd of about seventy-five turned out for the initial January 1994 meeting. The group quickly developed bylaws and elected officers. Although attendance has since varied from month to month, a dedicated membership has continued to meet for programs on a variety of Internet-related topics as well as to share ideas and experiences.

Access

A patron can connect to the Wendy's Connection by using one of the library's terminals or by dialing in from a personal computer with a modem. By either method, anyone can use the library's catalog or reach, via the Internet connection, the Montana State University — Billings and University of Montana library catalogs.

Figure 2: Telneting to the Parmly Billings Library online catalog opens this screen for the user. Telnet **Billings.lib.mt.us** or **198.207.189.1**, login: library, and select VT100 emulation.

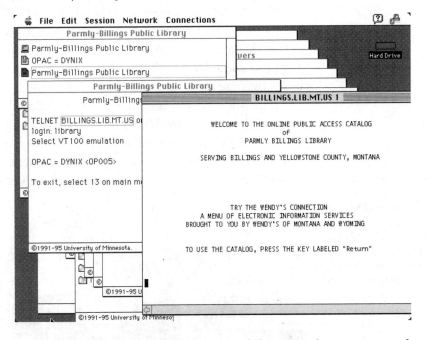

The 42,640 holders of free library cards have simply to enter a card number to gain free access, again via this transparent Internet connection, to a menu which includes the IAC databases, WLN's regional bibliographic database, Internet Gopher, the Library of Congress, and many other library catalogs.

16

We conducted a user survey in January 1995, in preparation for the library's long-range planning and role-setting process. It indicated that approximately 6,300 Yellowstone County residents had used the Wendy's Connection via dial-up from home or office personal computers during its first year of operation, a remarkably high five percent of the total population of the county. Another large, but unknown, share of the county population has accessed the Connection using library terminals.

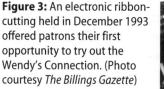

Figure 3: An electronic ribbon-cutting held in December 1993 offered patrons their first opportunity to try out the Wendy's Connection. (Photo courtesy *The Billings Gazette*)

The project also has supported individual Internet accounts for 26 library staff. These accounts are used both for reference and professional development purposes. They greatly diminish the need for paper-based internal communications such as memos, agendas, and similar documents formerly word-processed, copied, and physically distributed throughout the library. Monthly use of staff Internet accounts grew from just over 150 hours in January 1994 to almost 570 hours in January 1995.

Since July 1994, a small number of accounts have been established for some municipal officials and departments, including the city administrator, city attorney, city clerk, airport, transit system, fire department, information resources department, police department, and public utilities department. These accounts were all budgeted for by the departments and paid for by interdepartmental transfer. Although training was still being conducted for these units, the six accounts in use in January 1995 tallied some 25 hours of connect time for the month.

Internet accounts

Also in July 1994, the Internet services contract between the library and WLN was amended to permit the library to offer individual, full-service Internet accounts to its patrons on a cost-recovery fee basis. Through January 1995, 50 public accounts had been established, with usage already running over 415 hours per month. Among those purchasing accounts have been educators, writers, at least one student, a journalist, an attorney, and many others representing a wide range of ages and interests.

Accounts provide telnet, file transfer protocol, and e-mail services. They are available for a $25 initial set-up fee and a minimum fee of $20 per month for 20 hours connect time, with additional hours billed at $2 per hour. These rates cover the WLN charges for account set-up, training materials provided to account holders, and monthly access. It also includes a small surcharge to contribute to future expansion of incoming telephone lines, ports, modems, and license fees anticipated as usage grows. A monthly orientation is held for new account holders, most of whom attend one or more of the sessions.

The decision to offer fee-based Internet accounts was not lightly made. The service is being offered for the convenience of patrons, just like other library fee-based technologies, coin-operated telephones and photocopiers. It is available on a cost-recovery basis rather than for profit. This strategy minimizes the economic obstacle to patrons and ensures that no other services would be impacted by its discontinuation, in the event that future developments might render it obsolete. In the meantime, the library continues to offer as much free access to Internet and other electronic resources as possible.

A school connection

The resources made available by the Wendy's Connection were cited frequently by the Billings District #2 School Board when it decided in November 1994 to automate its school media centers. These centers, at Senior, Skyview, and West High Schools, will be linked to Parmly Billings Library's Dynix system. The intergovernmental effort was jointly developed following a successful pilot project, automating the media center at the Career Center, a vocational high school campus, through a leased telephone line link to the library.

The network will bring to the media centers the library's strength in automation, significant print resources, and a means to reach the Wendy's Connection. The convenient neighborhood location of the media centers, which will serve the public, and the District's courier delivery service to better serve users are distinct advantages gained by the library. The project is expected to be in full use when classes start in autumn 1995. Preliminary discussions are already underway to explore the potential for expanding the network to include middle and elementary schools.

The library also is developing plans to upgrade the telecommunications link with WLN from a 56 kbps line to a partial or full T-1, to install a SLIP connection, and to add at least some smart terminals, all to provide enhanced Internet access. Plans are also being discussed to add incoming dial-up lines to accommodate increasing traffic and to install incoming toll-free lines to provide free access to Yellowstone County residents living outside the local calling area.

Conclusion

The Wendy's Connection has brought Internet access and other electronic information resources to thousands of users throughout Billings and Yellowstone County, Montana. The project's impact on the community will only grow as the services it has initiated continue to evolve in coming years.

Monica Ertel

Internet and the Corporate Library
Creating New Opportunity at the Apple Library

 ibraries are increasingly being seen as the local Internet experts within corporations, institutions, universities and schools. They are aggressively accepting this challenge by offering training classes on the Internet, acting as clearinghouses for the latest network resources, and designing World Wide Web home pages, while surfing the Internet to meet their users' information needs. The Corporate Library at Apple Computer, Inc. has undertaken a variety of projects which involve the Internet. This chapter focuses on how the Library managed this new charter and discusses how libraries, overall, will meet the Internet challenge.

20

Monica Ertel was hired by Apple Computer, Inc. in 1981 to establish its corporate library. While doing so, she also founded the Apple Library Users Group, which has nearly 10,000 members from every corner of the world. In her current role as Manager of Technology Operations at Apple, Monica is responsible for the Apple Internet Program, Apple's External Research Program, Computer Operations, Apple Global Standards, and Strategic Programs, as well as the Apple Library. She is actively involved in several library associations including ALA, the Special Libraries Association (SLA), and the International Federation of Library Associations and Institutions (IFLA). You can reach Monica at Apple Computer, Inc., 4 Infinite Loop, MS 304-2A, Cupertino, CA 95014. Phone (408) 974-2552, fax (408) 725-8502, e-mail ertel.m@applelink.apple.com

We're in a highly competitive global marketplace. The company (or library) that can reach and satisfy customers (or patrons) will have an advantage. The Internet can help in maintaining relationships with customers, patrons, developers, students, providers and the public. By creating a corporate presence on the Internet, organizations can participate in all the benefits of online marketing, publicity, and sales. It is possible to use tools such as NCSA Mosaic, Gopher, FTP, Telnet, electronic mail and Usenet to build a virtual storefront, create catalogs that can be browsed online, announce products, take orders, and get customer feedback.[1] A quick check of the home pages of many corporations illustrates this phenomenon. In order to be competitive, organizations will be getting on the Internet in a B–I–G way.

The Internet is where business is beginning to happen and thus, this is where business *must* be. With the current growth of corporations on the Internet, it may not be long before *not* being on the Internet will be considered a sign of a hopelessly outdated company.[2] I don't believe that Apple Computer, Inc. or the University of Michigan or the Liverpool (New York) Public Library or any other institution has any other choice but to actively participate and thus learn about this vital information resource.

This chapter will discuss the role of the Corporate Library at Apple Computer, Inc. in helping our patrons find their way on the Internet. While this chapter specifically discusses what's been done at Apple, I believe that any library can take on some or all of these projects as well.

Why did we get interested in the Internet?

Someone recently told me that the Chinese character for warning is a combination of the characters for danger and opportunity. This seems particularly apropos when talking about our role with the Internet. For the first time in over 100 years, libraries truly have a chance to reinvent themselves. With the increased power of technology, we have a greater opportunity to bring service to wherever the potential users of library services happen to be. At the same time, technology is changing the way that people access and use information. This is creating many challenges and opportunities for libraries today. At this critical turning point for libraries, the Internet presents itself as a threat and as a wonderful opportunity.

I discovered the Internet about twelve years ago when one of the researchers at Apple suggested that I use my Apple IIe and modem to access a system called ARPAnet, developed originally by the Advanced Research Projects Agency (ARPA) of the U.S. Department of Defense. He said that he communicated with many of his colleagues using this system and that I might be able to

---

1. Jill Ellsworth. *The Internet Business Book* (New York: Wiley, 1994) 38–9.

2. Ibid., p. xxii.

use it to talk to my colleagues in other libraries. Using a rather arcane set of instructions, I found myself on the fledgling information superhighway. About six years later, I really began to use this system, as it had evolved, to exchange electronic mail with other libraries for interlibrary loan and general information sharing. About that time, the library began to receive requests from Apple employees to have information sent to them via the Internet, rather than through Apple's own internal e-mail system. In addition, in recent years the library has focused on the Internet and its impact on community networks, through a series of grants called the Apple Library of Tomorrow (ALOT) program.[3] Through ALOT, I began to appreciate what this new avenue of communication could mean to libraries.

However, as in most situations which affect a significant change, the event which really pushed the Apple Library into the Internet was a crisis. In the summer of 1993, the library was told that we had to recoup some of our expenses. Prior to that time, the library was fully funded and we were able to offer our services free of charge to any employee. In order to recover some of our costs, we began to charge employees for literature searches and document delivery.

We expected the usage of these library services to drop because of these new charges. However, we were fully unprepared for the massive impact this had on our usage. These charge backs (as well as the fact that we had loaded a significant number of bibliographic databases on our internal network for employees to search themselves) resulted in a drastic and sustained decrease in what had traditionally been our largest services. Our initial response was close to panic.

However, these events turned out to be a blessing in disguise because it gave us some much needed time to reflect on the services offered by the library. We used this extra time to put together a long overdue strategic plan to deal with changing uses of the library and to design a plan for the future. As part of our strategic planning exercise, we looked at the library's strengths, weaknesses, opportunities, and threats. This helpful exercise made our future path clear.

The area which appeared to present a great opportunity in offering needed services to the company, and in using the library's expertise, was — guess what? — the Internet. This was also the area which posed the most threat. There was a lot of talk within the company about the Internet but not a lot of support infrastructure to help people figure out how to get onto the Internet or learn what to do once they got there. We eagerly but tentatively embraced this exciting new challenge and began to slowly test the waters.

3. For more information on the Apple Library of Tomorrow program, contact Steve Cisler at Apple Computer, Inc., 4 Infinite Loop MS 304-2A, Cupertino, CA 95014; e-mail: sac@apple.com

What are we doing?

There are several projects and experiences in the Apple Library that are noteworthy as we've become involved with the Internet. I will examine a few in detail. While I will be discussing specific projects at Apple, I believe that most of these could be easily done at other types of libraries. We've done almost all of these with virtually no increases in head count or budget. The hardest part has been changing the way we think about library services and re-prioritizing our efforts.

►*Internet training*

In 1992, the Apple Library organized an Internet Teach-In. We wanted to see what kind of interest there was within the company regarding this area without investing a lot of money or time. We decided to hold a three–hour seminar in which we invited staff from other parts of the company, as well as the library, to talk about the Internet in general. We reserved the auditorium, sent out some flyers, advertised via inter-company e-mail, and waited in anticipation. We were thrilled when the room filled up. It was standing room only, as the audience filled all the seats and aisles. With very little initial investment, we knew we were on to something big.

What kind of feedback did we received from the initial "Teach-In?" Our colleagues wanted to see the Internet for themselves. They wanted to use Internet tools and get some guidance. As a result, we held a day–long Internet Fair. At the Fair, we set up computers, borrowed from the library, in a large conference room. Signs on various computers indicated specific demonstrations for NCSA Mosaic or FTP. The Library staff as well as other experts from within the company found themselves swamped by interested employees, anxious to learn more. Feedback from the Fair indicated that while people enjoyed being shown the tools, they wanted more. They wanted in-depth training classes, where they could sit down for a couple of hours and actually learn how to use the Internet in a more structured format.

We realized at this point that there was an opportunity for the library to take a leadership role, but the library staff didn't feel qualified to teach Internet classes or workshops. We felt that we were just learning about the Internet ourselves. However, we knew that if we didn't act soon, someone else or some other unit would. So, we decided that we didn't have to do it ourselves. We hired a consultant to conduct the actual training. We started learning about the Internet along with the other employees, so that eventually the library staff would conduct the training on their own.

We felt that the important thing was to get started and establish the Apple Library as the place to go for Internet information and training. We are now offering hands-on, half-day training workshops on topics such as "Introduction to the Internet," "Gopher, WAIS and AppleSearch," "World Wide Web," and "Strategies for Finding Information." We rent classrooms from Apple's Developer Support group, which are set up with sixteen workstations and Internet connections. These classes generally fill up within a half-hour of being advertised!

Figure 1: Internet classes which offer hands-on experience are popular with Apple employees.

In addition to more formalized training, the Apple Library has set up public access stations for Apple employees to take a test drive on the information superhighway. The latest Internet navigational software is installed on these machines. Staff provide the same sort of support on these computers as they would on any of the library CD-ROM stations or with any reference tool. These public access stations provide a simple, risk-free trial of what the Internet can offer without a lot of investment on the part of the user.

▶ Internet information clearinghouse

A center with printed information on the Internet is something that most libraries can easily do. Our collection contains books, periodicals, videotapes, technical reports, and databases on the Internet. It takes few resources to pull together a bibliography and keep it on hand at the front desk of the library. The Library also sends out updated bulletins on new materials acquired by the library via company e-mail. The Apple Library also maintains a server on the company network with copies of text files such as "The Big Dummy's Guide to the Internet," "EFF Guide to the Internet," and "Cool Tools." In addition, copies of the latest public domain, shareware, and site-licensed tools such as NCSA Mosaic, MacHTTP, MacWeb and Netscape Navigator are on the Apple Library server. It is now widely recognized in the company that if you want the latest Internet software, you simply go to the Apple Library's server and look in the Internet folder.

► *World Wide Web*

The Library's early interest in the Internet led to it having one of the first home pages at Apple on the World Wide Web. One of the library's information specialists found that he could answer many reference questions by going on the Internet. He began to collect sites that contained quality information. It wasn't long before he designed a home page for the library with these resources organized by general topic such as "Information about Apple," "Competitive Intelligence," "International Business Resources" and "Computer Engineering." As an internal resource, it has generated quite a bit of use and given the library its next big opportunity.

CommerceNet is a consortium of a growing number of U.S. companies who have a strong interest in electronic commerce on the Internet. Apple was one of the charter members of CommerceNet. At its introduction in the Spring of 1994, Apple wanted to show some of the possibilities of what a company could offer over the Internet. Because the Apple Library had been so active in Internet activities within the company, and because the library had designed a useful home page, we were asked by the Vice President of Apple's Advanced Technology Group to design Apple's corporate presence on the Internet via the World Wide Web.[4]

This assignment has been quite a challenge for the library with no additional head count or resources. However, we have been able to successfully implement a home page by creating a team, built with staff from different units and groups within the company to work with us on this project. This cross-functional team includes members of the Creative Services Group, which has designed the actual graphics for Apple's home page; members of the Computer Operations Group, providing technical support; staff from various product groups, giving the actual content; and colleagues in the Advanced Technology Group, supplying cutting-edge demonstrations and technologies. This highly leveraged model has worked extremely well. We've discovered that other corporate libraries are doing similar projects. This effort has also positioned the library within Apple Computer as an important Internet source.

---

4. To access Apple's Web home page, go to **http://www.apple.com**

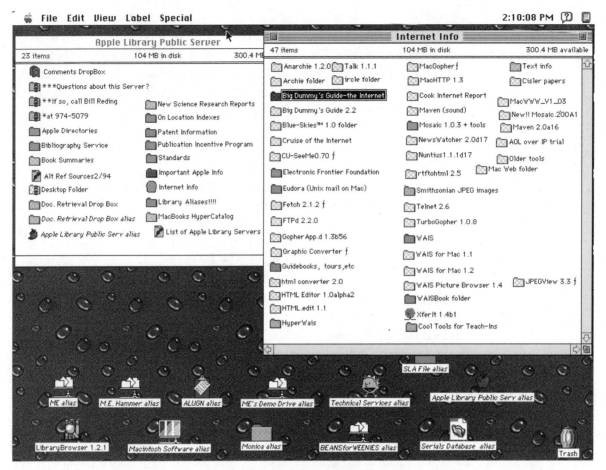

Figure 2: Numerous Internet tools are available on the Apple Library public server.

►Internet Interest Group

The Library is not the only group in the company working on Internet projects. We have found that many other units are designing home pages on the World Wide Web, distributing information to developers and customers over the Internet, and designing products to assist customers to use the Internet. With that in mind, the Apple Library, along with some of the scientists in the Advanced Technology Group, decided to organize an informal biweekly meeting called the Internet Interest Group. This *ad hoc* group is open to all Apple employees who are interested in talking about what they're doing or who simply want to learn more about what's happening inside Apple with the Internet. The group is very informal, but meets regularly. Sometimes there is an agenda with a speaker and thirty people show up. On other occasions, there may be a brief discussion about some new information, and just three staff appear for the meeting. The group costs absolutely nothing to organize or host but creates a forum for the exchange of information. It also helps to create powerful allies for additional support.

►House Calls

In addition to our Internet training, the Apple Library also offers what we call "House Calls" or one-on-one support for employees who want additional tutoring. We realize that not everyone can get to one of our classes. Some simply want some help getting started so that they can teach themselves. A Library staff member will go to an employee's office or alternatively they can come to the trainer's office. This tutoring could get out of control and consume a lot of Library staff time. There is a limit to the number of hours per week devoted to this training. It has proven to be a very effective way of getting people on the Internet.

Challenges

Along with opportunity comes challenges. The Apple Library has done all of the above without any additional head count or budget. We have had to take a critical look at what we've been doing and at services we've offered to reevaluate their usefulness in order to address the Internet challenge. This is more difficult than it sounds. It requires staff to give up some things in which they have invested a great deal of personal energy and to refocus their efforts. This shift has brought with it the reward of learning new skills and meeting new needs.

Working with the Internet requires, for some Library staff, different skills. Some were trained as librarians over twenty years ago, before personal computers or online databases were even used in libraries. Skills have kept pace with

Figure 3: The address for Apple Computer's home page on the World Wide Web is **http://www.apple.com**

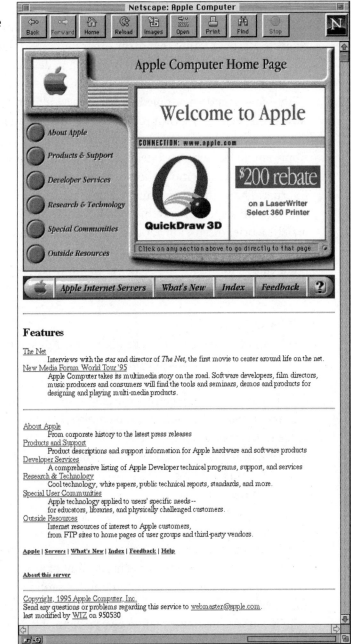

the changes over the years but the Internet requires even more stretches. Working with the Internet requires the ability to manage cross-functional teams representing different groups within the company to learn new languages and technologies such as the HyperText Markup Language (HTML) and server maintenance and to teach workshops and classes.

Figure 4: An Apple Library staff member makes a "House Call" to offer one-on-one Internet training.

Some staff may not find this shift attractive. After all, they were not hired as Internet experts when they joined the company ten years ago. However, these skills are simply extensions of what they have been doing for years. It's a matter of looking at them differently and being open to change. Given appropriate training, encouragement, and support, the library staff has eagerly approached these new assignments and excelled at implementing them.

Another challenge may come from another department within the company. Another unit may feel that the Internet is more in line with their charter than the library. This sort of in-fighting is particularly true as the Internet gains more visibility both within and outside of the organization. Politics is a necessary part of doing business. The Library has found that its cross-functional teams and the Internet Interest Group work as allies in these battles. In addition, the library's understanding of the importance of creating a service-oriented organization has gone a long way in making people happy and satisfied with our work.

Finally, changing the way that people think of and use the library may be difficult. I call this smashing the stereotype. Even today you will find some who think that the library is simply a quiet and musty smelling place to go

29

and read. We still have a lot of work to do to make patrons realize that the library is an exciting place for interactive information discovery, staffed by people who can not only help you find what you want but design the tools to help you get there.

What's next?

The Library is being seen more and more as a place with information gathering expertise. The Internet is still unfriendly and still very difficult to use for many. Librarians know how to organize and categorize information. They know how to determine valid and quality information sources. Librarians intrinsically understand the importance of offering a supportive and useful information service. This makes libraries a natural entry point for the Internet in many organizations.

In the near future, I see corporate librarians' roles changing quite drastically. Organizations are no longer going to fund a large information center in which the library staff expects their colleagues to come to them for information. Organizations are going to expect information specialists to be proactive and add value to the organization in a different manner than they have in the past. I see some new roles, such as the following:

► *Internet specialists*

These individuals will be responsible for preparing, creating, and maintaining HTML documents on the Internet. These staff will devise home pages for groups and departments as well as build their own home pages. They will be used as consultants by other groups ready to use the Internet to conduct their groups' business.

► *Teachers and guides*

These staff will work with users to determine their information and research needs, designing training seminars and classes. Library staff will find that their role in finding information for their users will change as they empower their users to find the information for themselves. Perhaps library schools and graduate programs in information science will begin to require more student teaching.

► *Resource clearinghouses*

An important role for the library staff will be to evaluate information resources, printed or digital. Collection development will take on a new meaning as librarians scour the Internet for useful databases and sources of information. Libraries will also be seen as the place to go for not only printed material on the Internet but also the tools used to access the Internet.

Conclusion

It is very difficult to write a conclusion because so much is in transition, changing every day. Are we doing enough? Are we doing the right things? Are we abandoning important things which we should still be doing? Most importantly, we need to remember that we should be making the most of our skills and expertise, and advertising our capabilities.

No one will come to us and ask us to take the lead within our organizations for the Internet. We need to promote our own skills and interests. I am reminded of the celebrated *New Yorker* cartoon in which two dogs are sitting in front of a computer with the caption "On the Internet, nobody knows you're a dog".[5] On the Internet, no one knows if you're a dog or a librarian! We have to make our colleagues aware of what we can do with the Internet.

---

5. Cartoon by Peter Steiner. *New Yorker* (July 5, 1993), 61.

Starting with old and second-hand equipment, the author turned a one-person library into a global resource.

Mary C. Pettengill

A Small Special Library in the University Makes Itself Bigger with the Internet

 pecial libraries greatly benefit from the resources that an Internet network connection provides for patrons and the librarian. The author's original interest in using the Internet was to support her own work as a librarian. She realized that an information server that directed users to important resources was a way to extend the library's special subject collection by including relevant Internet resources. As a result, the library gained users and visibility.

Mary C. Pettengill is Alumni Reading Room Supervisor at the Department of Petroleum and Geosystems Engineering of the University of Texas at Austin. She previously published an article about the Reading Room (then the Carter Reading Room) in the FARNET publication, *51 Reasons: How We Use the Internet and What It Says About the Information Superhighway*. She can be reached at the Department of Petroleum and Geosystems Engineering, CPE 3.158, University of Texas at Austin, Austin, TX 78712. Phone: (512) 471-3226, fax: (512) 471-9605, email: maryp@ mail.utexas.edu and Server URL: *http://www.pe.utexas.edu/Departmental_Information/Reading/*

Beginnings

Where are networks needed most? Small special libraries are cut off from the resources and communication systems of a large library. For this reason, small libraries need the resources that a network can provide for patrons and the librarian. The Alumni Reading Room is a departmental library for the Department of Petroleum and Geosystems Engineering at the University of Texas in Austin. During the last three years, the reading room has used the Internet to enrich its resources for students, staff and alumni.

The reading room has a collection of 3,600 cataloged books, journals, theses, and other petroleum engineering materials. It supports faculty and graduate research, and undergraduate education. The reading room is not a unit of the University General Libraries. As a result, the librarian is close to the users and receives immediate feedback regarding reading room policies and purchases. As the Supervisor of the Alumni Reading Room, I can be flexible in planning and using new technologies. On the other hand, as the reading room's only librarian, I do not have the nearby support of colleagues and staff that I would in a larger library.

During the past four years there was an average enrollment of 168 graduate students and 136 undergraduates in the department. Graduate students come from all over the world. During 1993–94, there were 46 from the United States, 28 from the Far East, 18 from South and Central America, 16 from the South Asia, 13 from Southeast Asia, 13 from the Middle East, 4 from Europe and 3 from Africa. They are a varied group with different backgrounds in computer use. However, even the least computer-oriented are motivated to use networks to communicate with far-off friends.

Use of the network started in a small way. As the new librarian in November 1990, I surveyed the status of the Alumni Reading Room. There was no record of any reading room policy. There was no record of how any task had been performed. There was no previous employee available to give me any information. There was no subject heading list. The reading room had no computers. There was a backlog of 450 volumes awaiting cataloging. Catalog cards were typed individually by department secretaries in their free time. I concluded that I needed some help.

Thus, my original interest in using the Internet was to support my own work as a librarian. In addition, since my position is only half-time and it is important to keep the library open as many hours as possible, I had to minimize the time spent doing searches away from the library.

Previously in the Geology Library, while working on a special project to catalog maps, I had learned to use the Internet in order to see how maps had

33

been cataloged at other universities. It was extremely helpful. I also became a reader of the PACS-L mailing list. I realized that these electronic sources would be valuable in my new position.

Network consumer

The Alumni Reading Room had a University of Texas General Libraries online public access catalog terminal that could also be used to read and send electronic mail. I encountered some resistance when I requested an e-mail account because I was not a researcher. I was persistent because I knew that by using e-mail, I could read about the experiences of others from library-oriented mailing lists and ask questions. As a result of getting the account, I received suggestions and information about filling in gaps in my periodical collection, using duplicates received from members of the GEONET mailing list. On the PACS-L list, I read about the Internet experiences of others, and I realized that with full network access I could do even more for my users.

I had requested a personal computer so that I could automate the production of catalog cards and start a local catalog. With an old personal computer and a shareware database program, I set up a catalog database. I was able to print catalog cards much more easily than before. Within the year, I cleared up the cataloging backlog. My success in using an old computer to solve a long-standing problem made it easier for me to get more computing resources.

After a year in the reading room, I was given an old Macintosh which was on an AppleTalk network that could access the Internet. Most of the faculty and staff used Macintoshes, so this made it easier for me to communicate with them. I also started using NCSA Telnet to go out onto the Internet to locate useful sources of information for petroleum engineers.

As students saw me using the Internet to verify citations or search in CARL's UnCover, they asked me more and more questions about network use. In early 1992, most of the Internet guides were aimed at those who already had some network skills. The students who had questions needed more than a one-page handout, or an address from which to download Brendan Kehoe's *Zen and the Art of the Internet*.[1] I wrote a guide to the Internet that focused on the information that would be most useful to novice users. *Mary's Quick and Dirty Guide to the Internet for Petroleum Engineers* explained the basics of Telnet and FTP. It also describes interesting sites for reading room users. It eventually grew into a 32-page booklet.

Students and faculty continued to ask me for help in learning to use network tools. I noticed two recurring themes. No one wanted to spend much time on the learning process. New users were overwhelmed by the amount of

1. Brendan P. Kehoe. *Zen and the Art of the Internet: A Beginner's Guide.* (1992) 1st ed.: *ftp.cs.widener.edu/pub/zen/zen-1.0.ps* or *zen-1.0.dvi* or *zen-1.0.tar.Z*

available information. It was not unusual to see students lose interest in the Internet when they took a good look at its breadth and complexity. I decided that setting up an information server that directed my users to key petroleum-related resources was a way to catalog the Internet for their benefit.

Becoming a network publisher

The next tool that I used to discover and organize network information was the University of Minnesota's Internet Gopher (URL: **gopher://gopher.tc.umn. edu/**). Gopher provides a logical menu structure within which to find and arrange information on the Internet. Information on a Gopher server is organized as a hierarchy of nested menus. When a given menu item is opened, it either provides information, or reveals another menu from which to choose a more specific topic. These menus or information files could be located on the same Gopher server, or on another server anywhere in the world. It would be difficult to overstate the assistance that Gopher provides for network travelers. Before Gopher, people who used networks had to know a variety of arcane commands and addresses. Gopher solved this information maze.

I set up a Gopher menu to point students to relevant Gopher sites. This was an alternative to continuing to rewrite and print my network guide. At first, I set up a Gopher server on my Macintosh. But I was never able to get it working satisfactorily. Our computer systems administrator suggested that I put my information on his new Unix server. My information, including the network guide, was incorporated on the departmental Gopher server. Unfortunately this server was set up so that I could not update it myself. The system administrator was too busy to make timely updates. Also I had no access to the server log so I did not know if I was providing a useful service.

Client access to the server was a problem especially during the times, once or twice a year, when I guide students to petroleum-related resources on the Internet. Following this orientation, some students ask to use my Macintosh for their own network exploration. I sometimes let students use my computer. But this is not satisfactory because I end up needing to use it myself.

That's not an indication of a lack of computers in the Department. There are network-connected machines in Departmental computer labs, but these machines are in heavy use. A CD-ROM workstation in the reading room (see Figure 1), featuring an index of papers published by the Society of Petroleum Engineers is heavily used as well. The workstation has been a big success, but it is not yet connected to the Internet. Departmental frustration mounts as some thirty computers await Internet connections.

Figure 1: The screen of the CD-ROM workstation looks like this when a University of Texas General Libraries online public access catalog session is in progress.

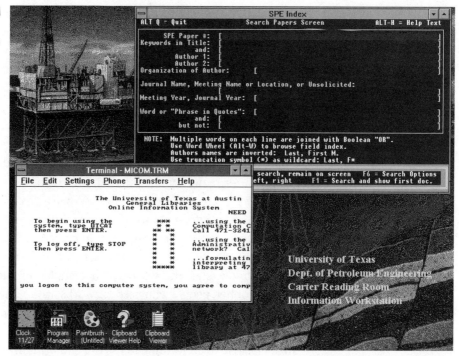

As network tools continued to evolve, I kept looking for ways to make it easier for my patrons to take advantage of the network resources I had located. For example, Gopher clients are easy to use but provide only access to information on Gopher servers. Many of my petroleum-related resources were on other servers using protocols such as FTP, WAIS, and NNTP (network news). In the fall of 1993, I learned about NCSA's Mosaic (URL: **http://www.ncsa.uiuc .edu/**) from a network newsgroup. Mosaic supports multiple Internet protocols so that it can retrieve information from many kinds of network servers. I tried a copy for myself and was very impressed, especially because users would use a single interface to reach network information sources.

In the Web, information access isn't organized by a hierarchy of menus. Web clients, such as Mosaic, can display hypertext documents marked up with HTML tags. HTML (HyperText Markup Language) is based upon the international standard, SGML (Standard Generalized Markup Language). HTML also allows any text or image in a document to designate a link to any other document available on the network. These links could be to text, graphics, sound, video, or any other kind of file. HTML documents are easy to write. The user can follow any cross reference simply by clicking on it. In addition to the older protocols, Web clients support a server protocol called HTTP (HyperText Transfer Protocol) that is optimized for hypertext documents. I found a share-

36

ware HTTP server that would run on my desktop Macintosh (MacHTTP's URL: **http://www.biap.com/**). With its instructions and online HTML guides, I was able to get the server up and running very quickly in June 1994.

After I had organized the server by rewriting my list of petroleum sources with HTML tags, I told my local users about it. The server (see Figure 2) was posted on the University of Texas home page. After the General Libraries put up home pages for their branch libraries in the fall of 1994, the home page was also linked from the Engineering Library home page. Because of the small size of my files and my sparing use of graphics, the operation of the server does not interfere with other uses of the computer.

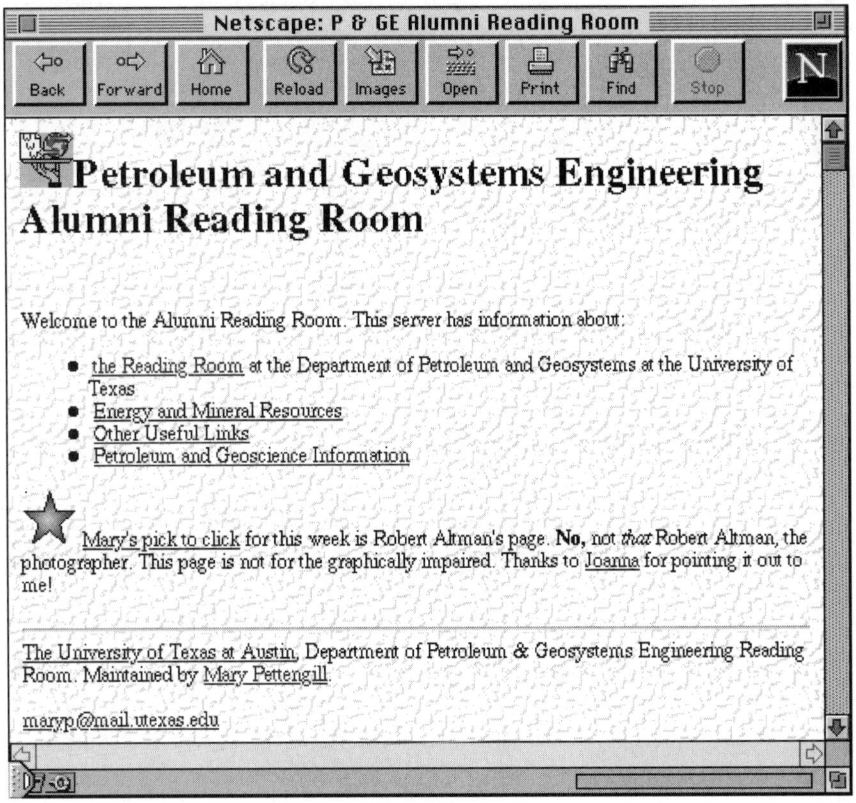

Figure 2: The WWW page with information about the Reading Room (**http://www.pe.texas.edu/ Departmental_Information/ Reading/**).

When the server was listed on such indexes as Yahoo (URL: **http://www. yahoo.com/**) and Carnegie Mellon's Lycos (URL: **http://lycos.cs.cmu.edu**), I began to see users from all over the world, from some 46 different countries. Use has averaged 43 requests per day. Originally, I had expected that the server would be used almost entirely by my own department. That has proved not to be the case; 27 percent of the log entries are from U.S. educational institutions.

The highest number, 29 percent, are from commercial sites, chiefly petroleum companies. From around the world, alumni, other universities, potential donors, and future students have all become users of the server.

As any network user can tell you, maintenance is the key to keeping a server useful. I have found that I must schedule time every week to find new links, check my old links, review the organization of my information, and make updates.

Figure 3: The WWW page that guides users to a variety of petroleum and geosystems engineering resources is constantly being updated.

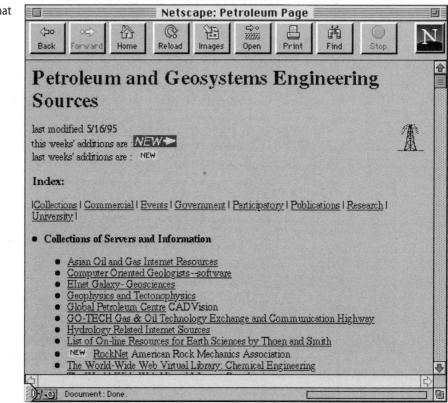

I use the log entries on the server, for example, as a way to locate new interesting resources for my users by following the addresses of those who connect frequently to see if they have good resources on their home servers. The chairman of my department, Larry Lake, has been supportive of my efforts, and has been pleased to see my work recognized and used by others in the field. Early in 1995 the reading room home page was moved to a departmental server. Now I can update my information easily.

38

Future

The tradition of naming years after animals seems appealing and reasonable to me. I named 1993 the year of the Gopher, and 1994 the year of the spider (Web); I am hoping that 1995 is not the year of the (bandwidth) hog, but it is too soon to tell. Network tools have changed and improved more rapidly than most of us could have ever imagined. Right now, organizing information on the Web so that it is helpful to my users is one of my primary goals. But in the future, I want communication to be a two-way street. The increasing popularity of forms prompts me to think that our network should become more interactive. Right now I have one form up on my server, but I am planning on more. I would like to set up a search tool, get requests for interlibrary loans, and collect recommendations for additions to the server as well. Electronic response is starting to come, but only in a small way. For my vision of the future to become a reality, I need to encourage my users to use the Web interactively, and to use it interactively myself.

section two

reach

riding the state and regional networks

• • • • • • *The Statewide Library Electronic Doorway*
(SLED) carries Internet to some 40,000 logins
a month, a model of access for the remote.

reach

Susan Elliott
Steve Smith

Mushing the Net in Alaska

n villages and towns throughout Alaska, where people hop bush planes *the way New Yorkers hail taxis, people ride the Infobahn as easily as their Outside neighbors. Online libraries, state government information, Internet searching, and more are available to most of the 600,000 residents at no charge through SLED, Alaska's Statewide Library Electronic Doorway. A project of the Alaska State Library and Rasmuson Library, University of Alaska Fairbanks, SLED is a connection machine with organized menu access to remote information resources. The advisory group of librarians and public users from around the state who evaluate resources and the well-staffed HELP desk give SLED its customer focus.*

As Information Technology Librarian at the Alaska State Library, **Susan Elliott** provides statewide consulting to libraries. She formerly worked as a systems analyst for California-based library automation vendors Carlyle Systems and Innovative Interfaces. She can be reached at the Alaska State Library, 344 West 3rd Avenue, Suite 125, Anchorage, AK 99501. Phone (907) 269-6567, fax (907) 269-6580, e-mail susane@muskox.alaska.edu

Steve Smith is Associate Director for Computing and Communications at Elmer E. Rasmuson Library, University of Alaska Fairbanks, Fairbanks, AK 99775. Phone (907) 474-6655, fax (907) 474-6841, e-mail steves@muskox.alaska.edu

Wildernet

Ellen Provost lives in Bethel, a community of 5,009 located on the Kuskokwim River in western Alaska. It is a cold, treeless, windy place, catching all the frigid air blowing in from the Bering Sea. It is about as far from the center of the vaunted Information Highway as you can get. In fact, you can't even get to Bethel on a normal concrete highway. There are no roads connecting this community to the rest of the world. Getting in and out of Bethel requires persistence and time and money. But Ellen, and other Bethelites, have local access to the Internet any time of the day, any day of the week for the price of a local phone call.

Figure 1: Map of Alaska overlaid on the United States.

In fact, throughout this large and isolated state, in cities viewed by outsiders as romantic tourist destinations, in villages where people fly as often as New Yorkers take taxis, access to online libraries, to state information, to World Wide Web and Gopher browsers and Internet searching is available to every resident. At no charge to the end user, except for small villages where a toll call is required to connect to any sort of computer network, Alaskans can drive the Infobahn as easily as anyone in California or Maryland, Japan or Germany. The vehicle for this access is SLED, the Statewide Library Electronic Doorway.

What is SLED?

SLED became available at no charge to Alaskan libraries and their patrons (and potential patrons) in April 1994. Developed and funded by the Alaska

State Library and the Elmer E. Rasmuson Library of the University of Alaska Fairbanks, SLED is an easy-to-use computer menu system connecting people to online information from libraries, federal and state government, community networks, and the Internet. SLED was designed to provide organized access to remote information resources. It is the Internet for the rest of us. When you connect to SLED's main menu, you see the subject orientation of the librarians on the statewide SLED Advisory Group.

Figure 2: SLED Opening Menu. For more information, learn more about SLED by visiting **http://sled.alaska.edu/ About_SLED.html**

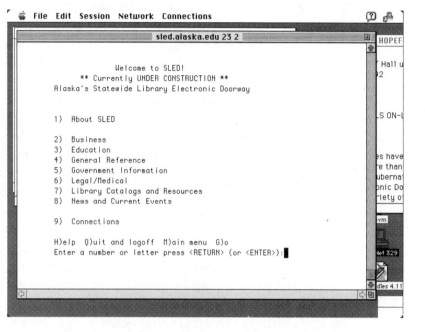

SLED connects to the usual popular Internet sites. Users can check the weather, read U.S. State Department Travel advisories, search articles with CARL's UnCover service, or wander through the Library of Congress. Through an agreement with NorthWestNet (the Internet provider via the University of Alaska), users like Ellen Provost in Bethel can search articles on Education Resources and Information Clearinghouse (ERIC) or Medline, the National Library of Medicine's database of journal articles, at the University of Washington.

Because the Western Library Network (WLN) database is Alaska's *de facto* union catalog, we also pay for a link to WLN's Easy Access. ERIC, Medline and WLN's Easy Access are available only to Alaskan SLED users, not to those who Telnet to SLED from outside Alaska. We'd like to provide more products statewide via SLED and are currently negotiating with vendors such as University Microfilms, Inc. (UMI) for statewide licenses to their databases. We do

45

provide Internet tools to SLED users, such as the Lynx client, a Gopher client, and WebCrawler.

SLED users are anonymous. That is, none of our users, neither librarians nor patrons, have individual accounts on SLED. This keeps access to the system simple. No pre-registration, no setting up accounts. Just visit your local library or dial up the local number to get access. We also intentionally started with a character-based system that works with VT100 emulation. SLED is software and hardware independent. Because of the anonymity of SLED's users, we do not allow open Telnet access *from* the system. We also run our Gopher browser in secure mode and the SLED Web browser in anonymous mode. A separate system called Muskox provides public librarians in Alaska with e-mail and unrestricted Internet tools.

SLED patrons are limited to one hour online per visit. Technically, there is nothing to stop a user from logging back in as soon as the time limit is reached and an automatic logout occurs, but it helps keep people from camping on the system. There is also a built-in time-out for inactivity after ten minutes. As a statewide resource, essentially available to anyone with a computer and modem, we've had to place some limits on sharing the resources. There have been lengthly discussions on what services and systems should be available via SLED. In particular, we ask whether some Internet resources are appropriate for a system as publicly and anonymously accessible as SLED. For example, access to network news, a popular Internet resource, is not available via SLED. There are those who would like SLED to police what users can access, but thus far we've resisted this approach. Sharon West, Director of Libraries at the University of Alaska Fairbanks, says she would rather shut SLED off than go down the path of censorship.

In December 1994, SLED was invaded by hackers who gained root access to the system and began adding programs and modifying system files. System programmers set up a Trojan horse program to catch the intruders. Working closely with the University of Alaska statewide network staff, we were able to trace the hackers to a high school in the state. A call was made to the school. Staff walked down the hall to the school computer lab and found several students logged into SLED. The authorities were notified, and, as this was written, the case was still under investigation.

Meeting monthly by audio teleconference and holding interim discussions on a LISTSERV, the SLED Advisory Group evaluates and tests new resources to add to SLED, debates policy issues that arise, and advises the two funding libraries on SLED matters. The Advisory Group began with 15 public, school, academic, and special librarians from around the state. We are slowly changing

46

the mix to add public members as well, though we are leery of making this working group so large as to be unwieldy. We consider the Advisory Group one of SLED's great strengths. They provide that important value-added component by selecting and organizing quality information resources of statewide interest. The group recently began discussing a formal collection development policy for SLED, a discussion that is proving thorny as we grapple with questions such as "Who is our audience?" and "What about MUDs (Multi-User Dimensions) and IRC (Internet Relay Chat)?"

SLED's contents

Alaskan information is a special focus of SLED. Like community networks before us, we are finding this more difficult than anticipated. Though we've worked hard to provide access to uniquely Alaskan resources, we're a long way from where we'd like to be. SLED links to ALECSYS, the Alaska Legislative Computer System which tracks bills and committee hearings. This system is old and the interface far from satisfactory. The information, however, is crucial to citizens around the state, so we provide the access and lobby in the background for a better system. During the 1994 election, all five candidates for Governor provided position papers on topics of their choosing. We posted these papers on SLED with candidate biographies and statements from a Division of Elections booklet. It proved a popular introduction to electronic democracy. More than 1,500 separate accesses were made to this material in its brief two-month tenure.

In September 1994, Alaska's state government officially connected to the Internet. While the agencies build familiarity with Internet publishing, the State Library is hosting a temporary World Wide Web server for state agency information. Tracy Swaim, Head of Technical Services for the State Library, has learned HyperText Markup Language (HTML). He will consult with state agencies who wish to provide public access to their information on the State's Web server. With budget shortfalls, it's not easy to free up staff time, but State Librarian Karen Crane recognizes that the future of libraries depends on our ability to make such innovative shifts in service.

SLED's use

Alaskan libraries like SLED. At the October 1994 Leadership Institute sponsored by the State Library, public library directors called SLED "the best thing that has happened for Alaska libraries in years." The State Library took the tack of allowing libraries to integrate SLED as they saw fit, at their own pace. From large to little, libraries around the state have been early and enthusiastic adopters. In May 1994, library director Dee McKenna hosted a free community workshop entitled "Internet Access for All" at Nome's Kegoayah Kozga Public Library. It was so successful, she has conducted two more workshops for the citizens of Nome.

Librarians around the state share workshop and handout materials for such efforts. At the Irene Ingle Public Library in Wrangell (population 2,639), director Kay Jabusch offered a workshop for the public and has made SLED available on a terminal in the library. Other libraries around the state, including Anchorage, Haines, Fairbanks, McGrath, and Ketchikan, are providing similar public access to SLED. In Willow, a local computer enthusiast has offered to donate a computer and modem for the library to use as a SLED station. Juneau's Capital City Libraries consortium added SLED as a menu item on all its Dynix terminals around the city. Their popular "Get Wired at the Library" workshops have waiting lists. The latest conversations involve putting SLED terminals in local homeless shelters.

In its short history, SLED has generated plenty of interest from the state news media. Public libraries took advantage of the sample press release provided when SLED went live in April 1994. Our files contain press clippings from Anchorage, Fairbanks, Haines, Juneau, Ketchikan, Nome, Petersburg, Sitka, and Wrangell, as well as the *Los Angeles Times*. TV news broadcasts about SLED in Fairbanks and Anchorage resulted in a flurry of patron calls and visits to local libraries.

SLED's HELP desk

The SLED HELP desk is a popular service. A rotating team of programmers and customer service representatives from the Rasmuson Library answers a statewide 800 telephone number, as well as electronic "Write to SLED" messages (under "About SLED" on the main menu). "Write to SLED" gives users an online option for comments and questions; the Web version of SLED (**http://sled.alaska.edu**) has an online form. We aim for a four-hour turnaround time for answering every message. The public is invariably impressed with the SLED HELP folks, who are friendly, intelligent, and patient. We review the "Write to SLED" comments and bump the policy level questions up for answers. We want to know what SLED users want and need. Future plans call for online surveys and more formal evaluation studies of SLED usage.

Getting to SLED

Because distances make telecommunications such a dominant issue in Alaska, the State Library used Library Services and Construction Act (LSCA) money to fund a direct connection to computers in the public libraries in Anchorage, Fairbanks, and Juneau for high-speed access to SLED. More than half of all Alaskans live in one of these three communities. With the help of the National Telecommunications Infrastructure Awards (NTIA), in partnership with the University of Alaska, we hope to provide high-speed access to several other communities' libraries. This is increasingly important as SLED becomes a World Wide Web server in 1995 and can be accessed by graphical browsers like Netscape Navigator and NCSA Mosaic.

For its first year of existence (1994-95), SLED was available via Telnet from the Internet and via dial-up as a host on Alaska's only X.25 network, AlaskaNet. AlaskaNet serves over 40 communities and about 87 percent of the population statewide with 9600-baud dial-up access. As a result of these connection paths, most libraries and citizens around the state can use computers and modems to connect to SLED without being charged for a long-distance phone call. This is a very popular feature, but an increasingly large chunk of the budget, since SLED pays by the hour for each AlaskaNet connection to the system.

The issue of ongoing telecommunication costs is one of the most threatening we face. We are considering several strategies to reduce our dependence on Alascom (the commercial X.25 provider) while holding firm to our commitment to statewide service. In Fairbanks, the University has initiated a partnership with other local entities, including the local community network, to provide a large, shared modem bank with one well-publicized phone number for public access. In Juneau, the Capital City Libraries, a consortium of University, public, state and school libraries, are increasing their dial-up modems to the online catalog, which includes access to SLED.

SLED's statistics

After nine months of use, we know something about how people use SLED. We respect people's privacy and don't collect information on who uses it. In January 1995, SLED had 33,186 logins, compared to 4,242 logins in May 1994. Considering Alaska's small population (just shy of 600,000), the word is clearly getting out, even if our marketing, except for an initial press release, has been almost nil.

The technical details? SLED runs on a Hewlett-Packard (HP) 9000 G40 at Rasmuson Library, University of Alaska Fairbanks with 128 MB of memory and one gigabyte of disk space, which is mirrored. The operating system is HP-UX. Communications hardware and software are also HP. The system is set to handle 64 concurrent sessions through the X.25 connection. So far, maximum sessions from that source have peaked at 32 and usually run between 15 and 25 sessions.

In addition to the World Wide Web and Gopher clients, SLED's initial incarnation used proprietary menu software developed at Rasmuson Library. Essentially it was a shell script which ran all the connections and masked the operating system from the user. From the beginning SLED has been designed with the average person in mind, the average library patron who may have little or no computer experience. Simplicity, ease of access, and ease of use are the guiding principles.

A place at the table

As the Web server version of SLED was designed, these principles were kept in mind. We started design with a character-based Web version of SLED. The majority of our users, even in many libraries in Alaska, are not yet able to work in a true client-server mode with a graphical interface such as NCSA Mosaic. We have been parsimonious with the images we have put on our graphical Web server. In surveying the Web landscape we found many innovative home pages, some so rich in graphics that access is painfully slow. We are designing alternative views of SLED much more dependent on graphics, but kept our primary home page quite lean and clean of extra flourishes. Our users want access to information; they don't want to see pictures of the programmers' children.

At this juncture, it's hard to predict the future of SLED. As the state gears up its own Internet access, and all the players from the Alaska Public Utilities Commission to the local phone companies agitate for a say in Alaska's telecommunications infrastructure, all we know is that things are bound to change. As State Librarian Karen Crane is fond of saying, "SLED bought libraries a place at the table." Librarians have an important contribution to make in the access to information and universal service debate, and SLED is a good example of "walking our talk."

The Lone Star State became far less lone when library principles were applied to the Net.

Mike Clark
M. Lisa deGruyter

The Texas State Electronic Library

Giving Texans "All They Need to Know" through a Single Source

he Texas State Electronic Library is an Internet information server that enables public libraries throughout Texas to provide their patrons with an organized, efficient and easy-to-use gateway to network information resources. The server is also used by the Texas State Library to make electronic public information available to the citizens and to extend the breadth and access of its own services. As a virtual library, the Electronic Library serves as a laboratory for the application of library science principles to networked information, with the aim of using telecommunications to deliver quality library services to patrons throughout the state. The server's careful organization and wide range of resources and services have helped it grow rapidly into one of Texas' leading information centers.

Mike Clark is the public information officer of the Texas State Library and Archives Commission and the editor of the quarterly magazine *Texas Libraries,* distributed in print and electronically throughout the state and nation. Clark holds degrees in communications theory and media studies from the University of San Francisco and the University of Texas at Austin. Mail to Texas State Library and Archives Commission, Austin, TX 78711-2927.

M. Lisa deGruyter is currently Manager, Electronic Library Services, Automated Information Services, Texas State Library and ArchivesCommission. She has worked in public libraries and regional library systems in West Virginia, Tennessee, and Texas. Most recently, she managed the Texas regional library and interlibrary loan systems. Mail to Texas State Library and Archives Commission, Austin, TX 78711-2927.

Spreading the wealth

The Internet has rapidly transformed from an arcane specialty tool to an essential vehicle for delivering library and information services. It has created a challenging imperative for the Texas State Library, charged with promoting the development of public library services throughout the Lone Star State. The State Library had to find a way to make the information riches of the Internet available, accessible, useful, and valuable to the staff and patrons of Texas' nearly 500 public libraries. Most of these people, in late 1992 when the Electronic Library project was born, had little if any experience with the Internet. Texas' vast distances, geographic dispersion, and traditionally below-median financial support for public libraries made it difficult for many libraries to justify spending scarce resources on a connection to a vague, confusing, and mysterious information network.

The State Library's mission

Beyond its responsibilities to public libraries and their patrons, the State Library also has to meet other information needs. The agency carries a mandate to make public information available to Texas citizens. This mission is fulfilled through a number of programs, including the Texas State Publications Depository Program, participation in the Federal Documents Depository Program, the Texas State Archives, and the State and Local Records Management Program. These activities involve both collecting and distributing government information statewide and making it available from the State Library's own collections, which number in the millions of items.

The State Library's programs and services have worked very effectively to ensure citizen access to public information on paper, in traditional printed formats. As the term "materials" became more commonly replaced by "resources," and more public-sector agencies moved toward paperless publishing, the State Library found it imperative to make electronic public information available to the citizens in a useful way. It also had to allow the State Library's own patron base — historians, genealogists and other researchers, state officials and employees, other Texas libraries, and the citizenry at large — to access the agency's services via the Internet directly.

How it started

In fall 1993, the State Library set out to create with available staff and resources an Internet-based information system that could fulfill the agency's extensive and diverse missions and meet the information needs of the citizens of the second largest state in the Union. This was all the more remarkable given

52

that the library had only automated its catalog a few months earlier, had spent the last ten years functioning in a "no-growth funding climate," and had never employed a staff member who focused exclusively on electronic library services. Even more remarkable was the goal of getting an electronic library off the ground within six months. The Texas State Electronic Library (TSEL), an Internet information server accessible through both Gopher and World Wide Web interfaces, was the result. In less than a year of operation, the Electronic Library has given millions of Texans a practical and efficient gateway to the Internet, provided the state's citizens with extensive access to public information in their homes and in their libraries, and established an admirable presence for the State Library as a networked information provider.

Figure 1: The Texas State Electronic Library can be accessed through both Gopher and World Wide Web clients (**http://links.tsl.texas.gov/**). At present, the services are identical, though the project plans to make use of the graphic and hypertext capabilities of the Web as the server continues to develop. At the time of the Electronic Library's creation, few Texas libraries had the hardware to provide full Web access to their patrons.

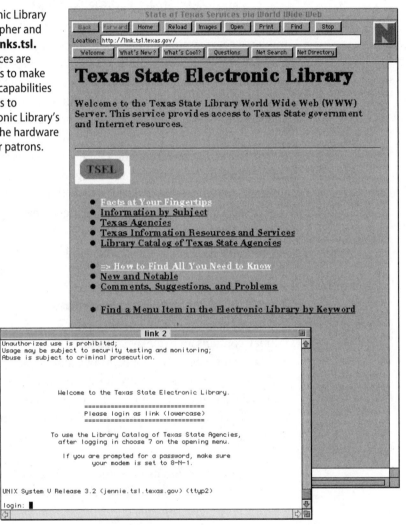

While the Electronic Library aims to serve the needs of information professionals as well as of the citizenry as a whole, each of the project's three goals involves a significant public-access component. These goals are to augment the state's public library services to provide ready access to public information and to expand the capabilities of the State Library's direct services. The majority of the Electronic Library's users are from the general universe of library users. However, State Library patrons were among the first to take advantage of the availability of Internet access to and within the institution, followed by public-information and public-library users.

What is TSEL?

The Electronic Library has provided the State Library with an easy way to consolidate and centralize electronic access to its resources and services. The public-access terminals located within the agency's collections (Reference and Documents, Genealogy, Library Science, Disabilities Reference, and the State Archives) provide patrons with a gateway to both State Library holdings and other resources throughout the network. For example, the agency's newly automated catalog, the Library Catalog of Texas State Agencies (LCTSA), encompasses both State Library and other agencies' holdings. It is available to users on-site via the Electronic Library, as well as via a Z39.50 server. This server allows patrons who are looking for a bibliographic citation on a specific title, but do not need to actually locate it in the holdings, to search LCTSA's bibliographic database without entering the catalog itself. Since the State Library's catalog is, in effect, a master list of everything published by Texas government (including state-supported academic institutions), this capability is a valuable one.

The State Archives comes online

Likewise, as the online home of the Texas State Archives, the Electronic Library contains an extensive selection of indexes and finding aids to the archives collection. That collection numbers many millions of items and includes materials dating from the 17th century through the present day. Bibliographic information for some of the archives' records series has also been included in the catalog. The archives finding aids first appeared in electronic format as part of the Electronic Library collection. The electronic versions have quickly become essential reference tools for patrons (and staff) within the archives reading room itself. Some materials, such as the archives' master list of Republic-era documents and the index to Confederate pension applications,

54

are used exclusively in electronic form. The Electronic Library also contains guides for researchers using both the archives and genealogy collections.

While these resources could certainly have been made available to State Library patrons as stand-alone services unconnected to the Internet, the advantages of providing them on-site through the Electronic Library go beyond the practical simplicities of maintaining one, unified automated information system. Users of these resources find the same information, and can access and use it with the same tools and techniques, whether they're on site, at another library, or working from their desktop. This greatly simplifies the research process for State Library patrons who often find themselves working on tasks at all three places.

Figure 2: The development of the Texas State Electronic Library involved marketing the server to its intended audiences: public libraries, state agencies, and users of State Library and other governmental resources. This figure illustrates the Electronic Library's initial marketing campaign ("Your Link to the Future"), targeted primarily to librarians.

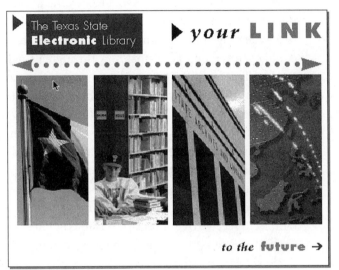

State reference services and resources

The Electronic Library also extends the reach of State Library reference services. Through the server, users can generate electronic mail reference requests to State Library collections and receive replies via e-mail, phone, fax, or photocopy, as appropriate. Users can also generate interlibrary loan requests for items from the State Library collections or obtain e-mail reference service from other sources at the same virtual desk. The project aims to expand this area of service by cooperating with other libraries in various reference specialties, allowing subject experts to serve the entire state.

In addition, by combining State Library resources with others available on the Internet, on-site users can follow links and threads beyond the confines of the State Library without actually leaving the building. For example, if patrons are searching for items not available in the LCTSA, they can search the University of Texas catalog, the Houston Public Library catalog, the catalogs of any other online Texas library, or a number of catalogs from around the world, with a few taps of the arrow keys. Along these lines, the Electronic Library is testing multiple-search tools that allow users to search for information. For instance, the LCTSA holdings are searched via Z39.50, the archives finding aids via WAIS, the server's menu items via Jughead, and the rest of the Internet via Veronica, and the user obtains one menu containing all the relevant links.

State Library patrons can, of course, use the Electronic Library to access Internet versions of materials traditionally included in the agency's collections, such as the *Texas Register*. This highlights the second purpose of the server, a vehicle for accessing electronic public information. Since its inception, the Electronic Library has put special emphasis on providing links to a wide range of Texas and U.S. government resources so that Texas citizens could exercise their right-to-know through a single, centralized, organized service. This is well expressed by the server's slogan, "All You Need to Know" (see Figure 3). Users from outside Texas can also learn what they need to know about the Lone Star State.

This task has been made easier by the increasing amount of public information available electronically, such as GPO Access. This service provides online connections to the *Congressional Record* and *Federal Register*. It is part of the Electronic Library's collection because of the State Library's status as a regional depository within the GPO network. This allows the Electronic Library to receive free subscriptions to GPO Access. While other regional depositories can provide the same service to their patrons, not all of them have established information servers.

The same trend has been seen in Texas government, and in fact has been helped along by the Electronic Library. Several state agencies, such as the Texas Commission on Alcohol and Drug Abuse and the Texas Music Office, have gone online for the first time. Texas was not among the very first state governments to embrace electronic public information. Indeed the Electronic Library was one of the first large-scale Internet projects of a Texas state agency. But the state has done an admirable job of catching up, and the Electronic Library provides citizens with access to most Texas state government information available online.

The virtual library

While several other Texas state agencies have their own servers and aim to provide a broad array of information services to Texans, the Electronic Library

56

Figure 3: This brochure is one of 10 informational pieces aimed at a variety of users of electronic library services.

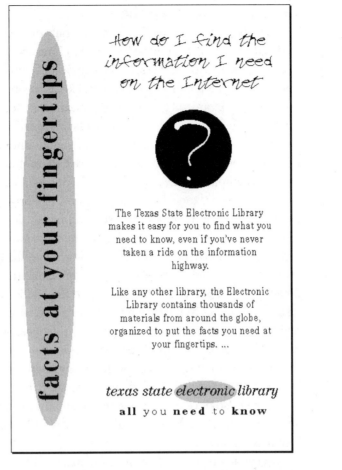

facts at your fingertips

How do I find the information I need on the Internet

?

The Texas State Electronic Library makes it easy for you to find what you need to know, even if you've never taken a ride on the information highway.

Like any other library, the Electronic Library contains thousands of materials from around the globe, organized to put the facts you need at your fingertips. ...

texas state electronic library

all you **need** to **know**

is the only Internet server in Texas that combines both government information and a full range of other kinds of Internet resources into a single, organized interface. This diversity of resources and efficiency of access, along with the State Library's responsibilities to public libraries, have made the Electronic Library an attractive and valuable way for Texas libraries to provide Internet access to their patrons. This, in turn, offers the State Library a way to ensure that citizens without computers or connections are able to use electronic public information.

In spring 1993, no public library in Texas had a direct Internet connection; by spring 1995, over fifty did. Users in many Texas cities and small towns can now walk into their public libraries and use electronic information world-wide through the Electronic Library. Some can dial-up their libraries' catalogs 24 hours a day, and use the Electronic Library through them.

Library principles applied

A basic premise of the Electronic Library project is the application of traditional principles of library science to Internet information. Unlike many Internet information servers, which can best be compared to encyclopedic publications, the Electronic Library is, like other libraries, a collection of publications organized for use. The project adapts collection development, cataloging, reference tools, and methods to the management of networked information sources; takes advantage of new technologies to develop new and improved tools; and distributes the work geographically.

For example, the Electronic Library features a number of adapted and custom electronic tools for acquisition and weeding. The Electronic Library's collection development policy, based on the Association for College and Research Libraries' (ACRL) model, served as a guide to the project staff as they browsed the Internet to build the opening-day collection. At the same time, the project constructed a review collection by automatically converting to Gopher directories server-based subscriptions to electronic lists highlighting new resources, such as Net-Happenings and NEWNIR-L. This allows users to review the featured resources and, if they so chose, build bookmarks to link to them. The Electronic Library uses such bookmarks to add items both to its subject collections and to its New Items shelf. Users can request specific items by filling out an e-mail request form accessible through the server itself. The project has also developed software which periodically checks selected sources on the Internet for subject-specific resources and automatically updates the Electronic Library's subject collections.

Serials acquisitions are more complicated. The server is subscribed to several hundred mailing lists dealing with library and information science, disabilities, networked information, and government. Project staff are still working to solve issues related to check-in, claiming, and subscription renewal. Since most electronic serials are irregular, and vary in frequency from more than daily to quarterly, devising a way to allow the computer to decide when new issues should have been received is difficult. These serials have one great advantage: they shelve themselves when they arrive!

The other half of collection development is weeding. The Internet changes rapidly. Links to remote resources may suddenly stop working. Each link must be tested, which is time-consuming. Recently installed software checks the Electronic Library's links and returns trouble reports; the project is developing software to allow staff to easily examine these dead links and either to restore or discard the items. However, it takes the better part of a week merely to check the entire collection, let alone weed it.

58

The Electronic Library's two major organizational tools are the menu hierarchy (equivalent to shelf order), and keyword indexing of the menu titles (an inadequate analog of the catalog). Subject classification of networked resources is just as labor-intensive as it is for physical materials. Descriptive cataloging is even more so, since most resources do not have a statement of responsibility, publication date, or even a standard title. Currently, the project's lack of cataloging staff has hindered attempts to develop authority files, or to assign Dewey Decimal numbers and subject headings to items in the collection, although the project has developed software to partially automate the latter task. Menu titles are assigned with keyword searching in mind (for example, prefacing all Texas state agency titles with "Texas"). Multiple-search tools, when properly tuned and aimed at particular sets of selected resources, based on subject and user, should be an effective way to build expert knowledge of the resources into the system in lieu of complete subject classification and indexing. But the latter will be needed throughout the Internet for users to make full and convenient use of electronic resources.

The Electronic Library's successes are not potential but actual, with more than 500 users a day accessing over 7,500 files. Both of these figures have tripled in the last six months of 1994. For a new and untried project, seeking to serve an audience with little exposure to the Internet, operating with limited resources in general and almost no resources to devote to promotion and awareness, the Electronic Library has within 12 months become a popular and respected element of Texas' information services. This speaks to the need for libraries to be involved in shaping Internet information resources and their delivery.

One of the catch phrases used to market the Electronic Library to the Texas library community is that the server "organizes the Internet so that you don't have to." In Texas, four out of five public libraries serve less than 25,000 people, but together these libraries serve more than 5 million people. Two out of three public libraries do not employ a librarian with an American Library Association-accredited master's degree. It was clear from the beginning of the Electronic Library project that in order for local library users and local governments to be convinced that the Internet was worth the trouble, the server would have to quickly, easily and effectively deliver information. Since 90 percent of public library funding comes from these users, the Electronic Library had to be more than a gateway to a chaotic and ill-defined network they had no idea how to navigate.

Conclusion

The success of the Electronic Library would seem to indicate that the server's organization is an effective one. The project is a product of library science, not rocket science. Most Texas libraries do not yet have the time, money or training to organize the Internet individually for their patrons. Though the Electronic Library's missions are resolutely practical, the project also has a theoretical dimension. As a work-in-progress, it aims to illustrate how the principles of librarianship are uniquely suited to working with networked information. The Internet provides a means for all libraries to broaden the availability, accessibility, and use not only of the materials themselves, but of the services that librarians provide that make that information useful and valuable to the citizens.

This award-winning effort is a model for both its solved problems and unresolved issues.

Rivkah K. Sass

Maryland's Sailor Project
A Library Gateway for Statewide Access to the Internet

 his chapter provides background on the Sailor Project initiated by the Maryland State Department of Education's Division of Library Development and Services. The project was developed as a statewide information access service and gateway to Internet resources, available to libraries and citizens throughout Maryland via a local telephone connection. The Maryland library community shares a vision to implement a service that will ultimately local, state, federal and worldwide resources to all communities in the state. Libraries play a crucial role in accessing electronic information.

Rivkah K. Sass has worked in and with public libraries since 1978 in a variety of positions. Prior to moving to Maryland in 1994, she contributed in the Washington State Library's effort to provide Internet training and access to public and community college librarians throughout Washington state, serving as a trainer and mentor in the Washington Libraries' Internet Project. She is currently chief of the Public Libraries and State Networking Branch, Division of Library Development and Services, Maryland State Department of Education, 200 W. Baltimore Street, Baltimore, MD 21201. Phone (410) 767-0443, fax (410) 333-2507, e-mail rs207@umail.umd.edu

reach

How Sailor began

Several years ago, a group of Maryland librarians met to discuss the future of the state library network. Included in that discussion were the hows, whys, and whos of interlibrary loan; continued cooperation among libraries; new services to the public; and how the network might look in the 21st century. Librarians, representing the division's various customer groups, were brought together by the Maryland State Department of Education's Division of Library Development and Services (DLDS). They discussed and debated new ways of delivering library services and developed a document called *Toward the Year 2000*.[1]

The Network Coordinating Council, a volunteer group of public, academic, special and school libraries, began meeting in 1990 to discuss possibilities for using new technologies effectively and to plan the future. What evolved from the planning discussions, debates, and visions was Sailor, a project of the Maryland library community to provide Internet access to the citizens of Maryland via a local telephone call.

How did a dream for creating a virtual library result in a telecommunications network stretching from the Chesapeake Bay to the border of West Virginia? What made it possible for users to connect to the Internet via a local call and browse through diverse information resources using a Gopher server? The simple answers are serendipity, cooperation, and good planning. The longer explanation reveals the spirit of cooperation that has previously established Maryland's reputation as "library heaven."

During summer 1992 the Seymour Working Group developed a plan for creating an electronic infrastructure linking libraries and users to information resources within and beyond the boundaries of Maryland.[2] *The Seymour Plan*, as it was named, called for the creation of a telecommunication backbone, allowing for local telephone access to nodes established throughout the state.[3] The plan also called for the use of fax and electronic mail to enhance communication among the libraries for resource sharing, for the development of community resources accessible to all, and for the system to serve as a gateway to Internet resources using the well-established Gopher protocol.

The reality of funding a project of this size prompted the Division of Library Development and Services to meet with Maryland's public library administrators. At this meeting, these administrators discussed the possibility of pooling a year's worth of Library Services and Construction Act (LSCA) funds in order to benefit all libraries and all communities. It is a testament to the cooperative spirit of Maryland's public libraries that this was resolved quickly and painlessly despite the fact that it meant a year with no competitive grants for special projects.

1. *Toward the Year 2000: A Strategic Plan for the Maryland State Library Network* (Baltimore: Maryland State Department of Education, Division of Library Development and Services, 1989).

2. Sailor's original name was to be Seymour but a trademark conflict resulted in a new name early in 1994.

3. The Seymour Plan, prepared by the Seymour Working Group (Baltimore: Maryland State Department of Education, Division of Library Development and Services, 1992).

The Sailor pilot test

Work toward making Sailor a reality began in earnest that fall. Several task groups were formed to plan for the various components of implementation. Among them were Find a Book, Internet, Interface, Grants and Development, and Marketing. However, it was the team known as "Network Cloud" that worked especially diligently during this time. "Network Cloud" designed the telecommunications backbone that made Sailor a reality. Staff from the University of Mary-

Figure 1: Maryland's "Lemon Law" is available in full text for Sailor users (**gopher://sailor. lib.md.us/00/FindInfo/.leg/ .law**).

```
                        Netscape: .lemon_law

  Back   Forward  Home   Reload  Images   Open   Print   Find   Stop      N


State of Maryland


MARYLAND'S LEMON LAW


A Guide to Consumer Rights and Remedies When a New Car Turns Out
to be Defective


Prepared by the
Department of Legislative Reference
Annapolis, Maryland


For additional copies of this pamphlet, please contact:

Library and Information Services Division
Department of Legislative Reference
90 State Circle
Annapolis, MD  21401
410-841-3810 (Baltimore/Annapolis area)
301-858-3810 (Washington, D.C. area)
1-800-492-7122 (Other areas)
410-841/301-858-3814 (TTY for Deaf)
Maryland Relay Service: 1-800-735-2258


In 1984 the General Assembly enacted the Maryland Automotive
Warranty Enforcement Act more commonly known as "The Lemon
Law." This law provides consumers with a number of rights and

  Document: Done.
```

land at College Park lent expertise, working with team members from the Enoch Pratt Free Library and the Division of Library Development and Services. The University of Maryland staff helped negotiate tariffs, determined the basic structure for transmission, and served as guides in uncharted territory.

It was determined that a pilot project would help in the planning process. Again the University of Maryland offered assistance, making available a Gopher server on which to mount "The Puppy," a testbed for staff and volunteers to load documents.[4] From this experience, they were able to determine the kinds of information that would be most helpful in establishing statewide access to information. The Puppy included documents relevant to the project, information such as Maryland's Lemon Law for automobile owners (see Figure

---

4. The original Seymour logo was a Chesapeake Bay retriever, a dog much loved in Maryland. It provided a whimsical but accurate representation as Maryland's "information retriever."

1), state agency telephone numbers, and of course, pointers to Gopher servers around the world. The Puppy was available to staff and task group volunteers via dial-in or Telnet, and to the greater world through Gopher access. Users were invited to react to the pilot via the "feedback please" mechanism, allowing planners to improve the system as it was being built.

A very important component in the success of the development of Sailor was an ever increasing public awareness about the information superhighway. A timely article in the *Baltimore Sun* appeared in November 1993, heralding the imminent arrival of Internet access for Marylanders. This resulted in many telephones calls and increased interest in the project's progress both from citizens and government agencies anxious to know more about the Sailor Project.

A front-page article in the *Washington Post* in June 1994 brought even more attention to Sailor, coming at such a time that it was both a blessing and a curse. Being in the news assured interest and success as the July implementation day approached. But that day was met with anxiety by libraries whose customers fully expected to have access in July that would not be available until much later. It was also during this period that some private Internet providers reacted to the news that Internet access would be "free" for all Marylanders. As the debate ensued, with cries of "foul" being uttered by providers, others expressed bewilderment at the fuss being made.

The staff of the project often stated that Sailor was a catalyst that would assure Maryland libraries a place in the future as information providers. This became more evident as Sailor went public in summer 1994. Some libraries added local funds to the project to increase the number of incoming lines available to the public. Libraries also worked to establish richer resources. Notable in these efforts were the Harford County Library, which worked with local officials to offer a variety of information via Sailor (URL: **gopher:// sailor.lib.md.us:70/11/CommInfo/Harford**), and the Carroll County Library, which worked to establish itself as the primary access point to local government information (URL: **gopher://sailor.lib.md.us:70/11/CommInfo/Carroll**). In November 1994 officials approved a proposal making Sailor the primary access point to the National Information Infrastructure (see Figure 2). These efforts to institutionalize Sailor within the local government structure have been met with enthusiasm and a desire to continue inventing the future.

Sailor's debut

Sailor went public on July 27, 1994, when the telephone number into the Enoch Pratt Free Library, Sailor's official home, was announced. Soon thereafter Sailor was accessible through sites around the state. Ten libraries were up and running by year's end, and complete implementation was scheduled for summer of 1995.

As Sailor was making its debut as a public information project, the discussion about its ultimate governance was lively indeed. The Network Coordinating Council, responsible for the concept and implementation of Sailor, created a subcommittee to study the issue of governance and to determine who should be involved with the running of Sailor. This was particularly interesting because Sailor was already installed on a server at the Enoch Pratt Free Library, Maryland's State Library Resource Center. Also complicating matters was the fact that the funds for the design and implementation of Sailor came from the state's portion of LSCA funds, the lion's share of which is designated for the development of public library services. Because Sailor had been a truly collaborative effort, it was recommended that governance be shared among all types of libraries including public, academic, and school libraries, with representatives from institutional and special libraries also participating.

After a great deal of debate, it was determined that because Sailor was really a pilot project, a formal governance structure would inhibit rather than enhance its development. Therefore, decisions regarding its growth and development would continue to be made by DLDS and staff at the Enoch Pratt Free Library.

Training

Essential to the sustained growth and success of Sailor is acceptance by front-line staff working in Maryland's libraries. These are the people who field the questions coming in from a public curious to know more and wishing to have access to the information superhighway. To that end a task group focusing on training was assembled to implement the suggestions made by an earlier task group working on Internet access. These volunteers, once again working with DLDS staff, developed a plan for training the hundreds of people who would ultimately need to know how to use Sailor and who would need to share their expertise with other library staff, government officials, students and the public. Borrowing from an idea developed by the Colorado State Library, it was decided to train a core group of master trainers who would receive intensive training both in using Sailor and in how to train others.

Nominations were sought, applications accepted, and fifty people were selected to receive several days of training, which included information on how to train others, how to access important Sailor resources, and how to develop effective training materials. Training also included a "dress rehearsal" in front of a video camera to allow for effective critiquing of presentation style. Master

65

Figure 2: The Sailor Gopher (URL: **gopher://sailor.lib.md.us**) provides Marylanders community information, Internet resources, state directories, and even the schedule for Maryland Public TV.

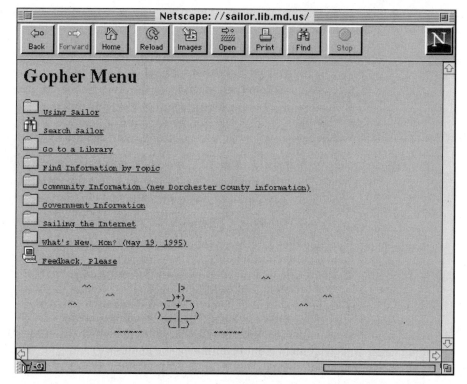

trainers came from all types of libraries and from all geographic regions in the state. All agreed to share the expertise gained with their home systems as well as with libraries requesting assistance. An excellent training manual provided the basic information needed. Trainers also developed specialized modules to be shared with others. Modules on basic Internet skills, using Sailor, and the Internet in reference services are currently under construction.

While the master training was being developed, it became clear that a stop gap was needed to meet immediate needs. Working with staff from the College of Library and Information Services at the University of Maryland, a small group of interested librarians developed what they called a module for "quick and dirty" Sailor training. These were sessions designed to give people basic information on the use of Sailor, the confidence to explore, and the skills to become effective users. These sessions were presented over a period of just a few weeks, and were specifically targeted to libraries whose Sailor connections were already up and running.

Marketing is also an essential aspect of the Sailor Project. The Sailor Marketing Task Group established a regular information mailing to interested stake holders. About 600 packets are mailed out every other month. Last summer volunteers and staff spent two days demonstrating Sailor and providing informa-

Figure 3: The Maryland Free home page provides users with access to various World Wide Web servers throughout Maryland.

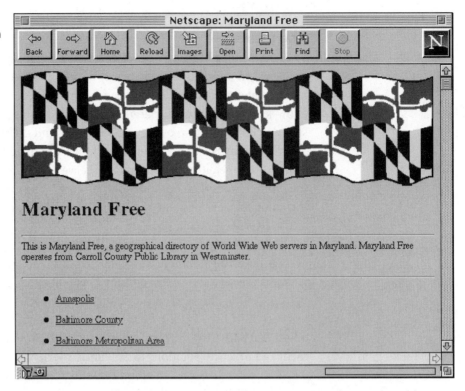

tion to county officials around the state at their annual conference. In addition, a short video, *Sailor: Maryland's On-ramp to the Information Highway*, was produced to provide an overview for training opportunities and to share with community groups, funding agencies and government officials. While initially planned by members of the training task group, it has become an effective marketing tool providing a somewhat light-hearted look at the possibilities Sailor presents to its users, while still imparting essential information.

Sailor was designed to provide basic access to the Internet using Gopher. As such, it does not take advantage of more robust Internet tools such as Mosaic, a graphical interface used to browse World Wide Web resources. However, in keeping with the spirit of innovation that is part of the philosophy of DLDS and Maryland libraries, additional pilot projects with the Maryland State Archives and the Carroll County Public Library are underway. We are developing Web servers to archival information. In the case of Carroll County, we are demonstrating library-government cooperation to local citizens (see Figure 3). Carroll County Public Library's Web server is designed to allow other libraries to replicate its success. Its home page and other HyperText Markup Language (HTML) pages include numerous pointers to the tools necessary for developing a Web server as well as information on how to train staff to create one.

The future

Still to come in Sailor's development is the interlibrary loan component that sparked the vision for a new way of doing business among libraries. Staff and volunteers are eagerly searching for that perfect seamless interface that will allow searching among disparate catalogs, and a one-touch button allowing staff and end users to request items from around the state or around the globe. The final result is yet unknown, but there are high hopes that a Z39.50 interface will provide the ultimate solution and serve as a model for others. In the meantime, any and all possible solutions are being explored and debated, including the development of a World Wide Web Common Gateway Interface to the diverse OPACs in the state.

Sailor is being embraced by the citizens it was designed to serve. An average day brings in more than 20,000 logins and growth has been steady. Analysis of usage shows that about 12 percent of Sailor's users go directly to the option, "Sailing the Internet," and out to the network from there. A help desk has been established at the Pratt Library, and two full-time staff working with additional part-time staff have their hands full providing advice, encouragement and practical solutions to new and experienced users.

The Sailor Project is an ambitious effort that is designed to accomplish several goals. It is essential that citizens in all communities have access to basic electronic information resources. Sailor will make that happen, as it brings the world of the Internet to the child in Accident, Maryland, as well as the state legislator in Annapolis. It provides a basic level of access for all, but one that can also be scaled to meet different needs for different communities. Sailor is the platform on which a variety of services will be built, not just those that help libraries do business more effectively, but also services that will enhance the lives of citizens, providing them with the opportunity to access resources formerly available only to more sophisticated users. Sailor has the potential to allow Marylanders to participate more fully in their communities, and certainly to have a world of information available at the touch of a keystroke. We believe that it will equip our citizens with the tools they need to conduct the daily business of living as well as satisfy their educational, recreational and information needs.

Unresolved issues

There are certainly issues that are yet unresolved. Unless state funding becomes a reality, Sailor's future is uncertain. LSCA took care of start up costs, but ongoing growth and development of the network, as well as staffing and other components require continued support. Sailor staff and volunteers are optimistic that Sailor will prove to be so useful that its funding will be assured, but given these uncertain times, there are no guarantees.

There are ongoing issues as we make Sailor fully operational. Most library systems use turnkey systems for automation and have little or no experience with systems administration as it relates to Internet access. Concerns have been expressed about the types of electronic materials so readily available to children. Staff are often asked about children accessing pornography or other materials deemed inappropriate for young eyes. The issue of libraries becoming Internet providers and charging for electronic mail, FTP, and Telnet access is a topic of continuing debate. And of course the governance issue unresolved a year ago is still unresolved today.

Another source of both joy and frustration is the feeling that Sailor represents a bleeding edge project for libraries. Networking is not new, nor is the desire to provide free access to citizens. However, the models that we have found on the Net are mostly those of local or regional areas. The reality of attempting to create a community network that extends beyond the usual geographic boundaries has been both exhilarating and frustrating. There would be less of a learning curve if more projects of its type were in progress along the highways and byways of the information superhighway. The opportunity to share the ups and downs with other libraries would be helpful.

Conclusion

The fruitful efforts of the Maryland library community to establish a statewide electronic information system are increasingly being recognized. In February 1995 Sailor staff were informed that the Maryland library community was to receive the 1995 James Madison Award from the American Library Association and the Coalition on Government Information for its work to bring local, state and federal information to the citizens of Maryland.

It is too soon to predict the impact that Sailor will have on Maryland. Staff and volunteers are examining early use statistics, hearing feedback from users, and assessing the results. We are interested in several questions: Will it make a difference to students and their information-seeking behavior? How will it affect the lives of rural Marylanders? Will it help local businesses and the local economy? Will libraries be viewed as more essential to their communities? Will libraries not be needed now that electronic resources are ubiquitous? We don't have the answers to these questions yet, but we are examining ways to gather the information that will help us plan our future as well as serve as a model for other libraries.

69

As we think about what success will look like for Sailor, we dream of a Sailor with adequate bandwidth to allow for growth and exploration of new and emerging technologies, of users who are information literate and understand how to make full use of the resources at their fingertips, and of libraries positioned as leaders in the electronic age as information centers essential to their communities. We think of a service that is crucial to government agencies and other funding bodies and one that has been integrated fully into citizens' perceptions of what having access to information means. We want every person who connects to Sailor to see the message, "A Project of the Maryland Library Community," and to understand that his or her local library is responsible for making this remarkable tool available.

To its thousands of dial-in and walk-in users, the consortium's new Internet connection looks deceptively simple. Here are the labors and costs behind that happy deception.

reach

Gerald M. Furi
Christine Lind Hage
Stephen A. Kershner

Metro Net Library Consortium

A Model of Public Libraries as Internet Providers in Michigan

even Michigan public libraries have formed Metro Net, a consortium, to acquire and share information resources electronically by implementing emerging technologies. A major consideration was connectivity to the Internet. This chapter details the process from choice of provider, equipment and costs, staffing and training, to system security and most importantly, public use and reaction to the Metro Net Gopher. Following this model, public libraries can become effective participants with their communities in the global information infrastructure.

Gerald M. Furi is Assistant Director at the Farmington Community Library in Farmington Hills, Michigan. He made an 180 degree turn from music to library science at the end of the 1970s. He conceptualized Metro Net and was the Project Manager. He now functions as the System Administrator. He can be reached at the Farmington Community Library, 32737 West 12 Mile Road, Farmington Hills, MI 48334-3302. Phone (810) 553-0300, e-mail gmf@metronet.lib.mi.us

Christine Lind Hage is the Director of the Rochester Hills Public Library. She has been a public librarian since 1971. She has served on the boards of the Michigan Library Association and the Public Library Association. She is a frequent contributor to several Internet LISTSERVs. She can be reached at the Rochester Hills Public Library, 500 Olde Towne Road, Rochester, MI 48307-2043. Phone (810) 650-7122, e-mail hagec@metronet.lib.mi.us

Stephen A. Kershner is Director, Bloomfield Township Public Library, 1099 Lone Pine Road, Bloomfield Hills, MI 48302-2410. Phone (810) 642-5800, e-mail kershnes@metronet.lib.mi.us

In 1993, seven public libraries in Oakland and Wayne Counties formed a new regional network to initiate technology projects for resource sharing. Metro Net Library Consortium (Metro Net), a Michigan nonprofit corporation, was born to take advantage of network pricing, grant opportunities, and to have a streamlined, workable governance structure.[1] The seven charter members were the Baldwin (Birmingham) Public Library, Bloomfield Township Public Library, Canton Public Library, Farmington Community Library, Independence Township Public Library, Rochester Hills Public Library, and Southfield Public Library. West Bloomfield Township Public Library joined as a subscriber in 1994. With ten facilities, the eight public libraries serve 500,000 people in 20 communities in southeastern Michigan.

Choice of provider

The Metro Net libraries wanted to establish a high-speed telecommunications network as the backbone for providing electronic resource sharing and information access for their patrons. The Metro Net libraries selected Merit Network, Inc. of Ann Arbor as the network provider. Merit brought a wealth of experience as a maintainer of NSFnet for several years. It provided Metro Net with the complete package of services, hardware, and software to get a metropolitan area network up and running. Additionally, Merit's MichNet subsidiary offered free dial-in access from almost any point in the state, translating a serial communication session from a home or office personal computer into a TCP/IP session without requiring SLIP or PPP.

We decided, in consultation with Merit, to implement a completely menu-driven system. Front-end menus were written by Merit in Perl, a Unix programming language. The Main User Menu (see Figure 1) provides basic Internet access to: electronic mail, available to staff only at present; Metro Net Gopher; World Wide Web servers; Anonymous FTP, Gopher and Web connections to addresses of choice; Lynx, the character-based Web browser; Telnet connections into the online catalogs of Metro Net member libraries; Telnet connections into external databases (for example, OCLC's First Search) to which member libraries subscribe; and a basic suite of menu choices of common Unix utilities (so users need not worry about Unix syntax or command prompts).

The technological underpinnings of Metro Net include the following and are described here to assist other libraries to emulate this model. Merit specialists configured a Sun SPARCstation 10/40 as the host machine. A Cisco 2500 router with a pair of DSU/CSUs was installed at each of the participating library sites. Each site is connected to the central host on an Ameritech 56 kbps

---

1. For more information on Metro Net, send electronic mail to: helpdesk@metronet.lib.mi.us

Figure 1: The welcoming screen of the Metro Net Staff Menu points to the major services available.

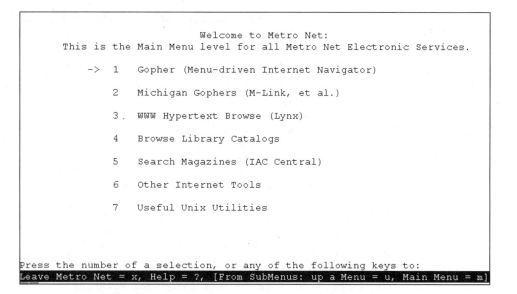

```
                        Welcome to Metro Net:
          This is the Main Menu level for all Metro Net Electronic Services.

          ->  1    Gopher (Menu-driven Internet Navigator)

              2    Michigan Gophers (M-Link, et al.)

              3.   WWW Hypertext Browse (Lynx)

              4    Browse Library Catalogs

              5    Search Magazines (IAC Central)

              6    Other Internet Tools

              7    Useful Unix Utilities



Press the number of a selection, or any of the following keys to:
Leave Metro Net = x, Help = ?, [From SubMenus: up a Menu = u, Main Menu = m]
```

data circuit. A central Cisco 4GS+ router was installed. The basic topology is a modified star with an Ameritech Frame-Relay connection to the Merit high-speed backbone. A block of C Class Internet IP addresses was obtained from InterNIC for Metro Net use. For the first 18 months, Merit agreed to provide Domain Name Services for Metro Net.

It took about three months to get all the sites up and running. By May 1994, Metro Net was a functioning entity on the Net. In October, we brought up our own fairly sophisticated Gopher server for in-consortium use. In March 1995, the server was registered for external access. All access to Metro Net services is obtained through free user accounts provided by the consortium. Our Gopher (see Figure 2) and Web (see Figure 3) servers are accessible at the following URLs: **gopher://metronet.lib.mi.us** and **http://198.111.64.10/**. VT100 Telnet service is also offered at **telnet://metronet.lib.mi.us** (login as "public" with password "library").

Working with library automation vendors

When Metro Net was being brought online in early 1994, most library automation vendors were just beginning to offer Internet connectivity. Nevertheless, the Metro Net libraries decided to place their library automation systems on the menu system offered to users. This decision was more difficult because the Metro Net libraries employed Dynix at four sites, Innovative Interfaces at two sites, and CLSI at two sites. In order to have the system function smoothly, it was decided that a second Gopher server, triggered from

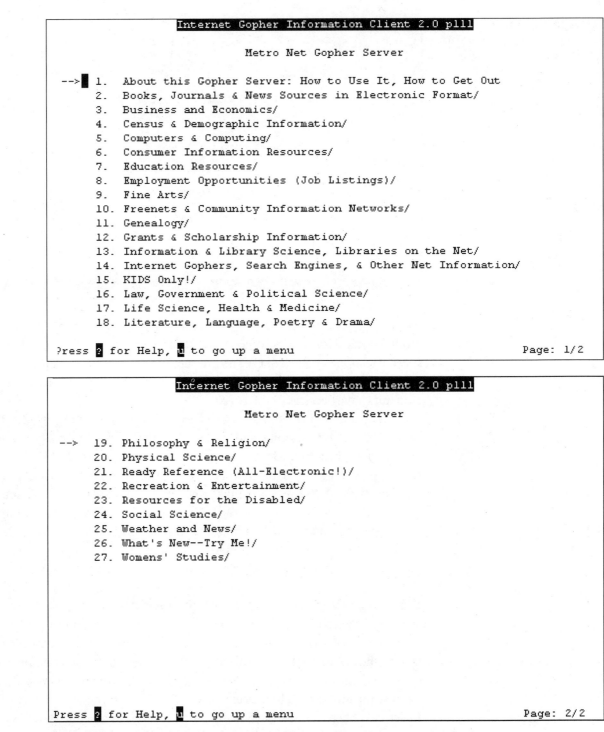

```
Internet Gopher Information Client 2.0 p111

                  Metro Net Gopher Server

  --> 1.  About this Gopher Server: How to Use It, How to Get Out
      2.  Books, Journals & News Sources in Electronic Format/
      3.  Business and Economics/
      4.  Census & Demographic Information/
      5.  Computers & Computing/
      6.  Consumer Information Resources/
      7.  Education Resources/
      8.  Employment Opportunities (Job Listings)/
      9.  Fine Arts/
      10. Freenets & Community Information Networks/
      11. Genealogy/
      12. Grants & Scholarship Information/
      13. Information & Library Science, Libraries on the Net/
      14. Internet Gophers, Search Engines, & Other Net Information/
      15. KIDS Only!/
      16. Law, Government & Political Science/
      17. Life Science, Health & Medicine/
      18. Literature, Language, Poetry & Drama/

Press ? for Help, u to go up a menu                    Page: 1/2
```

```
Internet Gopher Information Client 2.0 p111

                  Metro Net Gopher Server

  --> 19. Philosophy & Religion/
      20. Physical Science/
      21. Ready Reference (All-Electronic!)/
      22. Recreation & Entertainment/
      23. Resources for the Disabled/
      24. Social Science/
      25. Weather and News/
      26. What's New--Try Me!/
      27. Womens' Studies/












Press ? for Help, u to go up a menu                    Page: 2/2
```

Figure 2: The top level menu of the Metro Net Gopher Server lists 27 starting points for the user.

74

the main menu, would open Telnet connections to each of the library systems via an IP address assigned to each library automation system's minicomputer. Thus each machine had to be given an IP address on the Metro Net system in addition to whatever networking the mini used to talk to the terminals and personal computers that were networked directly to it.

In this situation, GEAC/CLSI proved the most difficult system with which to work. On the other hand, the Dynix Gateway software handled access smoothly, and even provided a "back door" into Metro Net via its own menus. The Dynix IBM RS6000 computers were very easy to work with, and configuration was accomplished and tested within a few weeks. Innovative handled access in its own way, with all configuration done remotely by Innovative Interfaces technicians.

To provide access in the local library, each automation system minicomputer includes an Ethernet card, which places the machine on an internal Metro Net Ethernet at each site. A flaw in this approach was that certain low end terminals could not support VT100 emulation, which is necessary for Net access. Personal computers with Ethernet cards and TCP/IP software were much more successful.

Central site costs

Metro Net members decided to implement Internet host services as well as to provide basic connectivity to the Net. The cost of technology changes so rapidly that the figures cited here are based on data that has already changed. Only the range of costs for a project of this scope can be given.

The total start-up costs for the central site came to nearly $20,000 and included a SPARCstation 10, a DAT tape backup unit, associated programming and setup costs, rudimentary systems administration training, the Cisco 4GS+ router, and a pair of DSU/CSUs. In the second year of operation, RAM on the SPARCstation was expanded, additional drives were added, and a final version of the Sun operating system was installed. These enhancements cost approximately $13,000. Metro Net also opened a hardware/software maintenance contract with Sun Microsystems, costing $2,500. Additional central site costs to be incurred relate to system security, installation of a firewall server, "choke" routers, and the closure of security loopholes in the Sun operating system and Internet services software (Gopher, FTP, Telnet, and httpd).

System administration

Metro Net was consciously designed to have no staff and offices; it is a virtual consortium. Nevertheless, a metropolitan network providing a full spectrum of Internet services requires someone to administer the software and the central site hardware. The System Administrator worked full-time on the setup for approximately the first year. Fifteen hours a week are required to administer the project on an ongoing basis. The System Administrator helps users; adds and removes users; adds, configures, and removes hardware within the central site; installs new software; maintains and enhances the Metro Net menu system, as well as the Gopher and Web servers; keeps abreast of new Gopher and Web sites; adds links to the servers; and maintains central site usage statistics. The administrator also monitors the system and does trouble-shooting at the central site; maintains local documentation; audits and monitors the system security; and acts as the postmaster for the system.

Individual library costs

There are two sets of costs for Metro Net libraries. The start-up costs ($15,000) included Merit affiliation fees, on-site equipment network monitoring, equipment installation, a router, a pair of DSU/CSUs, a 56 kbps data circuit and a share of central site costs for each library. Overall Metro Net costs totaled $130,000 for the central site and seven libraries at eight sites. A second cost is ongoing telecommunications and maintenance. It varies from library to library depending on how many access points they desire and the ability of existing systems to support Internet access. The second year telecommunications and maintenance costs are expected to be $10,000 for each library. Future costs for faster lines such as T-1, more sophisticated security software and telephone modem pools will increase that cost by $5,000–$10,000 per member.

Local library staffing needs

Although all Metro Net libraries have the same level of access to the Internet, each library has been responsible for its own internal equipment purchases, and staff and public user training. Each site designates a site coordinator responsible for hardware, telecommunications and local area network (LAN) troubleshooting. In many cases, this is the same person who coordinates staff training in the local library.

Once the hardware was installed and running, in-house staff training started. It has proven to be very successful and a tremendous morale boost. Many staff members did not know what the Internet was, so a series of classes (Introduction to the Internet, Introduction to E-Mail, Introduction to Gophers, Introduction to World Wide Web) were offered. Staff reaction to the classes has been fantastic! In the eight libraries, over 400 staff members have completed the classes, which are offered as a staff training benefit. Many staff successfully use

76

electronic mail, sign up for LISTSERVs and practice Internet surfing. Online discussion groups have been set up for youth service, adult reference and readers' advisory librarians.

System security

Security is a primary consideration when running basic Internet services. There are three primary areas of concern: threats from outside the network; threats from abuse by users; and security "holes" present in the Sun operating system, Gopher, httpd, Telnet, FTP, e-mail, etc. In late 1994, Metro Net experienced an attack by a cracker. Cleaning up after the attack, restoring services and implementing preliminary enhanced safeguards to forestall future attacks took several weeks of intensive system work. The mass media is full of accounts of systems being compromised, almost on a daily basis. Public-access systems such as Metro Net are often vulnerable.

Metro Net has implemented enhanced security measures. A firewall server and appropriate security software has been installed, addressing the external threat. Two "choke" routers protect the library automation systems from "back door" invasions via Telnet. Users now have contracts making them accountable for account usage. Acceptable usage policies have been ratified by the libraries. Individual public accounts have full authentication. System and Internet software has been strengthened to close off common security holes. System monitoring programs eject any public user who breaks out of the menu system.

Public access

On May 2 1994, the first Metro Net library began offering free public access to the Internet. The Internet is available on a walk-in basis in each library. People can also dial into the system from their home or office computers. The public has access to the basic menu, which leads them to Gopher and Web servers (Figure 3). In an effort to expand accessibility, one library connected a voice module and large print screen to a public terminal in their Outreach Services area. As yet, there has not been a great call for Internet use by persons with impaired vision, but access is available.

Image and public reaction

Several newspapers ran stories on the new service including the *Detroit News*, which covers the entire metropolitan area. Presentations have been given to local municipal officials, service clubs, school districts and community leaders. Public response has been wonderful! There is strong interest in dial-in access and moderate interest for in-house use. Some Metro Net libraries offer

Figure 3: The Metro Net Home Page (**http://198.111.64.10/**) provides a graphical view of Metro Net's services, including the Metro Net Gopher Server.

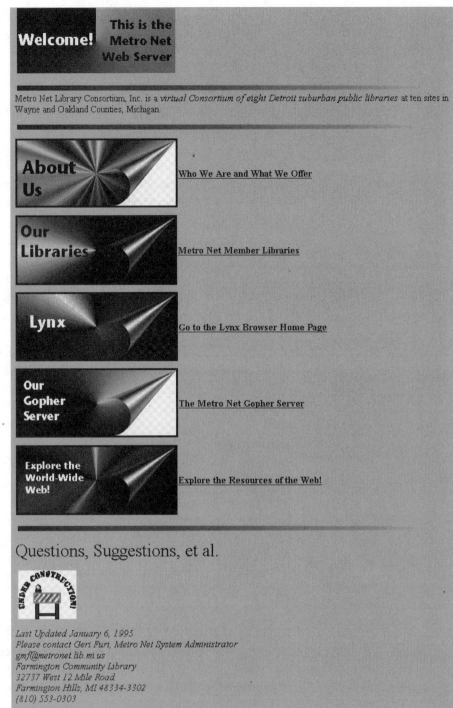

public training sessions that have been very popular. Others allow patrons with no special training to sit at terminals. There are seldom queues to access the workstations, but there are always people surfing the Net. Before being registered for global access, the system was being used approximately 50,000 times each month by Metro Net members.

Impact on collection development and reference use

For years, many librarians have espoused a philosophy of ownership-over-access toward collection development. With electronic delivery of vast quantities of data now possible, libraries can take a giant step toward truly becoming virtual libraries. Libraries can form new consortiums such as Metro Net to negotiate with vendors to deliver electronically more information for a better price. Librarians must think of the traditional Book Budget as an Information Services and Materials Budget. Expenditures for electronic services will cross departmental lines, with greater required cooperation among librarians on purchases. Librarians will weigh format options in delivering information quickly and cost-effectively. There is the opportunity for the smallest library or individuals at home or office to access global resources.

Staff members use the Internet on a routine basis as one of their reference tools. Patrons are very impressed with information retrieved from the Internet. Sources such as *Taxing Times* have provided specialized federal income tax forms. Documents such as the *Contract with America* have been provided on demand. OCLC's First Search has been particularly helpful for verifying authors and titles. As more and more staff become comfortable with the Internet, its use is assimilated into routine reference service.

Patrons, too, are successful using the Internet in their research. A Metro Net patron was concerned that Latvian family members may have been aboard a ferry that sunk in the Baltic Sea. Via Internet Relay Chat (IRC), the passenger list of the ferry was obtained and the patron was relieved that no family members were on the boat. Several patrons have located medical information via the Net. Tremendous amounts of software are being retrieved for personal use by patrons. Students use the Internet for school work relating to foreign countries. In particular, the U.S. Department of State's Background Notes (URL: **gopher://dosfan.lib. uic.edu**) and other reports are very helpful as a research resource for middle and high school students.

Community networking

The Internet world provides wonderful opportunities for libraries to offer greater service to their constituencies. The public library can reach out electronically to its residents and businesses; the college or university library beyond the campus to the surrounding community; and the special or corporate library can network throughout the whole institution or corporation. Libraries will serve as hosts and access points to global networks. Metro Net links municipal officials and staff, chambers of commerce, community groups and organizations. From online community calendars and information on government services to business and economic development information, citizens connect to resources, enabling better decision making and a better quality of life.

Summary

Following the Metro Net model, public libraries can become major participants in the Internet world. Not only can libraries be access points for the public and recipients of information but also as providers of information generated locally to be shared globally.

section three

change

reengineering the old ways

The Internet can help upgrade the rural library, but there's a price.

Denise A. Garofalo

Internet Use by Rural Public Libraries
An Examination of Two Programs in the Hudson Valley of New York State

oes access to and use of the Internet act as a hindrance or a help to small rural public libraries? Two grant programs have tried to answer that question, and both have discovered there is no clear-cut answer. A description of the two programs precedes an examination of the impact of Internet use and access in four small rural public libraries.

**Denise A. Garofalo** is the Automated Systems Manager at the Mid-Hudson Library System in Poughkeepsie, New York. She has served on committees such as the New York State Biennial Review Committee, the COSLINE Networking Committee, and the New Hampshire Automated Information System Board. She has been an invited speaker on technology and automation topics at the New York Library Association, New Hampshire Library Association and the Computers in Libraries Conferences. Her writings have appeared in *Library Journal, LITA Bulletin, Information Technology and Libraries,* and *Footnotes.* She can be reached at Mid-Hudson Library System, 103 Market Street, Poughkeepsie, NY 12601. Phone (914) 471-6060, fax (914) 454-5940, e-mail mhls@transit.nyser.net

Assumptions

Right or wrong, there has long been the hope that technology will help small libraries do their jobs with less effort. With all the talk and hype about the Internet, an assumption developed about its potential impact on rural libraries. If rural libraries like those in the Mid-Hudson Library System (Mid-Hudson) of New York State had Internet access, it was assumed that they would access reference data that they could not store or afford to purchase. Mid-Hudson hoped to prove this assumption true.

Mid-Hudson is an agency chartered by the State of New York to serve 65 public libraries and their branches in a five-county area bordering the Hudson River, midway between Albany and New York City. Population in the counties of Columbia, Dutchess, Greene, Putnam and Ulster totals almost 600,000 and is spread out over an area of 2,937 square miles. Most of the libraries are in communities of 10,000 people or less. These libraries have collections of 20,000 items or less. Some of the library buildings are recycled old municipal buildings or private homes. Space is a big constraint on use. Many of the libraries receive little public tax funding and must rely on fund-raising efforts such as bake sales, fairs, and the like to raise operating and capital monies. Budgets are therefore small, and many reference collections consist of encyclopedias, an almanac, and a few directories.

Project GAIN

While Mid-Hudson was planning a grant program to test the impact of the Internet, another project was already underway. NYSERNet, the mid-level Internet access provider for New York State, had launched Project GAIN. Project GAIN was a pilot project to study the idea of connecting selected rural libraries in New York State to the Internet. It provided libraries with training and education, and determined if the Internet was useful to rural libraries. NYSERNet worked with the J.M. Kaplan Foundation and Apple Computer, Inc. to provide equipment and funding to connect six project sites to the Internet. One of the sites selected for Project GAIN was the Woodstock Library in Ulster County, a Mid-Hudson member library.

The Woodstock Library, in the words of its director, D.J. Stern, "serves a rural community of well-educated people with sophisticated information needs, people who have always used the library to meet those needs." Project GAIN provided the Woodstock Library with another means of serving the community and meeting the needs of the citizens of Woodstock. Once word was out that the library had the Internet, interested citizens arrived at the library's doorstep with the expectation that everything was on the Internet. Education became a key component of the Woodstock Library's experience. The staff learned how to use the equipment and navigate the Internet. Users were educated in what could be found on the Internet.

Through Project GAIN, library users in the community had access to full Internet connectivity (FTP, electronic mail, Veronica, Archie, Gopher) via a Serial Line Internet Protocol (SLIP) connection. Efforts were made to inform the community about this new service. The library began to be regarded in a new and positive light for providing Internet access. A users group was formed to share experiences. As new connections, both traditional and electronic, expanded, library staff observed that providing this new service supported their opinion that libraries must have a role in connecting people if libraries are to continue as a viable institution.

Mid-Hudson's Internet Workstation Grants

As Project GAIN progressed, staff at Mid-Hudson finalized plans and criteria for a similar venture. Mid-Hudson receives a share of RBDB (Regional Bibliographic Data Bases) monies from New York State. These monies are earmarked for resource sharing and other efforts. In order to test our initial hypothesis, Mid-Hudson decided to use RBDB monies to fund a two-year competitive grant program. This program, called the Internet Workstation Grants, would provide three rural libraries with everything needed for dial-up Internet access.

Recipients of an Internet Workstation Grant would receive a modem-equipped personal computer and printer, an additional telephone line, access to the Internet, training, documentation, and support for telecommunications costs. Mid-Hudson held an informational meeting for interested applicants prior to the distribution of the grant applications. The grant program was described and suggestions were solicited from attendees. One suggestion that met with great approval was to provide a notebook computer to allow more portability, take up less precious desk space, and make demonstrations to community groups much easier.

The 24 applications were evaluated on four criteria:
► Does the library have the physical space to house the printer and to use the notebook computer?
► Does the library indicate a commitment to the project through specific hours in the library's schedule for Internet access and training?
► Does the library have a staff member or volunteer available and willing to be the chief Internet searcher?
► Does the library have a specific plan for publicizing the service?

85

The choice of recipients was a difficult one. Mid-Hudson regretted that we did not have more workstations to award. Our three recipients were the Philmont Public Library, the Cairo Public Library, and the Beekman Public Library (see Table 1).

Table 1: Location and population served by Internet Workstation Grant recipients.

Library	County	Population served
Beekman	Dutchess	10,400
Cairo	Greene	5,418
Philmont	Columbia	3,031

Dial-up Internet access through NYSERNet was provided via a text-based service for nonprofit institutions called TRANSIT. Telecommunications considerations and costs have been a major stumbling block to the project. The additional telephone line was included as a part of the grant because the majority of our member libraries have one voice line. Using that one line for dialing into the Internet would have a negative impact on the library's ability to provide service to the community. The Cairo and Philmont libraries must make a long-distance call to reach the closest point-of-presence to access the Internet. Over half of the 65 libraries Mid-Hudson serves are in the same situation as these two libraries. Efforts are currently underway at Mid-Hudson to examine methods of providing dedicated data lines to an Internet access point as a means of reducing the burden of expensive long-distance toll calls.

Listening to the experiences of the Woodstock Library, Mid-Hudson knew that training and education were crucial to the success of the project. One-on-one training was provided at each grant library over several sessions. The grant recipients were more or less technology neophytes. Early training sessions covered using a computer and using a modem and telecommunications software. Later sessions covered navigating the Internet, evaluating resources located, and downloading information. Training is very important, but hands-on experience is truly the only way to learn the Internet. Grant funds purchased books for each grant recipient. The libraries purchased some titles on the Internet too.

In order to relieve pressure on the library staff, each grant recipient was to designate a chief Internet searcher. This searcher — a volunteer, an intern, a Board member — was to be responsible for time-consuming aspects of the project. In reality, however, the director at each library became the *de facto* searcher, relying on support from other staff, Board members, volunteers, interns or the users group.

Each library established a users group. The success of this effort varied from library to library. Nevertheless, each grant recipient felt that a users group was essential to the project. The group was a means of reaching out into the community, publicizing a new service, and spreading the concept of "each one teach one" to users.

Providing free public access to the Internet helped account for the project's success in attracting users. There are few restrictions for public use of the workstation. Users are cautioned not to subscribe to newsgroups or LISTSERVs, since there is only one account at each library. To subscribe to a LISTSERV would have an impact on all users. If there are others waiting to use the Internet, users are asked to limit their time to 30 minutes per session. For security reasons, the library staff logs on to the Internet. The user is then free to use the Internet without staff intervention. If users are not knowledgeable or feel uncomfortable being on their own, the staff or the Internet searcher will provide help.

Evaluation

As a Project GAIN participant, the Woodstock Library was involved in quantitative and qualitative evaluation methods. Structured interviews, evaluation forms, logs, background data, questionnaires and site visits were all used in an attempt to discover how the Project GAIN libraries were using their Internet access. When asked, "What might you do differently?" The Director of the Woodstock Library replied, "I see an importance for potential economic development of our area, and the ability to tell people about our area." Also mentioned was the reality that Woodstock was far from Project GAIN's headquarters in Syracuse, which made the library and its staff feel "odd man out."

The three libraries that participated in the Mid-Hudson Internet Workstation Grant project were asked to have users complete a brief evaluation form. Overall, almost everyone who used the Internet and completed the query, "Did you accomplish your purpose?" answered "Yes." Many of these users had been curious about what the Internet was. Having the opportunity to sit down and see it for themselves was enough to elicit the positive response. There were many instances of users who had specific information needs which would have been impossible to answer at the library without access to the Internet. For example, one patron came into the library one evening and requested detailed information he needed that evening about a prostate cancer drug. The library did not have any medical reference texts, and could have sent the query to the system's central reference library via our surface delivery system. An answer would have arrived in about a week. By using the Internet the patron found an answer before the library closed.

When the three grant recipients are asked to evaluate the project, they tend to evaluate the Internet itself. Access speed, the quality (or lack thereof) of Gopher servers, and the lack of a graphical connection have been cited many times by the libraries. But the prevailing opinion is that Internet access is an advantage, making the libraries more visible in their communities.

On a broader note, after telecommunications costs, a major stumbling block for our four member libraries with Internet access (Woodstock, Beekman, Cairo, and Philmont Libraries) has been attitude and expectations. The public has the assumption that the Internet contains everything. They can become testy when they or the staff cannot put their hands on specific information in a few seconds. Even with such a high expectation level, most of the public who have used the service indicate that they are satisfied with the experience.

High pride, low aggravation

The Woodstock Library is seen as progressive as a result of having Internet access. Director Stern says "the Board is proud of the library being in the first wave of rural libraries on the Internet." Although Project GAIN is over, the Woodstock Library has continued to provide access to the Internet to its public. Stern cites the opportunities for teachers and others to gain a valuable means of communication by using the Internet. To quote Stern, "In the past, slow uncoordinated channels of communication have meant that essential information has often been out of date or redundant by the time people in rural areas hear it. The Internet can change all that. The bigger question, however, is not how do we use it, but how do we participate in it? The Internet is expensive, time-consuming, and you can't always see the benefits."

Another potential problem cited by the libraries is censorship. Although librarians have discussed the content of the Internet, there has not yet been an instance of the public clamoring to shut off Internet access to anyone. There have been no horror stories of parents outraged over children having access to strange or bizarre newsgroups. One Mid-Hudson participant mentioned that she was more concerned about the potential of a group demanding to know why the library had Internet access but not more copies of a new Stephen King novel.

The libraries with Internet access have gained recognition and status in their respective communities because they have Internet access and other institutions in the community do not. These libraries have gained more recognition among their fellow member libraries because of their access to Internet. Libraries in communities near the grant recipients have come for Internet demonstrations. As part of the reciprocal borrowing arrangements in Mid-Hudson, these libraries send users interested in Internet access to the grant-recipient libraries.

The assumption that Internet access in rural public libraries would aid the libraries in providing information to the community has been proven to be true. Access to the Internet provides new and different information. The telecommunications situation in rural areas is far from ideal and needs much improvement, but efforts are underway to correct that situation. Both Project GAIN and the Mid-Hudson Internet Workstation Grant project have demonstrated that small rural libraries with Internet access allow library users quick access to reference material and other information that the library may not have in print form.

The bottom line is that the service is valuable. Participating in the projects has made these libraries different from neighboring libraries, different in a very positive way. In the words of one of the grant recipients, "Access to the Internet has been a help and not a hindrance to the staff and the public." Mid-Hudson is now in the second year of the project. We are cooperating with another agency to establish our own Internet Gateway so that the benefits available to the grant recipients will be available to all 65 small rural libraries which Mid-Hudson serves.

Library staff at depositories of government information are coping with huge opportunities and wired nerves.

Doreen L. Hansen

The Internet in Depository Libraries
Better Service, Higher Stress

s the Internet becomes the primary means for disseminating government information, it is critical that federal depository libraries be equipped with knowledgeable staff and appropriate computer resources to provide easy electronic access for their patrons. Depositories in particular are poised at the forefront of this electronic transition to potential paperless or "virtual" collections. As a result, depository librarians and staff will find themselves in new and changing roles as the Internet's revolution continues. Concerns abound regarding exponential growth of information, evolution of current technology, and mutability of the Internet, as well as about the future of depositories in general. For now, as we move from traditional to digital formats, depository libraries must use available tools to utilize the Net's resources, enhance Internet searches, and provide user assistance. Finally, librarians must take the lead and advocate for up-to-date electronic access facilities and equipment.

Doreen L. Hansen is the Federal Depository Office Manager at the University of Minnesota Library in Duluth. She began work in government documents in 1992, and is codeveloper of this library's CD-ROM workstation system known as "Electronic Data & Documents (EDD)." In addition to CD-ROM technology, she is much involved with the Internet, especially in areas of government information. Her interest in digital communication is more than just computers. She has been a licensed Amateur Radio Operator for 12 years, callsign AAOMAJ. Mail will reach her at the University of Minnesota, Duluth, 10 University Drive, Duluth, MN 55812-2495. Phone (218) 726-7881, fax (218) 726-6205, e-mail dhansen@d.umn.edu

The Internet is profoundly affecting the way libraries conduct their business. The electronic information explosion is shifting emphasis from what a library owns to what the user can access. This is especially true for government depositories, where electronic conversion has already affected services. Due to their public origin, most government documents are free of copyright which in turn facilitates their digital distribution. "Federal agencies are spawning bulletin boards, Internet servers, and CD-ROMs at a dizzying pace," wrote the Superintendent of Documents.[1] These changes force depositories to adapt to this virtual environment.

Documents librarians need to weigh different formats to determine which best fills a need. They must also understand technology and regularly reassess systems and equipment, as electronic information is positioned to replace more traditional formats. Implications of these changes on the role of the depository system and staff are still unfolding, but one thing is clear. To uphold their commitment to free and open public access to government information, depository librarians will face increased demands in keeping up with a massive electronic conversion. After all, a depository's key role is to serve as an access point to government information, including electronic resources.

Transition to electronic information from the government

The movement of government information into electronic formats has been highlighted by several major initiatives. They will transform government information as we know it. Some of the more significant developments include the Government Information Locator Service (GILS), GPO Access, the Federal Bulletin Board (FBB), Fedworld, and Gophers and Web servers from federal and state agencies.

One of the federal government's major contributions to this electronic revolution is the Government Information Locator Service (GILS). GILS was established to create a virtual card catalog of government resources. It is a decentralized locator for agencies that identifies, describes, and provides help in accessing information.[2] Depositories furnish free public access to this expanding directory of federal electronic information. Until streamlining of the many components of electronic access takes place, depositories will continually be presented with new and changing information sources.

The Government Printing Office (GPO), in its initiative toward electronic publishing and access, made great headway in the summer of 1994 with the introduction of GPO Access. This service currently offers full text of the *Federal Register*, *Congressional Record*, the U.S. Code, and other resources. As a foundation for the eventual goal of complete electronic access, wide availability is

---

1. Wayne P. Kelley, Jr. (Text of letter sent to all directors of depository libraries, dated January 4, 1995), *Administrative Notes: Newsletter of the Federal Depository Library Program* 16 (January 15, 1995):1–4.

2. Eliot J. Christian, "Helping the Public Find Information: The U.S. Government Information Locator Service (GILS)," *Journal of Government Information* 21 (July/August 1994):305–14.

important. To ensure broad dissemination of this information, the Model Gateway Library program was established between GPO and selected depositories, allowing users in homes and offices to freely utilize the resources of GPO Access via Telnet.[3]

The GPO also offers the Federal Bulletin Board (FBB), where the public may obtain free or low-cost federal information via Telnet or dial-up. Depositories are given free access to all files on FBB as part of recent legislation. In turn, the depositories promote and provide free public access.[4]

Another major electronic initiative is Fedworld, an Internet service operated by the National Technical Information Service (NTIS). It provides subject access to large databases of scientific and technical documents. Fedworld also contains a gateway to many sources of government information not directly on the Internet.

State governments are also moving toward electronic outreach. For example, Minnesota's Legislative Gopher, expanded in October 1994, contains the full text of the Minnesota Statutes and pending bills, plus journals, laws, biographies, directories, and press releases. Similar electronic schemes for distributing state information are underway in California, Michigan, New York, Texas, and other states. State government information, once slow to be printed and sent, arduous to process and shelve, and difficult to use, is becoming far more accessible to patrons.

Electronic publishing has revolutionized the logistics and costs of producing information. Networking has expedited the access and distribution of government documents. The Internet has exposed depositories to the full potential of this revolution. Recent electronic initiatives have produced Internet resources essential to day-to-day operations (see Appendix). Many federal and state agencies are already providing information through their own Internet connections.

Technical skills and requirements

Despite the Internet's technological complications, constant metamorphosis, and uncertainty, its powerful resources can be tapped with the organizational skills and knowledge of practiced "cybrarians." However, it is taxing to maintain skills as servers proliferate and changes occur so swiftly. Ongoing training becomes crucial in the electronic age.

Depository staff now cope with a modern malaise called technostress, defined as "…a modern disease of adaptation caused by an inability to cope with the new computer technologies in a healthy manner…"[5] It is the result of the need to become adept with so many complex systems, software, CD-ROMs,

3. *GPO ACCESS: Information for Depository Libraries* (Washington, D.C.: U.S. Govt. Print. Off. 1995):6–9.

4. GPO ACCESS: The Federal Bulletin Board," *Administrative Notes: Newsletter of the Federal Depository Program* 15 (May 20, 1994):27–8.

5. Craig Brod, *Technostress: The Human Cost of the Computer Revolution.* (Reading, Mass.: Addison-Wesley, 1984):16; and, John Kupersmith, "Technostress and the Reference Librarian," *RSR: Reference Services Review* 20 (Summer, 1992):7–14.

and Internet databases while meeting day-to-day responsibilities. Staff must perform at more sophisticated levels in areas of both reference and technology.

In addition to professional expertise, depository staff will have to come to terms with the ever-changing technical requirements of electronic information. As the Internet advances, so does the sophistication of hardware and software, requiring at times frequent equipment upgrades. Equipment needs to surpass minimum requirements or it will operate too slowly for practical purposes. To meet government objectives, the GPO suggests high specifications for computer standards in its "Recommended Minimum Technical Guidelines for Federal Depository Libraries."[6] By 1998, depositories not complying with minimum standards will be subject to lowered ratings during official inspections. In order to avoid these predicaments, resource allocators in libraries need to follow technical developments and purchase equipment and software upgrades as necessary. To do otherwise would jeopardize a depository's capability and services.

Net searching needs librarians!

As depository librarians contemplate their future, they often worry that they might become irrelevant, supplanted by emerging technologies. Nevertheless, human creativity cannot be replaced by robot searchers in cyberspace. Besides managing technology, depository librarians advise users who are vague about their needs, those who don't know how to start their research, and those who lack understanding of the workings of government. On another level, they also assist sophisticated researchers with the more complex questions involving legislative, regulatory, and statistical matters.

Librarians are creative in finding answers on the Internet, but the sheer quantity of material of electronic information is staggering. Information overload makes it difficult to choose the most useful material. The Superintendent of Documents, Wayne P. Kelley, Jr., noted that on the Internet, sources are not cataloged. He remarked, "Surfing the net can take time — It is like a huge, constantly expanding warehouse with books piled everywhere and no system for finding the one you want."[7]

Until a more universal search system is developed, Internet search engines continue to appear as locators for information. Usually they require a combination of experience, creative keyword searching, perseverance, and luck. The experience and knowledge of documents librarians helps in locating electronic sites that best meet the needs of patrons.

6. "Recommended Minimum Technical Guidelines for Federal Depository Libraries," *Administrative Notes: Newsletter of the Federal Depository Library Program* 16 (January 15, 1995):5–7.

7. Wayne P. Kelley, Jr., "Remarks to Depository Library Directors at the American Library Association Midwinter Meeting in Philadelphia, Pennsylvania, February 4, 1995," *Administrative Notes: Newsletter of the Federal Depository Library Program* 16 (February 15, 1995):6.

One search, 236 options

On the Internet, choosing the right server is a large part of the challenge. Which works best? Various sites occasionally provide access to the same information. Using a Web search engine or Veronica searcher can lead to many sites, yielding a perplexing number of possibilities. For example, see Figures 1 and 2, for the results of a search for the *Federal Register*.

Figure 1: Wandex, a search engine for the World Wide Web, looks for servers with the *Federal Register*.

Figure 2: Wandex locates 236 occurrences of the *Federal Register* in its search.

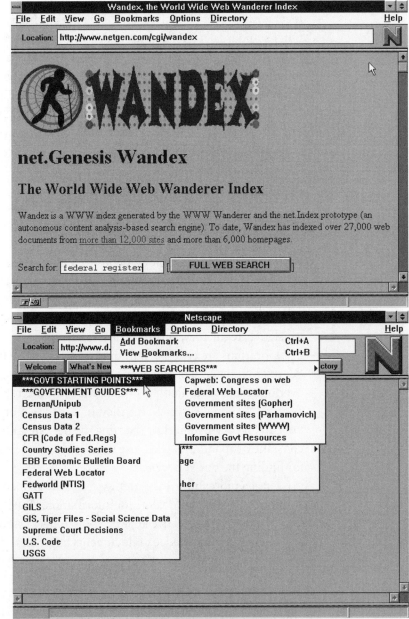

A Wandex search on the World Wide Web netted 236 sites for the *Federal Register*. We will contrast just four of these sites, demonstrating the need for a librarian's familiarity with a resource to guide patrons toward better choices. Significant differences in otherwise comparable looking sites would surely confuse most users.

Counterpoint Publishing's Gopher offers the *Federal Register* by subscription. This Gopher provides tables of contents and parts of notices and articles from several prior months free. The LEGI-SLATE Gopher, another subscription site, offers the means to search the full text of the *Federal Register* from January 1994 forward, with a capability to narrow by agency, day, words in caption, words in text, and page number. At another server, the *Federal Register* is free but only contains information related to the Occupational, Safety, and Health Administration (OSHA). This site provides information from 1971 on, with free full text for recent years, and short citations for earlier years. A fourth site offers only the 1994 and 1995 *Federal Register* through GPO Access. This particular site is unique in that it uses WAIS to explore the actual text of the *Federal Register*. These examples illustrate the differences between the *Federal Register* at just a few servers on the Internet. They prove the value of librarians' expertise in leading the patron to the best possible servers.

Depository staff are playing a key role in making electronic information available. As the electronic revolution progresses, depository staff should look beyond software and hardware, and reassert their roles as experts in government information. Staff should make use of their personal expertise coupled with these new technologies for improving services for their patrons.

New sites, new roles

Modern information, available through networks, is fundamentally changing the way libraries, and especially government documents depositories, conduct their operations. The Internet is having a profound impact on documents librarians and it is providing exciting new opportunities for improved services to our patrons.

As we become more accustomed to the Internet, we become even more aware of buzzwords such as the virtual library. We cannot help but speculate about the future. Nevertheless, the Internet, at present, has not entirely replaced traditional sources but just added new alternatives. These electronic variables, and the constantly changing technical environment, have placed added stress or "technostress" on documents staff. For the foreseeable future, we need to adjust by seeking training in the use of hardware, software, databases, protocols, and search strategies.

In addition to coping with stress, government documents staff are struggling to understand and redefine their roles, while worrying over the future of the federal depository system.[8] Recent political shifts in Congress have spawned legislation that could greatly alter the GPO and the Depository Library Program. Without some other agency to promote the centralized dissemination of federal government information, libraries could face major obstacles in making information available in the near future.

In the long term, however, these political problems will be resolved. We will find that the electronic revolution is an inexorable force in libraries.[9] Librarians working with government information must keep pace with the ongoing developments in information technology and adjust accordingly. Library directors and other resource allocators must be kept abreast of new developments and changing needs. Equipment, software, and network connections must be continually upgraded, or libraries will lose their ability to properly serve the public.

Finally, librarians working with government information must reassert the value of their professional expertise. The electronic revolution will greatly improve access, but it also brings new complexity and confusion for library patrons. As in the past, the knowledge and capabilities of library staff will continue to be the key to quality library services in the future.

8. Gary Cornwell *et al.*, "Problems and Issues Affecting the U.S. Depository Library Program and the GPO: The Librarians' Manifesto," *Government Publications Review* 20 (1993):121-140.

9. Steve McKinzie, "Bad News/Good News: Have the Documents Prophets Outstated Their Case?" *Documents to the People: DTTP* 22 (June 1994):95.

Appendix

Examples of government Internet sites used at the University of Minnesota, Duluth Library Depository

Code of Federal Regulations (CFR)
http://www.pls.com:8001/his/cfr.html

Federal Bulletin Board (FBB)
telnet://federal.bbs.gpo.gov:3001

Federal Web Locator (one-stop shopping for numerous federal sites)
http://www.law.vill.edu/Fed-Agency/fedwebloc.html

GPO Access
http://www.access.gpo.gov (free through depository)
http://thorplus.lib.purdue.edu/gpo/ (free Web version through Purdue University)
telnet://bigcat.missouri.edu (login as "guest")

Library of Congress
http://lcweb.loc.gov/

National Technical Information Service's (NTIS) Fedworld
http://www.fedworld.gov/

NorthStar (State of Minnesota)
http://www.state.micro.umn.edu/state/index.html

Stat-USA
gopher://stat-usa.gov or **ftp://stat-usa.gov**
http://www.stat-usa.gov/stat-usa.html (free through depository)

U.S. Supreme Court
http://www.law.cornell.edu/supct/supct.table.html

Students get a chance to be the library's Internet gurus, and rise to the challenge.

c h a n g e

Terry Metz

Student Employees Enhance Internet Expertise for a Liberal Arts College Library

t Carleton College, two librarians are responsible for identifying Internet resources and for teaching users how to access them. It is increasingly difficult for these librarians to keep abreast of the wide range of new Internet information tools and resources while at the same time meeting the demands of traditional reference service, bibliographic instruction, and other administrative duties. To better balance these competing demands for time, effort, and talent, the librarians are using skilled students to expand the library's pool of Internet expertise. Delegating selected Internet-related duties to these students permits librarians to be more productive at a time when the size of the professional staff is not growing.

Terry Metz is Systems Support & Instruction Librarian at Carleton College in Northfield, Minnesota. He manages delivery of electronic information services for the Carleton Library, including the online catalog, CD-ROM products, external database services, and Internet resources. He also shares responsibility for Internet training and for promoting its use as part of the library's mission to deliver electronic information. He can be reached at: Carleton College Library, One North College Street, Northfield, MN 55057. Phone (507) 663-4530, fax (507) 663-4087, e-mail temetz@carleton.edu and URL: *http://www.carleton.edu/campus/library/staff/terry/terry.html*

A particular benefit of employing technically savvy students is that it allows professional librarians to devote more time to attaining and retaining greater Internet expertise themselves. The ultimate goal is to be able to provide a better informed, more highly-skilled, and less-stressed cadre of library staff to meet the information needs of students and faculty.

GIRDing for student help

During the 1993-94 academic year, two Carleton College librarians began using a select group of student library employees to increase the library's depth of Internet expertise, as well as to expedite a transition toward greater use of computer information technology in the library. We were interested and willing to use student library employees for technology duties because of another library experiment launched that winter. That experiment eliminated the traditional reference desk model in favor of a General Information and Referral Desk (GIRD) and created a "tiered" or "layered" reference service. Physically adjacent to the GIRD are two rows of computer workstations; some of these support CD-ROM products while others are network stations serving as portals to Internet resources.

Figure 1: Students use network workstations in the Carleton College Library.

Under the GIRD model, reference librarians no longer staff a desk. Instead specially selected and trained student employees serve at the GIRD. They are available to assist Library users who have routine or noncomplex information needs. Students refer more difficult questions to an on-call reference librarian. By serving in an on-call capacity rather than waiting passively at a reference desk, professional reference staff are able to focus their energies on more advanced and complex service. Such service includes consultation for term papers and senior comprehensive exams or personal appointments with students and faculty who have specialized information problems or needs.

The GIRD system, in turn, is a direct outgrowth of the college administration's directive to seek imaginative ways of serving students and faculty without additional funding. In a nutshell, we were informed that change, substitution, experimentation, and innovation were easier to come by than dollars for additional library staff.

The Internet expertise crunch

At the Carleton College Library, a group of six librarians participates in responsibility for on-call consultation service. Due to the relatively lean staff size, each of these librarians holds two and sometimes three other professional and administrative responsibilities within the library. As the two professional staff members among this group whose additional duties also include overall responsibility for library instruction, the Government Documents and Instruction Librarian and the Systems Support and Instruction Librarian began offering *ad hoc* fundamental user training for retrieval and interpretation of networked information sources in early 1992. We grew increasingly frustrated in an attempt to cope with rapid changes in our field given the rapidly expanding universe of Internet resources and retrieval tools; a small, but growing, demand for assistance with Internet navigation among library users; and the time commitment of other duties. Not surprisingly, we concluded that we had to redesign our jobs to achieve the objective of becoming the campus Internet information retrieval experts.

Clearly, it was impossible to carry out all of our "conventional" responsibilities and still devote substantially more resources both to training and retooling ourselves, as well as to locating, selecting, retrieving, interpreting, and in many cases packaging Internet information for our users. Still, we were determined to find some way to maintain and expand the technological capabilities because we were convinced of its importance to our profession and to the future success of our graduates. The need to master more and more technology in less and less time with no opportunity for additional full-time staff to assist us was the primary motivating factor in the decision to draw more heavily on student talent.

100

Identifying and hiring student employees

Ideally, we wanted to hire students with whom we could consult on a broad range of information technology topics; who could tutor us on specific skills we lacked and wanted to acquire; who complemented the repertoire of Internet computing skills we already possessed; and who demonstrated the motivation and responsibility to follow through on projects assigned to them. The first two students helping us with Internet-related work were already working for other departments in the Library, in government documents processing and in copy cataloging. Purely by accident, we learned about their experience and interest in Internet computing. We arranged with their work supervisors to have them reassigned to work for us.

Eventually, as we began to realize how invaluable technologically-adept student employees were toward meeting the long-term objectives, we drafted a more formal job description for this type of position. This description has evolved over the past two years. Some changes result from foreseen needs such as seeking a candidate who possesses a specific skill which we want transferred to us with as short a learning curve as possible. Others result from our becoming more aware of the relatively sophisticated technical capabilities of students available for library employment. A copy of the job description as it existed at the time of this writing appears at the end of this chapter. Readers may also review a current copy of the job description (URL: **http://www.carleton.edu/campus/library/studentworkers/jobs.html**).

We recruit technology students through the campus student employment office, via word of mouth, and by means of postings on the campus Gopher and World Wide Web servers. To date, the first two methods have generated the majority of applications. In the future, we expect more candidates will learn about us through the network postings. We are hopeful that the students who respond to the electronic job postings will be already interested in using network technology.

We recognize we are competing with the campus academic computing department for talented student employees. However, our computing colleagues have welcomed our attempts to make library staff more computer savvy because this reduces our reliance on them for assistance. That reduces the demands on their already overworked staff.

Dispelling any notion that the cadre of technology students are congenital "netheads," it is reassuring to note the varied academic majors of those students who have or are still employed by us for technology-related responsibilities: American studies; history; anthropology; international relations; art; mathematics; computer science; physics/astronomy; English; political science;

geology; and religion. Although technology students must meet the minimum position qualifications, their varied backgrounds and interests occasionally are useful in helping us tailor presentations or guides for information seekers from various disciplines.

Creating a workspace for our student employees

Finding and adapting the physical space for a work area for the technology students stemmed from several physical changes in the library during the summer of 1994. As part of an overall technology improvement plan, we migrated to a new local automation system (Innovative Interfaces), and upgraded and expanded the voice and data cabling for the Library building. As a ripple effect of these changes, library staff agreed that workspace relocations were needed to support anticipated changes in work flow and staffing assignments, after we had successfully completed the system migration.

The Systems Support and Instruction Librarian's office was relocated adjacent to the Government Documents and Instruction Librarian's office. Both are now part of a suite of offices housing other reference librarians. This office suite serves as one boundary of the GIRD area. Thus, the two of us who are primarily responsible for assistance with network navigation are immediately accessible to students and faculty using the workstation just beyond the office doors. Doors leading from the rear of the Government Documents and Systems Librarians' offices provide access to the newly-formed information technology work area. This area, formerly used for government documents processing, is now devoted to workspace for the technology students.

Some of the hardware housed here includes:

► DEC lpx 486 PC running Windows with an attached Hitachi TCDR-7000 external CD-ROM drive;
► Macintosh 7100/66 Power PC with internal CD-ROM drive;
► Hewlett-Packard Laser Jet 4 laser printer;
► Hewlett-Packard Scan Jet IIcx scanner;
► 325 MB external hard drive cannibalized from our previous Carlyle online catalog system;
► 386 PC cannibalized from the Carlyle system;
► Macintosh SE computer; and,
► DEC 333c 386 PC running Windows with an attached Hitachi TCDR-7000 external CD-ROM drive.

Occasionally, we also use public network workstations (Macintosh 7100/66 Power PC computers with internal CD-ROM drives) near the GIRD Desk if they are not in use.

During the building-wide cabling project, we piggybacked electrical and data cabling for the technology work space at very little expense. We also found some spare furniture and shelving, purchased some basic tools for repairing and upgrading computer hardware, and hung a large grease board for jotting down ideas, planning assignments, and noting problems, etc. Each student is provided with a space for in-baskets, file folders, floppy diskettes, and other materials.

Figure 2: Student employees in technology work area.

Nurturing student expertise

Understandably, only the most outstanding candidates arrive on the job with most of the skills they will need to serve successfully as one of the technology students. Therefore, in addition to receiving an orientation from us about our operations, newcomers are apprenticed to veteran students who demonstrate how to use the hardware and software tools.

We have used a portion of the Government Documents and Library Systems departmental funds to build a working collection of books, periodicals, articles, and video tapes for the technology students. Student employees are encouraged to refer to these materials for assistance with projects that are assigned to them. They are also welcome to browse through these resources

103

when they don't have other specific duties to perform, or to borrow these items for their own personal reading.

Technology students occasionally subscribe to or retrieve archived messages from relevant LISTSERV mailing lists to support projects they may be working on for us. These lists include NETTRAIN, GOVDOC-L, PACS-L, Web4Lib, BI-L, and INNOPAC. The exchange of information on these lists exposes them to the issues of the profession and gives them an opportunity to see the big picture beyond the library.

The Government Documents and Instruction Librarian and the Systems Support and Instruction Librarian consult with the technology students almost daily and include them in planning sessions. We encourage the students to ask questions, of us and of their peer workers. The standard operating procedure among the technology group is that one must share new discoveries or successes with other members of the group as a way of enhancing the skills of all group members.

Lastly, but most significantly, we sanction and encourage the technology student employees taking time for exploring new Internet tools and technologies as part of their normal work assignments. In our experience, we have seen that giving technology students time to invest in practice, experimentation, and serendipitous discovery pays enormous dividends toward improving student employee skills, toward effective joint problem solving, and toward maintaining high morale and esprit de corps among the technology team.

How we've applied our students' expertise

▶ *Internet station maintenance*
Several of the students have taken responsibility for maintaining the public Internet workstations, such as creating user-friendly welcome screens, keeping current versions of client software mounted and functioning properly, and investigating hardware and software security concerns.

▶ *Net scouts*
Much of the students' efforts are devoted to learning about the latest Internet software tools and exploring with them. They also use these tools to locate network resources relevant to our needs. Delegating this task to students releases time for professional staff to prepare for classroom presentations, for one-on-one appointments with students and faculty, or to attend continuing education opportunities to stay abreast of new technologies and resources.

104

Figure 3: Opening screen display from one of several Power Macintosh computers used as a network information workstation in the Carleton College Library.

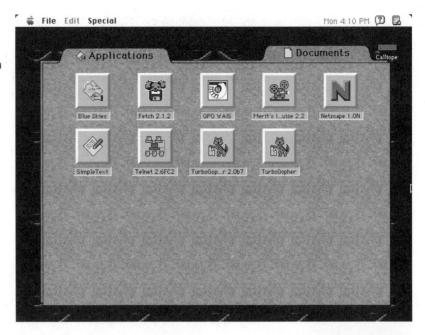

Figure 4: Screen display of Government Printing Office WAIS client installed and maintained by student employee on a network information workstation in the Carleton College Library.

Metz/Student Employees Enhance Internet Expertise for a Liberal Arts College Library

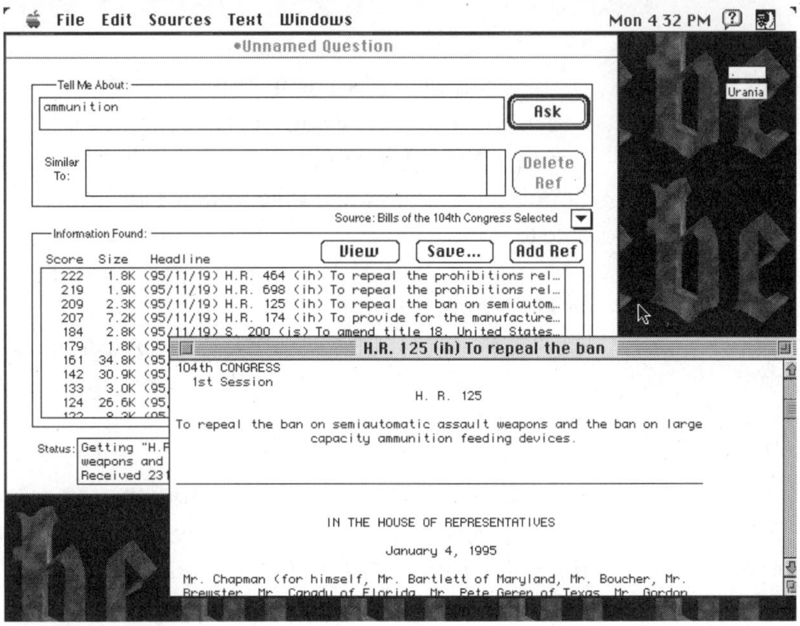

Here are three examples of Net reconnoitering tasks performed by the students:

▶ Students will verify that a new version of Eudora or TurboGopher exists, retrieve it via FTP, examine it for new features and enhancements, and report on its advantages and potential pitfalls. If staff so wish, they may request that a student mount the newer version onto their computers.

▶ A political science faculty member approaches a librarian to request a presentation two days from now on how to locate information on environmental pollution issues facing thirty developing nations around the globe. We assign a technology student to scour various Gophers and Web servers to help us identify potential Internet resources to include in this presentation.

▶ A student searches through the archived messages of relevant LISTSERV discussion lists to identify useful advice about how to manage public network computer stations in libraries; she summarizes the salient details and reports her findings in an e-mail message to us.

▶ *Net trainers*

The technology students train and consult with other library professional and support staff on using Internet applications such as e-mail, FTP, Telnet, Gopher, Web browsers, etc., whenever the Systems Support and Instruction Librarian or Government Documents and Instruction Librarian are unavailable to do so.

▶ *Handout creation*

Technology students use desktop publishing software, drawing programs, and scanning equipment to help prepare paper handouts used for Internet instruction.

▶ *Bibliographic instruction demonstration setup*

Students assist us with preparing for bibliographic instruction demonstrations by verifying that projection equipment, hardware, and software are functioning properly; that aliases and passwords are current; and by crafting, adapting, or editing presentation software "slides."

▶ *Hands-on bibliographic instruction demonstrations*

When their work schedules permit, technology students assist with bibliographic instruction presentations held in the college's computer presentation

106

lab by joining the professional librarians in the role of roving troubleshooters and coaches during hands-on time.

► *Newsletter contributions*

Students occasionally contribute articles describing a particular Internet resource or technique to the library newsletter.

► *Board of Trustees presentation*

In May 1994, the technology students helped plan and participate in a presentation before the College Board of Trustees to help librarians educate the board about the library's information technology achievements as well as our future plans and funding needs.

► *Conference presentations*

In September 1994, a technology student created artwork and images on a home page used as part of a World Wide Web presentation for Oberlin Group library directors held at Carleton College: URL: **http://www.carleton.edu/ campus/library/obegroup.html** We are also planning to have some of the students attend a professional conference with us so that they can participate in offering a conference presentation.

► *URL and bookmark management*

Recently, we have begun using a student to maintain a library of URL bookmarks for us. When potentially useful URLs appear in our LISTSERV e-mail discussions, we send these messages to a student, who verifies the accuracy of the URL address and places it into the appropriate location in the URL bookmark library for future use.

► *Maintaining Gopher and Web presence*

One of the most coveted assignments among the technology students is being asked to create and maintain files on the campus Gopher and Web servers. Composing Web pages is particularly popular. Nearly all of the students have some proficiency in composing HyperText Markup Language (HTML) documents and scanning images to illustrate them. Some are becoming particularly adept at this technique.

Keeping technology students motivated

We are very proud of the skills the technology students are developing and the responsibilities they are accepting. College policy does not allow the library to differentiate pay scales among student employees based upon skills, experience, or seniority. Therefore, we cannot increase the technology students' direct compensation. To date, however, we have successfully retained most of the technology students by offering other intangible competitive benefits, such as:

▶ access to newer hardware and software tools not generally available to the campus student population at large;

▶ authorization to create personal Web pages; and,

▶ field trips to Minneapolis to chat with the developers of Gopher at the University of Minnesota; to experiment with Geographical Information Systems (GIS) mapping software in the University's Map Library;

▶ to meet with distance learning technology experts in the University's Extension Department; and to tour the School of Communications Arts to see demonstrations of computer-generated animation.

We also share selective professional library job announcements which appear on the Internet with the students. We look for those in which employers are seeking candidates who have experience with computing technology and Internet tools because we want the students to be aware of how the skills they are developing by working for us could transfer to future career opportunities.

Conclusion

Because much undergraduate scholarship is becoming digital, we are relying more and more on networked systems and services. We believe it is imperative to have sufficient, knowledgeable, and well-trained library staff members to assist and educate users so that they can become information-literate, independent learners and researchers. Effective use of expensive technological assets requires a highly-skilled library work force. Keeping up with rapid changes in these important technologies is time-consuming. Yet, at institutions such as Carleton College, staff sizes remain lean. At Carleton College, we have been fortunate to receive the support of the library director in taking some bold, unconventional, and perhaps controversial steps to deal with these challenges. One of these approaches utilizes the talent and enthusiasm of student employees to increase the library's overall Internet expertise.

Use of technology students has accelerated the library's exposure to information technology, freed up time for librarians to conduct Internet training, created more opportunities for one-on-one consultation with users about their information needs, and allowed librarians to become more visible on campus.

"All indications are that the future will be the past on fast forward."[1] Looming on the horizon are changes in information technology the magnitude

1. Dennis Dickinson. "Academic Libraries on the Cusp," *Library Issues* 15, no. 3 (January 1995):3.

of which will severely challenge college libraries. Experimentation, risk taking, and making difficult decisions to shift resources away from some library operations to support innovative ones are necessary to ensure that libraries successfully meet and survive these challenges. Tapping the technological talents of the student employees is helping us avoid being left behind as the train pulls away from the station.

Appendix

Recruitment Announcement

```
Openings Available for Information Technology Assistants
during 1995-96 Academic Year

Job Description:
Information Technology Assistant — Support operation of
library automation technology (online catalog, CD-ROM
stations, staff computers, peripherals,etc.) as directed
by the Systems Librarian. Typical duties will likely
include (but are not necessarily limited to):

• conducting routine maintenance of library automation
  tools (e.g., performing hard drive backups, upgrading
  virus protection software, running file maintenance
  applications, cleaning hardware, etc.)
• installing software; organizing and deleting files
• performing backups for Muse (online catalog)
• maintaining hardware and software inventories
• maintaining/updating library information on library
  World Wide Web server
• testing and experimenting with new electronic resources
  (including surfing the 'Net!)
• drafting and/or proofreading user documentation for
  electronic resources
• performing hardware and software troubleshooting tasks
• performing some clerical tasks (photocopying, filing,
  typing labels, etc.)
• occasionally lifting +40 lbs items will be necessary

Other challenging automation projects may be arranged if
employee is interested and qualified.

Schedule: Must be available to work a minimum of 6 hours
per week; It may be possible to schedule some work in the
evenings or on weekends, but the majority of work hours
will fall in the 8-5, Mon-Fri time frame.
```

Essential Qualifications:

- must be thorough, show attention to detail, and have aptitude for linear problem-solving
- must be a reliable self-starter who is comfortable with working independently
- must have patience and poise in trouble-shooting situations
- interest in computers, networking, and/or library automation essential
- inquisitiveness and enthusiasm a plus

Other Qualifications:

- getting and using a VAX e-mail account required
- previous DOS/Windows or Macintosh experience required
- preference given to those with previous experience using Internet tools such as:
  e-mail, VAX notes, Telnet, Usenet news, FTP, Gopher, World Wide Web

- preference given to those having experience with one or more of the following:
  CD-ROM technology, Macintosh networking and file sharing, file compression, image and OCR scanning, desktop publishing, trouble-shooting with computers, terminals, printers, and barcode scanners
  hardware upgrades such as:
    changing hard drives, changing floppy drives, installing CD-ROM drives, adding circuit boards, adding RAM, etc.
  composing HTML documents for the World Wide Web

- preference given to those with experience using any of the following Macintosh software:
  Microsoft Word, Microsoft Excel, Microsoft Powerpoint, Claris FileMaker Pro, Claris MacDraw Pro, Adobe Photoshop, Aldus Freehand, Aldus PageMaker, Caere OmniPage Pro

How to Apply:

Interested applicants should contact:

    Terry Metz, Systems Support and Instruction Librarian
    Library #467
    x4530
    temetz@carleton.edu

*In a security-sensitive corporate setting,
selling the library as an Internet center
took talent, guts — and a thick firewall.*

Pamela Jajko Leslie Fisher
Becky Barber Ann Hubble
Greg Bassett Bill Putney
Jenny Chu

Implementing the Internet at Syntex
Collaboration between the Library and Information Systems

*he Internet is not just a technical connection. It is a way for people to
interface and exchange information. Organizations will find that
the most successful implementation occurs when both the Information Systems staff [IS] and the library staff work in close collaboration. Each group will use its unique expertise to support organiza-*
tional applications of the Internet. At Syntex, the perceptions of the respective roles
of these two groups, in an Internet implementation, differed substantially. The

Pamela Jajko, Manager of Corporate LInC and Corporate Record Systems at Syntex, is the
stargazer, creator of prime directives, and central router in the LInC universe. Mail will find its way to
her at Syntex Corporate LInC, 3401 Hillview Ave., A2-060, Palo Alto, CA 94303. Phone (415) 852-
1794, fax (415) 354-7741, e-mail pam.jajko@syntex.com

Becky Barber, Systems at Corporate LInC, is the cyberkitsch of LInC, specializing in weirdnews,
arcane facts, and spam. Send mail to Syntex Corporate LInC, 3401 Hillview Ave., A2-060, Palo Alto
CA 94303. Phone (415) 855-1740, fax (415) 354-7741, e-mail rebecca.barber@syntex.com

Greg Bassett, Network Engineering, is a natural-born teacher, lecturer, and lynch-pin in networking collaborations. Send mail to Syntex, 3401 Hillview Ave., MS: A5-6, Palo Alto, CA 94303.
Phone (415) 423-5825 or fax (415) 855-5103, e-mail greg.bassett@syntex.com

process of accessing the Internet created numerous opportunities for acknowledging and discussing these different perceptions and for renegotiating responsibilities. The outcome was a better understanding of, and increased respect for, each group. This chapter examines the introduction of the Internet to the staff of Syntex. It examines the process of administrative acceptance, stages of negotiation between IS staff and library personnel, corporate-wide marketing of Internet resources, skill development, and delegation of responsibilities within the library.

Implementing the Internet in any organization, regardless of whether it is a for-profit corporation or a public library, requires close collaboration between the library and the technology experts. Initially, the perceptions of these two groups may differ substantially. Information systems professionals often assume that once the technology is in place and the network connected, users will learn to use the Internet on their own or through colleagues. Librarians, on the other hand, tend to believe that providing physical access to the Internet is only the first critical step. Librarians recognize that training and navigational assistance should be provided to help people use the Internet more effectively and locate resources relevant to their work more easily.

Implementing the Internet at Syntex created numerous opportunities to acknowledge and discuss these different perceptions, and to renegotiate responsibilities. These discussions led to a better understanding of, and increased respect for, what each group could offer to a successful implementation.

About Syntex

Until recently, Syntex was a midsize international pharmaceutical company, with operations worldwide. Its well-known products include Naprosyn, a prescription pain killer; ALEVE, a new over-the-counter formulation of Naprosyn; and Torodol, a non-narcotic pain killer. In fall 1994, Syntex was bought by Roche, a large Swiss pharmaceutical company. Syntex, now one of five Roche Research and Development Centers, specializes in the discovery and development of new medications in the therapeutic areas of immunology; bone and joint disease; gastrointestinal disease and urinary tract disorders; and pain reduction.

History of the Internet at Syntex

Beginning in early 1991, Syntex provided limited access to the Internet. However, access was not easy and required that employees register, in advance, any non-Syntex electronic mail recipients. Needless to say, few employees bothered to become connected. Network Engineering made several proposals to Corporate

Jenny Chu, Systems, is the archon of web pages and the preceptor of PCs in LInC. Send mail to Syntex Corporate LInC, 3401 Hillview Ave., A2-060, Palo Alto, CA 94303. Phone (415) 855-5491, fax (415) 354-7741, e-mail jenny.chu@syntex.com

Leslie R. Fisher, Information Research Analyst, is a web surfer, ontological adventurer, and poet laureate of LInC. Send mail to Syntex Corporate LInC, 3401 Hillview Ave., A2-060, Palo Alto, CA 94303. Phone (415) 855-5434, fax (415) 354-7741, e-mail leslie.fisher@syntex .com

Ann Hubble, Team Leader for Systems, is the leader of the pack in LInC systems with 21 years on the Internet (in dog years). Send mail to Syntex Corporate LInC, 3401 Hillview Ave., A2-060, Palo Alto, CA 94303. Phone (415) 855-5492, fax (415) 354-7741, e-mail ann.hubble@syntex. com

Bill Putney, Network Engineering, is a ham operator, private pilot, and swell guy with 18 years on the Internet. Phone (415) 423-1259, fax (415) 855-5988, e-mail bill.putney@syntex. com

Information Services, their parent department, to improve access, but the proposals were repeatedly rejected. There was a fear that hackers would penetrate Syntex's internal systems and obtain access to proprietary research information.

In 1991, Corporate LInC (the Corporate **L**ibrary and **In**formation **C**enter) decided that the Internet was an extremely important aspect of future information management. Instead of using Syntex's limited system, it contracted with an external vendor to provide full access to the library staff. LInC then submitted proposals to Corporate Information Services to expand the use of this commercial vendor campus-wide to encourage more employees to access the Internet. These proposals were turned down.

Finally, in fall 1993, Networking Engineering was able to demonstrate a plan for an effective firewall. This firewall would prevent hackers from entering Syntex's internal systems. The plan was accepted and Network Engineering moved rapidly to establish access to a local node.

Syntex's firewall

A firewall may seem a concern more pertinent to corporations than to other types of libraries. Nevertheless, all librarians responsible for bringing the Internet into their organizations must be very aware of the potential for disruption and destruction resulting from unauthorized access into local networks.

A firewall controls access into and out of the Internet from a private network. In the case of Syntex, the corporation made a decision that it would place no restrictions on what employees on the Syntex network could do out on the Internet. On the other hand, very stringent controls were placed on what could come into the Syntex network from the Internet. The fire wall at Syntex consists of several key components (see Figure 1).

BARRnet is the service provider, providing access to the Internet from a single communications line. The DSU/CSU, a type of modem, connects to a small ethernet segment with two routers and two Sun Unix-based computers. This area is called Syntex's safe zone, a place for public access to some services and information. A router is the primary access control device, limiting almost all public access. The router allows all outbound — to Internet — connections and all electronic mail into the mail gateway.

The result is a very robust service for Syntex staff and very tight security to prevent break-ins. Several months after access to the Internet was implemented, Syntex's Information Systems hired a professional group to try to break into the system. This team of hackers was unsuccessful in its efforts to penetrate the firewall.

113

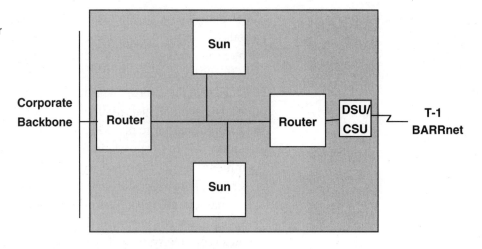

Figure 1: Several Sun workstations provide a barrier between the Internet and Syntex's network.

Negotiating collaboration

Following successful implementation of the firewall, an Internet proposal was finally approved in fall 1993. A company-wide roll-out of the system was planned for January 1994. LInC was approached for involvement in the roll-out.

Initially the scope of LInC involvement, as envisioned by Network Engineering, was quite limited. LInC would provide bibliographic information on books and materials that employees might want to check out and borrow. Syntex's network engineers had used the Internet extensively without much support or training. They felt that most of Syntex's employees would be able to do the same. LInC did not see the capabilities of the Syntex staff in the same light, seeing instead a real need for Internet support. There was a need for Internet literacy and end-user support for utilizing Internet services. LInC could have a role in providing this support. In other words, LInC wanted to become "Internet Central" at Syntex.

Immediately, the LInC staff began to ask questions on the process of the Internet roll-out. Numerous discussions were held with Network Engineering. LInC started by examining a brief guide, compiled by Network Engineering, and making extensive recommendations for revision. Additionally, more discussions were held on the content of the Internet seminar to be presented to all employees. Eventually, the discussions lead to new and altered roles and responsibilities for all parties in this project. LInC's role expanded from organizing the resource collection to being responsible for the preparation and publication of a manual that would be distributed to all participants at the roll-out seminar.

Just weeks before the scheduled roll-out, Network Engineering unveiled an internal home page using NCSA Mosaic. This home page added a whole new dimension to the roll-out. The LInC staff's excitement over this new resource was matched by the angst of completely revising both the content of the seminar and the manual in a short time period.

"I just wanted to thank you for yesterday's Internet overview. I think it was outstanding." a Syntex toxicologist

Introducing the Internet to Syntex

By mid-January 1994, announcements concerning the roll-out seminar had gone out to all employees. This seminar, presented jointly by LInC and Network Engineering, was an overwhelming success. The lecture hall was packed, with people standing several deep in the back of the hall and sitting on every step. During the course of the presentation, employees continued to try to enter the room, only to give up and leave in disappointment.

The audience was very interested and listened intently to a basic overview of the Internet, a description of some Internet tools, and an explanation of the firewall. Live demonstrations were enthusiastically received. The audience particularly enjoyed virtually examining a soda machine at Rensselaer Polytechnic Institute in New York and learning how many cans of Jolt Cola were at hand. Although Gopher and Archie were shown, the highlight of the demonstration was the World Wide Web browser, NCSA Mosaic.

Employees who had attended the lecture returned to their departments and quickly spread the word. Requests poured in for additional seminars and several more were scheduled. In less than a month, some 600 employees attended the first wave of these presentations. An announcement was made at each seminar that hands-on training classes would be available shortly. The phone at the LInC reference desk was extraordinarily busy for days, as employees called to schedule classes.

LInC staff

By this time, it was obvious that a major commitment would be required from LInC staff to successfully support the Internet. A decision could have been made at that point to hire trainers to come in and teach the classes. But the LInC staff decided instead to use this as an opportunity to increase their own knowledge of the Internet. This allowed LInC to work more closely with Network Engineering and to increase the visibility of LInC to the rest of the organization.

Of course, regular library work was ongoing. Temporary help was brought in to take over more routine tasks. The immediate consequence was a doubly expanded workload while temporary staff was located, interviewed, and trained. All the while, business proceeded as usual and work on the Internet project continued. In retrospect, this was an excellent decision. The LInC staff is now recognized as Syntex's experts on the Internet with responsibility for ongoing resource development, training, and support.

"Great hands-on intro. I had tools including Mosaic on my desktop, but didn't know how to get going." **a clinical coordinator**

Training

At this point, LInC staff began working more closely with other groups in Corporate Information Services. These efforts included coordination with the site-wide computer training facilities as well as the desktop support staff to enable workstation connectivity for individual users.

Before training could really begin, our Internet manual was reevaluated. A critical review showed that the flow of information as well as the layout of the manual, which had been distributed at the seminars, could be improved. A member of the computer training documentation staff helped revise the manual for future presentations.

In addition, the structure and content of the classes were analyzed. In about three weeks, after an intense investment by LInC, the first class was given. It didn't take long to discover a serious problem in the training program. Training both Microsoft (MS) Windows and Macintosh users in the same class was very difficult for the trainer and very confusing for the students. There was no alternative but to contact hundreds of employees already signed up for classes, and assign them to either MS Windows or Mac classes. Training materials were once again reevaluated and a separate Mac version of the manual was rapidly created along with appropriate class supplements.

Video production

When Syntex's international units learned that Internet access was being offered, they requested training for themselves as well. Although a video had been made of the roll-out lecture, it was unsatisfactory for off-site training. To provide orientation to multiple locations, a better approach was a training video which would supplement other training materials. This video was designed to coordinate as a self-study program with LInC's Internet manual.

To expedite this process, an independent consultant was hired to put together two video versions for MS Windows and Macintosh, corresponding with Syntex's dual-platform environment. LInC staff provided the script, production, and talent for this endeavor, adding another layer of work to the

116

already burgeoning Internet workload. The video took about a month to script, shoot, edit, duplicate, and move into circulation.

Mosaic development

Meanwhile, a committee was formed consisting of staff from LInC, Network Engineering, and computer desktop support to discuss the next steps on the Internet and the future development of Mosaic. It was obvious that continuous development would be needed on the Syntex internal home page, a home page initially constructed by Network Engineering. In addition, a LInC home page was needed as a focal point for specialized information services and resources. Instructions and support were also needed for other departments wishing to develop their own home pages. LInC assumed responsibility for all of these areas.

During this time, Human Resources was becoming increasingly interested in the potential of using Mosaic to post job openings and to provide potential employees with information about Syntex. Over the next few months, discussions were held on the best and quickest way to implement a Syntex external home page. A decision was made to support LInC staff development and in this case develop literacy with the HyperText Markup Language (HTML). With this expertise, LInC would assume a leadership role in the utilization of Mosaic in the organization.

A consultant experienced in developing commercial home pages was hired to provide an optimal layout that would be both graphically appealing and easy to navigate. Revisions to the Syntex internal home page were postponed until the external home page was completed, in anticipation of a new layout. Unfortunately, with the acquisition of Syntex by Roche, much Mosaic development has been delayed. The external home page has not yet been released.

Future directions

The Internet is exciting because it is dynamic and always changing. LInC's initial involvement to implement the Internet at Syntex has expanded into a major commitment to continually stay on top of Internet changes, to better support the staff. The Internet training courses require continual revisions. A new modular organization of classes and materials is being developed with some subject specialty classes, such as highlighting resources most valuable to chemists or molecular biologists.

With Syntex now part of Roche, both the Syntex internal and external home pages need extensive revisions. LInC, along with Network Engineering, continues to be centrally involved in these revisions and provides technical support to other departments developing their own home pages. Meanwhile,

LInC maintains its traditional role as a repository for published information by expanding its collection of books, journals, video materials, and resources downloaded from the Internet.

Conclusion

The Internet is not just a technical connection. It is a way for people to interface and exchange information. Both novice and experienced users usually navigate the Internet with ease when they are just browsing. Both alike are challenged when trying to locate specific information quickly. Organizations will find that the Internet will work most effectively when both the information systems staff and the library staff work in close collaboration. Each group can then provide its unique expertise to support the use of the Internet resources.

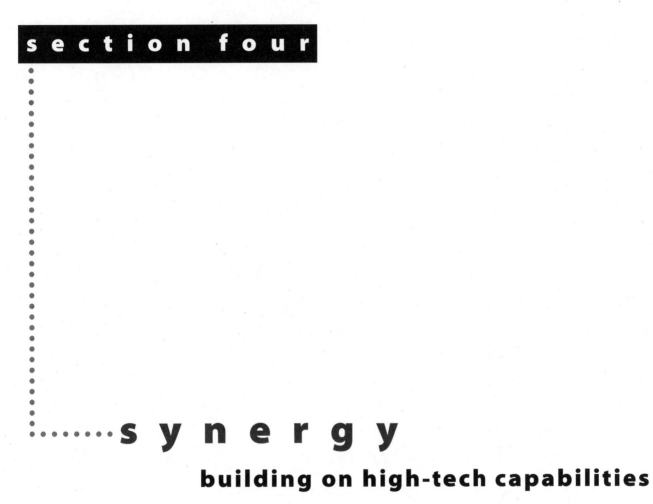

section four

synergy

building on high-tech capabilities

synergy

Robert E. Mayer
Suzanne Sweeney

Finding a Place in an Advanced Networking Environment

The Library of the Stanford University Graduate School of Business

he Internet has become an integral part of access to information in the
Jackson Library at Stanford. It provides an essential backbone for
dispersed files and documents and enables the library to function as a
true gateway to information. While other functions of the Internet are
used, it is access to the World Wide Web that has most dramatically
stimulated new services and products. The Stanford Business School and the
Jackson Library are moving to use these new opportunities in order to develop
innovative products and services for their communities.

Robert E. Mayer is Head Public Services Librarian/Assistant Director in the
Stanford University Business School's Jackson Library. Mail to J. Hugh Jackson
Library, Graduate School of Business, Stanford University, Stanford, CA 94305-5016.
Phone (415) 725-2002, fax (415) 723-0281, e-mail smayer@gsb-peso.stanford.edu

Suzanne Sweeney is Library Systems Manager and Manager of Staff Client Services in the Stanford University Business School's Jackson Library. Mail to J. Hugh
Jackson Library, Graduate School of Business, Stanford University, Stanford, CA
94305-5016. Phone (415) 725-2005, fax (415) 723-0281, e-mail ssweeney@gsb-
peso.stanford.edu

The Jackson Library setting

The J. Hugh Jackson Library (Jackson Library) is one of five autonomous coordinate libraries at Stanford University. Together with the main campus library system, known as Stanford University Libraries (SUL), it constitutes part of that collection of institutions known as the "Libraries of Stanford University." Informal means of interactive cooperation, as well as a common technical infrastructure, exist across the campus to facilitate coordination between these quite distinct institutions.

The Jackson Library was founded in 1933 and has since developed into the second largest academic business library in the United States. It has a Library of Congress classified collection of well over 400,000 volumes, about 1,900 current periodical and newspaper subscriptions, hundreds of thousands of corporate reports in various formats, and access to numerous electronic information sources. In recent years, it has completed a successful renovation of its main floor into a functioning business information center. Founded through a gift as the Rosenberg Corporate Research Center (RCRC), it was designed not only to provide access to extensive traditional on-site material, but also to serve as a gateway to information in an emerging world-wide virtual library. The RCRC has been very successful in integrating a variety of information resources and formats. Intermingled with traditional print collections and study spaces are numerous workstations, both networked and stand-alone, which provide access to data in various electronic formats and services. In this environment, the Internet is an integral connective link between many different components.

Stanford's computing and networking environment

The Stanford campus physically consists of many buildings located over several square miles. The Stanford University Network (SUNet) connects these facilities, and the almost 20,000 mainframe and host computers, terminals, workstations and personal computers that they contain, with a high-speed data network.

This network is part of the Bay Area Regional Research Network (BARRNet) and thus of the Internet. Like the Internet, SUNet is composed of interconnected local networks. It allows diverse centers of computing to exist and provides easy access throughout the campus to Stanford's Campus Wide Information System called Folio. Folio includes the University's online catalog, Socrates. Connections to other locally created, mounted, or shared files are available in Folio, as well as connections to various external Internet sources. Support for Internet use is shared between individual departments, schools, the main campus computing organization and the libraries.

The local Graduate School of Business (GSB) network consists of a mostly Ethernet backbone (except for a Fiber Distributed Data Interface between a two-building complex) that connects to the SUNet. This backbone links individual computers throughout the school's two buildings to local hosts in floor-by-floor connections. The computers in the Jackson Library are part of RCRC and are connected via hubs to the GSB backbone. Other computers in the school are connected by hubs and repeaters.

Use of the Internet

The Jackson Library uses the Internet as a gateway to electronic information resources beyond those heavily used ones already in the local information consortium of Stanford and the University of California, Berkeley. Thirty public Microsoft (MS) DOS workstations in the Library, together with an additional forty in the Student Computing Lab, provide access to a full range of these networked resources. An additional thirty-five Macintoshes in the Lab provide access to all but the local CD-ROM databases. Additional workstations are supplementally dedicated to remote resources, including databases such as Bridge and Reuterlink.

Each of the library's networked MS-DOS computers uses a main menu to point to three main groups of applications. First, there's a collection of applications and utilities including Microsoft (MS) Windows; the World Wide Web browser, Netscape Navigator; MS Windows and MS DOS applications including Microsoft Word and Microsoft Excel; and miscellaneous software and data. In the second group are communications tools such as gateways to Folio, Telnet, FTP, and the Jackson Library Internet Gopher. Finally there are reference resources. These consist of CD-ROM databases; online services such as Lexis/Nexis and Dialog; and other local information files.

Uses of the Internet in the Jackson Library fall under a number of functional areas, described in the following paragraphs.

▶ Online services

The Internet acts as a communications gateway to vendor-supplied online services. Beginning with Lexis/Nexis in 1992, most have migrated from leased lines to the Internet. The Internet has proved an excellent communications technology for online services.

▶ Local databases

The Internet is an interactive communications gateway connecting local databases and services. SUNet links diverse campus computing sites and provides

123

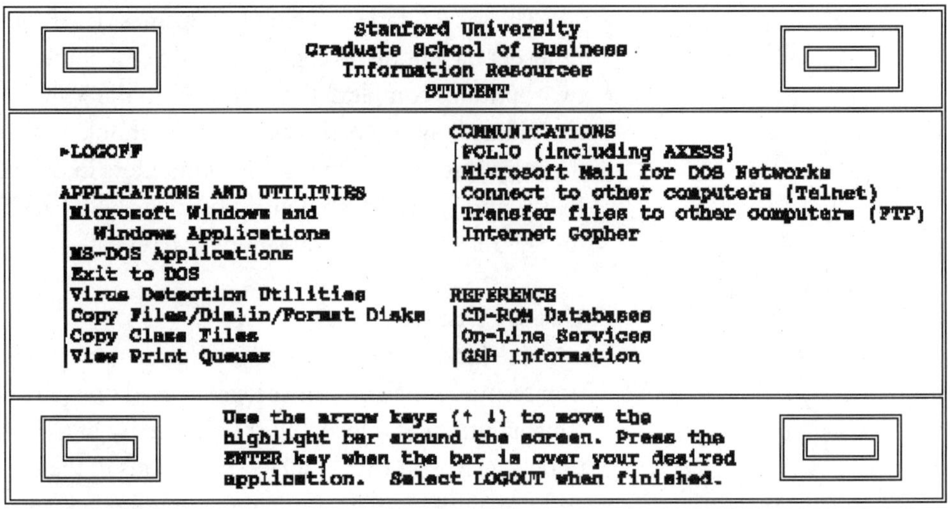

Figure 1: The main menu provides access to many resources from a single point. These include both direct access to the Internet as well as brokered access to other resources and databases.

```
                    Stanford University
                Graduate School of Business
                  Information Resources
                        STUDENT

  ▶LOGOFF                    COMMUNICATIONS
                            FOLIO (including AXESS)
  APPLICATIONS AND UTILITIES  Microsoft Mail for DOS Networks
  Microsoft Windows and       Connect to other computers (Telnet)
    Windows Applications      Transfer files to other computers (FTP)
  MS-DOS Applications         Internet Gopher
  Exit to DOS
  Virus Detection Utilities   REFERENCE
  Copy Files/Dialin/Format Disks  CD-ROM Databases
  Copy Class Files            On-Line Services
  View Print Queues           GSB Information


            Use the arrow keys (↑ ↓) to move the
            highlight bar around the screen. Press the
            ENTER key when the bar is over your desired
            application.  Select LOGOUT when finished.
```

a way to reach Stanford administrative applications, Folio, and the University of California library catalogs (Melvyl), which include many of their own special resources. Together with the Jackson Library's own print and networked electronic databases, patrons find almost unimaginable and unequaled information resources, able to satisfy the vast majority of their information needs.

▶ *Electronic mail*

Internet e-mail is pervasive in the culture of Stanford and, most particularly, of the Business School. It has revolutionized communications both internally and externally. It has also led to a dramatic increase in the sheer quantity of data communicated. The qualitative aspects of this change are still not entirely clear, since quantity has, at the very least, not always translated into quality. E-mail is also used to capture and transmit information from many databases in Folio and Melvyl to the desktop. For example, screen dumps of Lexis/Nexis searches are sent to a user's local e-mail account. Additionally, the University of California provides an awareness service from its Information Access (IAC) files, covering popular magazines, major newspapers, and computer-related journals. With a single command, users create a search on a specific topic and have new search results electronically mailed to them as databases are updated. Similarly, CARL's UnCover table of contents service is available to users through e-mail reports.

▶ *Gopher*

The Jackson Library Gopher site serves both as a gateway to other Gopher sites and as a repository for several locally produced data files. Along with

124

typical Gopher information, there are locally created bibliographical indexes and records for some items that previously existed only as a single paper list. These files include holdings of the Working Paper Collection at the Jackson Library as well as listings of both GSB and other business school cases, some of which are available at the Stanford Bookstore. The GSB Gopher has also been used as a repository of guest speaker transcripts to "Creativity in Business" classes. In the past it also served as an archive/bulletin board of class discussions. The indexing capabilities in these applications are inadequate and problems associated with the ongoing enhancement and maintenance of the databases remain unresolved.

On the whole it would have to be acknowledged that the real potential of the Gopher has not been fully realized. As an effective repository for information resources and user services, the school's Gopher seems likely to be replaced as a central resource by the GSB World Wide Web Home Page. The Gopher will continue to provide basic access to Internet and GSB Information for those without more sophisticated computers.

▶ World Wide Web

The Stanford Business School's World Wide Web Home Page is an object of unceasing discussion, speculation, experimentation, and development. Probably more than any other recent development on the Internet, the Web has achieved recognition in the school as the single most innovative and sophisticated instrument currently in use. Its capabilities enable the school to immediately address some existing practical needs and offer exciting prospects for new kinds of electronically enabled processes and initiatives. While there are certainly many questions about its ultimate form and shape, some fairly ambitious concepts and plans for its future development are also coming into place.

▶ The Web site

The first GSB home page was created in summer 1994. This pioneer effort was designed and implemented by the school's News and Publications Office. It was notable for making available the school's first ever online publishing venture, an issue of the *Stanford Business School Magazine*. The page itself is blessed with a strong basic conceptual outline and notable architectural and graphical elegance. With continuing support from key faculty and the administration, it became clear that a substantial commitment had emerged within the school to exploit the potential of the home page.

A number of other Web pages (with particular emphasis on those from academic business institutions) were studied, in hopes of identifying features which made some more effective than others. This process of evaluation resulted in the development of some core assumptions about the design and function of the Stanford Business School's Web server. These assumptions pointed to a wide range of objectives.

First, the home page would serve as a public relations arm of the school. It would place on the Internet information about the school, its mission, programs, and details about its faculty, staff and students. It would link the school to its alumni through the online publication of the school's alumni journal, the *Stanford Business School Magazine*. The home page would act as an electronic publishing forum for faculty as well as a tool to explore new kinds of instruction, for individual and interactive exploration and learning.

The home page would replace some paper archives and provide for electronic, rather than print, distribution of faculty working papers, articles, works in progress, case studies, and other files. It would function as a gateway to online services, designed to meet the specific needs of the school's clienteles. Links would be organized to databases on the Internet such as the U.S. Securities and Exchange Commission's EDGAR database (**http://town.hall.org/ edgar/edgar.html**). The home page could recognize publicly accessible files and services and those which are accessible only to certain groups and patrons within the school. Finally, it would lead to the development of expertise within the school, in creating and translating files into readable formats.

Some architectural principles for the home page seem to be emerging. There is a focus on elegance in order to fully exploit the graphical capabilities of the Web. With an emphasis on simplicity, the home page will be easy to use and encourage user interaction. Files of actual utility and functionality are being preferred over a sheer mass of information and a large variety of content. In addition, there is a commitment to a clear and logically constructed set of hierarchies.

Overall editorial control of the local Web site has developed into a fairly decentralized set of operational processes. The school's News and Publications Office has played a key role in creating the initial home page and in establishing its overall design. In practical terms, many other school departments are now, or eventually will be, developing their own home pages within the school's Web site. These departments will exercise a considerable degree of control over their own design and contents. For example, individual home pages are being created for each faculty member, as well as for selected staff. It is probable that some sort of overall process of editorial control and responsibility will emerge, in order to ensure some basic uniformity of style, design, and functionality.

►*Library home page*

The Jackson Library is currently developing its own home page, with references to those of its own resources and services which are available to users. The library is also playing a role in the development of the school's overall home page by collaborating with individual faculty as well as with the News and Publications Office. The library is positioning itself to serve as the electronic publishing agency for faculty who write for the school's own working paper series as well as for those who produce case studies. In this way, the current focus on print products with relatively slow and limited distribution may give way to a much more dynamic process of interactive scholarly communication.

The ease and convenience of desktop publishing on the Web has even led one faculty member to devise the concept of a work in progress on his own Web home page. Colleagues are invited to interact in the creation of this scholarly work through communications directly over the Web. The work will develop organically in this fashion and is intended to have no other "published" manifestation.

As of this writing, the basic outline of the GSB's Web site is nearing completion. The GSB home page (**http://gsb-www.stanford.edu/home.html**) provides a basic index to many subsets of data. Each link may lead to many subsets of links. For example the home page link labeled "Faculty" will lead to a full listing of faculty names. Each name, in turn, will lead to an individual home page for each faculty member, including a photo, a brief biographical text, and a list of publications. The list of publications may lead to the actual publication itself when it is available on the Web, either as a GSB file or in another electronic publication elsewhere. The overall concept provides for any number of GSB departmental offices to have their own home pages. In this decentralized scheme, individual units will have the ability to design their own Web site within the constraints of the design of the Web site for the GSB as a whole.

As an aside, the Stanford Business School's Web site has just this year been given a top or four-star rating, together with three other business schools. This rating was made in Wayne Marr's *BSCHOOL Web: Marr's Official Rating Guide to Business School Webs*. The rating is based on the "design and usefulness of its Web pages.

Other Uses

▶ *Partnership with a vendor*

The Stanford Business School hopes to leverage the Web to support interactive and vendor-like services. Such services are already being developed by some commercial enterprises for a fee. The Jackson Library currently enjoys a special partnership with a local document retrieval and delivery vendor, Information Express. This partnership enables the library to provide comprehensive document retrieval and delivery services to school faculty and staff at minimal direct cost by extracting added value from collections and information resources.

Information Express is currently developing programs using the World Wide Web as a vehicle for marketing specific products and services. These will enable end users to interactively acquire and pay for specific products and services. The Web's graphically sophisticated displays, as well as its forms capabilities, make it an ideal online environment for user-friendly interactive network transactions. Information Express is in the process of developing systems to develop the Web as a product which not only passively purveys information but also provides interactive services. This developing expertise has proved to be a good match for the needs of the Stanford Business School. In addition to providing free document retrieval and delivery services, Information Express has also been providing the school with programming assistance in designing and preparing documents for its Web site, as well as helping to train staff. It has lent an additional element of design and functional sophistication to the school's home page that would otherwise have been difficult, if not impossible, to obtain in so short a time. This creative collaboration between a nonprofit academic organization and a commercial enterprise continues to be a key element in the school's commitment to create a truly visionary information and service node on the Web.

Faculty and staff information services

One of the most interesting online products that Information Express has developed for its World Wide Web site is an interactive Table of Contents (TOC) Alerts and Document Delivery module. This system is designed to allow Web users to set up an account, browse an index of periodical titles from which contents are provided, and then design a profile of periodicals for which the TOC service is desired. Paper or e-mail notifications are sent to customers, who may then request the documents. Still in development, this module is currently being tested. It is being designed to function within specific customer sites or as a widely available Internet resource. Should this system prove to be successful,

128

it is very likely that Information Express will be asked to make its TOC service available as a node on the GSB home page. As a node, it will then become the vehicle for faculty and staff requests for document delivery through the existing on-site Information Express document delivery system. The entire alerts and delivery process will then be fully integrated into a single operation.

Additionally, it may be possible for Jackson Library to collaborate with Information Express in providing a mechanism for browsing and ordering GSB Research Papers and case studies published on the Web. Information Express already has agreed to maintain access to the *Stanford Business School Magazine* at its Web site and to serve, in effect, as a distribution and subscription agency. Another project currently under development is to convert the Jackson Library's *Selected Additions List* into an electronic publication and to incorporate it into Information Express' overall TOC service on the Web.

▶ *Ariel*

The Jackson Library is at last on the verge of creating an Ariel workstation for document transmission over the Internet. As of this writing there is at least some confidence that it has potential beyond the obvious interlibrary loan applications, particularly as more libraries and vendors make use of it for high quality document delivery over the Internet. The entire workstation will be in a public area and the document scanner will be available as a stand-alone to those who need to digitize images for use in computing applications.

▶ *Surfing for information*

Particularly with the World Wide Web, the Internet has begun to emerge as a unique and powerful resource for supplying information to library clientele. Skills and interests in this aspect of Internet use vary widely, however, and no single pattern of use is discernible at this point.

Immense potential

The Internet has become a fully integrated component of the Jackson Library communications and information infrastructure. It enables the library to serve as a gateway to information and thereby to realize one of its most important missions. The single most significant commitment is clearly to the ongoing implementation of the local World Wide Web site. The Jackson Library views this as a development with immense potential to provide resources and services with a significant impact on the library. While much remains in the realm of development, sufficient results have already indicated that the Internet will enlarge the role of the Jackson Library as an information intermediary.

synergy

David R. Clark

Pikes Peak Library District's MAGGnet

*y creating an open and freely accessible Internet interface, the Pikes
Peak (Colorado) Library District broke new ground, maintaining its
reputation of using technology for the public interest. This service,
called MAGGnet, gives the Colorado Springs community access to
portions of the Internet from Maggie's Place, the district's public menu
system. MAGGnet is in the first wave of such interfaces offered by public
libraries in the United States. The success of MAGGnet means that this number
will grow substantially in the near future.*

**David R. Clark** is the Systems Officer for the Pikes Peak Library District in Colorado Springs,
Colorado. He is experienced in developing and managing online network systems. He has
been successful also as an independent producer of specialized software applications and as a
consultant in all aspects of computer systems and software operations. In his spare time, he
dabbles in art and woodworking and developing his expertise in producing customized
multimedia applications. Mail can be sent to 5550 N. Union Blvd., Colorado Springs, CO 80918.
Phone (719) 531-6333, x1100, fax (719) 528-2800, e-mail dclark@ppld.org

Introduction

The Pikes Peak Library District (PPLD), against the backdrop of the majestic Pikes Peak in Colorado Springs, is proud of its reputation for using technology to fulfill patron needs. Technology-based services already in place include an electronic catalog, dial-in lines to check holdings from home, and several community databases.

Several years ago, as the Head of Technical Services was retiring, the district installed an electronic catalog. Since her office was being vacated, it was procured as the new computer room. In honor of the departing Maggie O'Rourke, the new public computer interface was named "Maggie's Place."

Figure 1: The main menu of Maggie's Place points to information resources available locally and remotely in the Pikes Peak Library District.

```
─────────────────────────────────────────────────────────────────
─                      Terminal - MAGGIE.TRM                  ▼ ▲
─────────────────────────────────────────────────────────────────
 File  Edit  Settings  Phone  Transfers  Help
─────────────────────────────────────────────────────────────────
 Imagination Celebration schedules are at all Pikes Peak Library  ▲
 District facilities & area Wendy's restaurants.
            ──────────────────────────

       1.  PPLD On-Line Card Catalog

       2.  Community Connections: Menu of Community Information Databases

       3.  MAGGnet:  Gateway to the Internet, including
                Access Colorado Library Information Network (ACLIN)

       4.  Reference Sources and Indexes:  Encyclopedia, Business,
                Magazine, Health, General Interest, and more!

       5.  Government Databases, including City Hall On-Line
                and Colorado Legislative Database

       6.  Other Library Systems

       7.  Help and Library News

       8.  Non-Public Databases

 Enter the NUMBER of your choice, and press the <RETURN> key >>█

                                                                  ▼
─────────────────────────────────────────────────────────────────
 ◄ █                                                            ► ▼
─────────────────────────────────────────────────────────────────
```

Since then, the district has aggressively added databases of local interest to Maggie's Place to complement our online holdings. Community databases on children such as the Colorado Springs Childcare database and others for local clubs and organizations have been added. The Colorado Legislative Database, containing all of the bills under discussion in the Colorado Legislature, is also available. Commercial databases, like the *Grolier's Encyclopedia*, have been licensed and are in use as well.

As a logical extension of these efforts, the district decided to see if we could offer selected files and databases from the Internet. This led to the district's free public Internet interface, available via Maggie's Place and called MAGGnet.

131

Figure 2: The cover of the brochure for MAGGnet describes the kinds of information available via the Internet.

Why we did it

Reinforced by the Director, Bernie Margolis, the district feels responsible to the community as a vital information resource. This responsibility traditionally has focused on print rather than electronic resources. As technology evolves, public libraries must provide access to information in any format. The Internet is just one form of information which the community needs to function in a modern world.

The district also invented a public Internet interface to give the community access to this important communication and research tool. The district's Internet interface gave patrons an opportunity to explore and use the Internet. Indeed, it gave the community a competitive edge. Their experiences with the Internet would transform their understanding of it as well.

What we decided to do

Once the decision was made to offer Internet access to the public, we began to think about what the district could reasonably offer to its community. The possibilities ranged from a kind of Free-Net to simply offering a single database. The actual delivery vehicle was also discussed. What form should the interface actually be — text-only or graphical?

Since the primary purpose of MAGGnet was to provide exposure to the Internet, we thought the most appropriate way to develop this service would be incremental. As the patrons became more comfortable, and experimented with the Internet, new functions would be added as necessary.

At least three companies in the Colorado Springs community offer fee-based Internet access. The district decided not to compete with them by offering a kind of Free-Net. Without a Free-Net, the district could not offer individual accounts. We would not offer individual passwords to patrons. That meant some Internet functions would not be available.

What kind of interface would be best? For example, Internet Gopher uses a series of menus to make text files and other documents accessible. Mosaic, from the National Center for Supercomputing Applications (NCSA) at the University of Illinois, is a graphical interface operating on a number of computer platforms. Mosaic uses hypertext to create links between files, connecting information on local or remote servers on the Internet. As a graphical interface, Mosaic includes graphics, videos, and audio files, allowing for complex and richer views of Internet-based resources. Mosaic is one kind of Web browser; Lynx is another Web browser that provides a text-only view of the Internet.

MAGGnet is based on a Gopher interface for several reasons. First, patrons are accustomed to the menu hierarchy of Gopher, based on their experiences with Maggie's Place. Second, a simple text-based interface made it possible to reach the MAGGnet from any point in the district. With eleven branches in the district, and hundreds of terminals, a more complicated graphical interface would have meant the replacement of most of the public terminals with personal computers and workstations. Funds were not available to make the sort of wholesale equipment change to do this, but a move to a graphical interface and new computers certainly will be part of the near future.

With a Sun Microsystems SPARC Classic workstation, the district was able to maintain all Internet user passwords and control the Gopher interface. The workstation gave the district ample freedom in defining Internet access, which would have been difficult working through an Internet service provider. Working with a provider would have meant a huge reliance on the provider for every detail of operation of the Internet host, even simply adding a new userid and password for a new staff member. With the workstation, the district's staff can add user passwords within minutes. The district's Internet connection is through Colorado SuperNet, with a dedicated line established between the Sun computer and a local SuperNet node.

What kinds of Internet destinations does the district offer? There are some Gopher servers that offer an option entitled "All The Gophers In The World" which in turn connect to thousands of Gopher servers. We decided not to overwhelm the district's patrons with too many options. A more structured interface to the Internet in MAGGnet's first release allowed our patrons a chance to become comfortable with the Internet and its resources.

The Nitty Gritty

With the design and interface decisions made, the staff of the district began to work on the details of MAGGnet and how it would be delivered to patrons. A committee was formed, pulling staff members from every department in the district. This group decided which Internet destinations would be offered on the first version of MAGGnet. Committee members were issued passwords to explore the Internet to locate interesting servers and resources.

We designed a framework to present several different categories of Internet-based databases and destinations. These categories ranged from General Reference to News and Weather to Medical Information. This list varied during development; at this writing it contains some fourteen major categories. The "About MAGGnet" option provides information about this Internet service and the library district.

In the district, patron response cards in printed form can be found in all of the branches. They simply ask "How are we doing?" Responses go straight to

Figure 3: The main menu of MAGGnet (**gopher://peak.ppld.org/**)indicates that there are 14 broad subject areas to explore on the Internet.

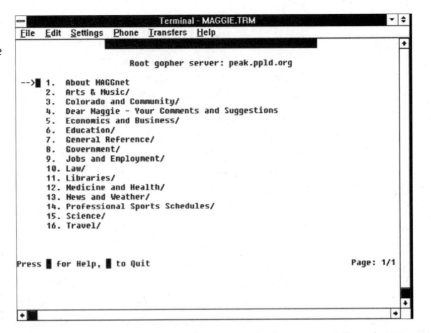

```
 ═                        Terminal - MAGGIE.TRM                    ▼ ▲
 File  Edit  Settings  Phone  Transfers  Help
                                                                      ▲
                     Root gopher server: peak.ppld.org

-->█ 1.  About MAGGnet
     2.  Arts & Music/
     3.  Colorado and Community/
     4.  Dear Maggie - Your Comments and Suggestions
     5.  Economics and Business/
     6.  Education/
     7.  General Reference/
     8.  Government/
     9.  Jobs and Employment/
    10.  Law/
    11.  Libraries/
    12.  Medicine and Health/
    13.  News and Weather/
    14.  Professional Sports Schedules/
    15.  Science/
    16.  Travel/


Press █ for Help, █ to Quit                              Page: 1/1
                                                                      ▼
 ◄ █                                                              ► ▼
```

the director, so these forms are known as the "Dear Bernie" cards. We needed a similar form on MAGGnet, and so a menu option was implemented, called "Dear Maggie." The electronic version sends a mail message to the Internet administrator, Ken Pratt.

The district's Internet committee met monthly, and in its deliberations, discussed several issues. What should be done about objectionable postings on MAGGnet? What kinds of resources would be best for MAGGnet? Members of the committee, in their Internet explorations, compiled lists of servers with valuable information. In particular, Lynn Harrison, a reference librarian, was especially effective in finding useful sites. Lynn became the lead Net surfer, spending many hours looking for every potential destination.

Since MAGGnet would be available from any public terminal, Internet training for the district staff was vital. For several weeks, Dave Doman, the district's full-time trainer, Lynn Harrison, and I conducted training sessions every Tuesday, Wednesday, and Thursday morning. Any district staff member could sign up. These sessions were nearly always full. Training and support of MAGGnet by the staff led to its rousing success.

The MAGGnet public release

The district and the staff all wanted MAGGnet to work as expected. Ample time was available to fine tune the service, before a big public splash. In

135

advance of the public announcement, MAGGnet quietly appeared on Maggie's Place one Monday in the autumn of 1994.

For about a month, the district made no public comments on MAGGnet. During that time, knowledge about and access to MAGGnet spread by word of mouth through the Colorado Springs community. We collected many Dear Maggie comments and talked both with patrons who enjoyed the new service, as well as those who had trouble. Suggestions were also made for different kinds of resources to offer, and the committee looked for servers addressing these needs.

Within a week of providing access to MAGGnet, all twelve dial-in lines for users at home were busy constantly. With this sort of traffic, the help desk began to receive calls from patrons wondering if the computer was down, since they could not access the system. We suspected that this problem would develop, but not so quickly. The installation of thirty new phone lines would relieve this difficulty.

At a press conference in November 1994 we announced MAGGnet to the public. By this time, MAGGnet was heavily in use, the second most popular option on the Maggie's Place menu, surpassed only by the online catalog. All the local media — television, radio, and newspapers — were present. At the press conference, the director made the official announcement about MAGGnet, and I gave a demonstration of it. The story about MAGGnet was carried by all of the media that night and the following day. A morning radio program talked about it.

Figure 4: MAGGnet made headlines throughout the community, and was featured even on radio and television.

Patron feedback

The overwhelming majority of comments collected through the Dear Maggie option have been favorable. Here's an example: "Thank you very much for giving me access to the Internet. There is no other way for me to get it, and I'm having a great time looking around."

There are others who say "You call this Internet access?" From skilled Internet users, we hear disappointment that the district does not offer a Free-Net. Of course, there are other comments I can't begin to print. Overall, the commentary has pointed MAGGnet to new destinations, such as genealogy databases.

Current status

The main menu has remained stable for many months at this point. We are in the long range process of finding and evaluating databases and destinations to add to the MAGGnet menus. The initial offering included some 60 to 70 databases. The district's Information and Reference (I&R) Committee is examining new Internet resources, with a new subcommittee specifically evaluating Internet databases and sites, hunting for new and interesting information on a wide range of topics. Some 100 possible new destinations are currently being discussed. Additions to MAGGnet will take place as frequently as every two weeks.

Mosaic and our next steps

With the initial work of creating MAGGnet over, the district is studying two main areas to improve overall service to patrons. First, work will begin on a Web home page. This will be for any Internet user with the appropriate hardware and software to support a graphic interface. It will position the district to eventually replace "dumb" public terminals with personal computers and workstations. Graphics of the branches of the library, of local attractions, and other illustrations can be added to this Web view of the Internet. Second, the systems staff and the I&R Committee will work together to develop a Gopher dedicated to reference, with much broader range of features than MAGGnet. This resource should allow reference librarians to answer patron questions quickly and easily.

Summary

The entire MAGGnet project has been a success for the library district staff and the local community. Patrons now have the opportunity to plug into an abundance of modern resources. We have also raised community awareness of new technologies. There's still administrative work for the district to complete, such as formal Internet usage policies. Statistics on the use of MAGGnet will help

137

develop these rules. MAGGnet has proven to be an important and interesting service, and we are proud to have the opportunity to offer it to the Colorado Springs area.

Figure 5: The development team of MAGGnet is justifiably proud of its work, and its contribution to the Colorado Springs community.

138

• • • • • • In this technology-friendly environment, the Library turns out new Internet services as fast as you can say Mosaic.

Eugenie Prime
Kathe Gust
Tony Carrozza

Wish Lists Come True at the Hewlett-Packard Laboratories Research Library

 *he Hewlett-Packard Laboratories' Research Library was the first HP library on the Internet. This chapter discusses the experience of the library with the Internet and the NCSA Mosaic browser for the World Wide Web. It describes the early development of the library's home page, the library services available to users at their desktops, the use of Mosaic as a reference tool for the library's information analysts, and plans for future library products and services using the Internet.*

Eugenie Prime has been Manager of Corporate Libraries at Hewlett Packard Company since 1987. Mail can be sent to Hewlett Packard Laboratories, Research Library – 2L, Palo Alto, CA 94303. Phone (415) 857-3094, fax (415) 852-8187, e-mail Eugenie_Prime@ hpl.hp.com

Kathe Gust has been with the HPL Research Library since 1986. Her mail address is Hewlett Packard Laboratories, Research Library – 2L, Palo Alto, CA 94303. Phone (415) 857-3094, Fax (415) 852-8187, e-mail Kathe_Gust@hpl.hp.com

Tony Carrozza is an Information Technology Engineer. He has been involved in software development at Hewlett Packard since 1988. His mailing address is Hewlett Packard, 1501 Page Mill Road – 2L, Palo Alto, CA 94303. Phone (415) 857-3620, fax (415) 857-2066, e-mail Tony_Carrozza@hpl.hp.com

synergy

Introduction

It all started on the Friday before Christmas 1993, when the manager of corporate libraries at Hewlett-Packard, Eugenie Prime, saw a demonstration of the NCSA Mosaic browser for the Internet World Wide Web. After just 15 minutes, she knew she had found a tremendous new tool for the Hewlett-Packard Laboratories' Research Library, and she knew that the library's users would love it.

Hewlett-Packard has had a relatively long tradition with the Internet. Every researcher at HP Labs has access to the Internet. However, use of the Internet as a research tool has been limited. This is probably because it is difficult for researchers to find information on the Internet and even harder to find it quickly.

The HP Labs Research Library

The HP Labs Research Library serves the Hewlett-Packard research community, including researchers in all product areas: computers, semiconductors, software, medical and other instruments, networking, printers, and many others. The library provides technical data, marketing information, patents, and other information.

At the library, the information analysts were all exposed to basic Internet training and were encouraged to explore the Internet as an alternate searching tool. They found searching to be very cumbersome and the results quite unproductive. Other than the occasional sortie online by a few enterprising souls, the Internet was ignored as an information source. It was much more frequently used as a communication device or a delivery mechanism. Analysts joined bulletin boards, mailing lists, and topical newsgroups. The library received a number of daily and weekly newsletters, reports, and other publications via the Net. Staff then redistributed these to local customers at the labs, and remotely to other HP libraries and employees elsewhere.

That encounter with Mosaic, however, was the beginning of an adventure for the library. Each new source, each new tool, each restructuring of the home page continues to be exciting. The Mosaic experiment has been extremely well received by our customers. At the end of the first four months, the library was receiving some 10,000 inquiries a month on its home page. Kathe Gust, an information analyst in the library, was the key player, not only in choosing Internet information sources but in the design and structure of the home page using the HyperText Markup Language (HTML). After the first year of the home page, the library hired a software engineer, Tony Carrozza, to provide technical programming support and wizardry. These people, plus the strong

140

support of the labs' management, were essential in creating access to the Web that met the library's two goals: increasing the amount of information available at the labs, and increasing the ease of searching it.

How we did it

▶ The Research Library Home Page

The first job was to develop the library home page, listing information products and services available through the library. The home page was designed for growth, to allow for the addition of offerings without changing the page's basic appearance. Subsequent pages give the user more information about a topic selected on the home page. The home page went online in January 1994 with three offerings; by August 1994 it had a full complement of fifteen resources. It is still growing.

Information selected for the home page must be available in an electronic format. A conscious decision was made not to rekey anything that was not already being typed for production by the staff. This means that some potentially popular items are not offered on the Web because we cannot get them in any format other than hard copy.

HP Labs as a whole has two home pages: an external home page for users outside the labs, and an internal home page available only to users within the labs. The library home page is accessible only to internal users with a link on the internal home page. We chose a graphic to put on the labs' internal home page to represent the library. It is about the size of a postage stamp and helps the reader quickly reach the library link. Within the library suite of pages, graphics are used to help users identify information sources. If the information is supplied by the library, the home page picture appears on the page. If it comes from another source, an attempt is made to recreate the supplier's logo or graphic on the page.

▶ First conversion efforts

We decided to start with the *Library User Guide* as our first online document. This guide was already available to employees using FrameMaker as the hypertext viewer. Although we had some previous experience with hypertext, we soon realized that the conversion process would take some time as Kathe Gust learned to use the new language. Some assistance was available from our Computing Services group, but we had to learn much by ourselves. Conversion of the *Library User Guide* was not completed until spring 1994.

To get information up on the library home page quickly, we knew we would have to look for some smaller documents that would be easier to convert.

141

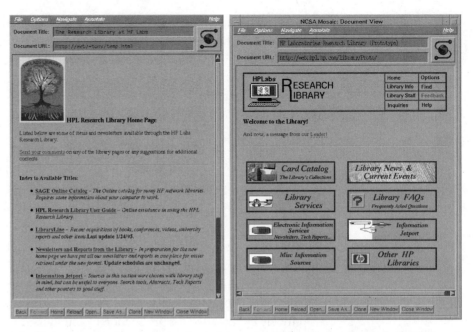

The library receives a number of newsletters in electronic format and produces others in house. These licensed newsletters are redistributed to the library's clients via electronic mail. We selected the new acquisitions newsletter, *LibraryLine,* to become the first item on our home page. It went online in January 1994. Since conversion was considerably less painful for shorter documents, we soon added other newsletters.

It was important to us that the home page should look professional, and we wanted our document offerings to look exceptional too. An early temptation was to do too much to enhance the newsletters. At first, we put contents lists and hypertext links in all the newsletters, but as the amount of information increased we began to publish the newsletters in a simpler format.

After the library suite of pages had been up for a couple of months, the Library Board of Customers met. We gave the group a talk with slides about the new pages. Several of them had already looked at what we were doing and liked it. They requested that all the electronic newsletters should be posted to the server, to put everything in one place. We were already offering two daily newsletters, two biweekly newsletters, and five weekly titles. Posting all the newsletters in a hypertext format required a great deal of time, so we decided to post the daily and biweekly newsletters in simple ASCII format. The weekly newsletters are longer and are produced with a hypertext table of contents at the beginning. Four to six issues of all the newsletters are left on the server, depending on title and frequency of the newsletter.

Some of the requested titles have licensing restrictions that do not allow us to share them company-wide. With support from the Computer Services group, we installed a secure directory on the server. This allows us to post the restricted newsletters in an area that can only be accessed by one machine on the network at the labs.

▶ *Leveraging our investment*

The highly successful deployment of the newsletters encouraged the library to find additional items of interest for our clients. We also wanted to leverage our investment to serve more of the company. Computing Services had already created an automated listing of the *HP Labs Technical Reports* for the server (URL: **http://www.hpl.hp.com/**). The library received report notices and abstracts from several membership organizations such as Sematech and these were added to our list. *Sematech Abstracts* was added in March 1994, *Recent HP Labs Technical Reports* in April, and the *Library User Guide* in May. Wide Area Information Servers (WAIS) searching capability was also installed by Computing Services. This was the last time the library was able to get assistance from them for something new. Many of the other service organizations at the labs were starting their own home pages, and free programming assistance was no longer readily available. We decided that the new library systems person would need to be familiar with Web issues. Tony Carrozza was able to provide technical support services, essential if we continued development of library electronic services.

Since images on the Web are quite clear on most users' large screens, we decided to enhance the electronic version of the *Library User Guide* by including photographs of the staff. Portraits were taken with a digital camera, and each person was encouraged to submit a short biographical sketch to accompany the portrait. One of our interesting statistics each month is discovering who has the most popular photo.

▶ *Mosaic as a reference tool*

At about this same time, the library staff discovered the value of the Mosaic browser as a reference tool. In the course of answering reference questions, we found information sources of many different kinds. We also discovered that many universities and some companies make their technical reports available on the Internet. So much material of value to our staff and clients began to turn up that we started a special page called the Information Jetport. It was modeled on the Teleporter, a collection of Internet pointers selected by Computing Services that are found on the HP Labs internal home page.

The Information Jetport contains pointers to Internet resources that we think may be especially valuable to our staff, clients, and colleagues at other HP libraries. We developed a set of informal rules similar to the collection development

Figure 2: One of the lists of Technical Reports available from the library's WWW pages (**http://www.hpl.hp.com**).

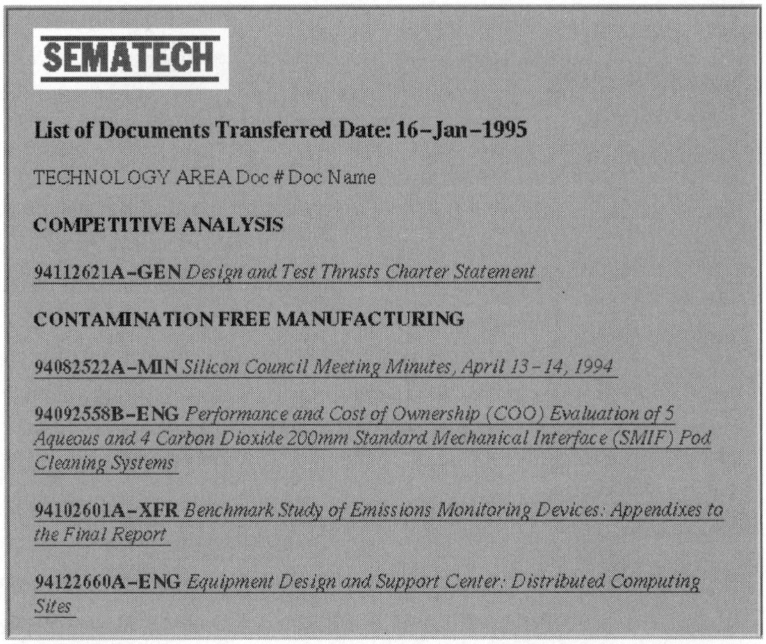

SEMATECH

List of Documents Transferred Date: 16–Jan–1995

TECHNOLOGY AREA Doc # Doc Name

COMPETITIVE ANALYSIS

94112621A–GEN *Design and Test Thrusts Charter Statement*

CONTAMINATION FREE MANUFACTURING

94082522A–MIN *Silicon Council Meeting Minutes, April 13 – 14, 1994*

94092558B–ENG *Performance and Cost of Ownership (COO) Evaluation of 5 Aqueous and 4 Carbon Dioxide 200mm Standard Mechanical Interface (SMIF) Pod Cleaning Systems*

94102601A–XFR *Benchmark Study of Emissions Monitoring Devices: Appendixes to the Final Report*

94122660A–ENG *Equipment Design and Support Center: Distributed Computing Sites*

Figure 3: *The Library User Guide* was transferred to the home page in May 1994.

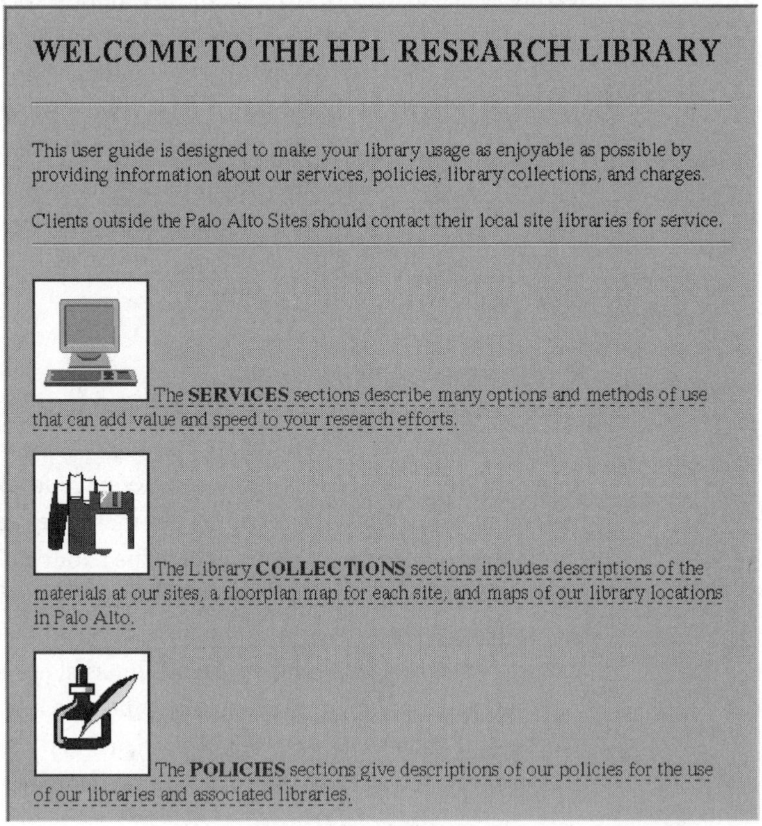

WELCOME TO THE HPL RESEARCH LIBRARY

This user guide is designed to make your library usage as enjoyable as possible by providing information about our services, policies, library collections, and charges.

Clients outside the Palo Alto Sites should contact their local site libraries for service.

 The **SERVICES** sections describe many options and methods of use that can add value and speed to your research efforts.

 The Library **COLLECTIONS** sections includes descriptions of the materials at our sites, a floorplan map for each site, and maps of our library locations in Palo Alto.

 The **POLICIES** sections give descriptions of our policies for the use of our libraries and associated libraries.

144

policy for the library to govern the content of the Jetport page. Items on the page must be currently functioning, readily available, and free of charge. We deliberately restricted the Jetport pointers to include only the kind of item that would have relevance in answering the types of reference questions received at the library. An example of such an item is EDGAR, the U.S. Securities and Exchange Commission (SEC) database. Library staff and clients are also encouraged to suggest specific URLs and types of information they would like to see on the page. The suggestions are evaluated and tested before a decision is made to add the items to the collection.

►*Improvements*

Both the Information Jetport page and the library home page have gone through a transformation since their first versions. In both cases, the listing of individual items grew too long for easy access. We made subsidiary pages, divided by subject, to handle the problem. Since we had designed the file structure to allow each section to stand alone, we were able to insert extra pages without changing the pointers. The subject breakdown on the Jetport page now includes web searching tools, business information, government sources, legal sources, bookstores and publishers, basic reference tools, technical reports, and other topics.

There has been a steady rise in usage of the items we offer to our users. There is also significant and growing usage from the rest of the company as word of mouth spreads beyond the Palo Alto sites. We were the first HP library on the Internet. We have not done any active advertising outside of our immediate area, except to inform the other HP libraries at our annual meeting. Several smaller HP libraries in the San Francisco Bay Area are suggesting the use of the library pages to their clients. In February 1995 we registered ourselves on the list of internal home pages for the company. We anticipate that the usage will continue increasing as a result of this action.

► *Tracking usage statistics*

The server at HP Labs uses the Getstats statistical package from Enterprise Integration Technologies to track usage of the documents on a monthly basis. The library tracks usage from both HP Labs and the rest of the company worldwide. The method used to collect the statistics makes it necessary to design documents creatively, to ensure that statistics are taken on the items the library wishes to track. Statistics are collected by server only, not machine connections, so the result is a lower limit of usage, not an exact count. Since none of the offerings has been available for a full year yet, we have not used the

145

statistics to help decide whether to remove certain items from the list, but we may in the future.

Where we're headed

Our long-term goal at the library is to deliver our services directly to our users. The HP network (which is a part of the global Internet) includes HP-UX workstations, and Microsoft (MS) DOS, MS Windows, and Macintosh personal computers. In the past, the software applications that let users access library services had to be developed separately for each kind of computer. Then the appropriate application had to be installed and maintained on each user's machine. Since HP has about 90,000 employees worldwide, the efforts — and costs — of this approach were obviously enormous.

Because it can be used by all types of computers, the World Wide Web provides a much more efficient way to deliver information services. The Web lets the library's applications and information reside on a single server machine at the library. Patrons can use any Web browser they choose, on whatever kind of machine they have, to access the information on the server.

We intend to take full advantage of these Internet capabilities by improving library services. The improvements will permit direct communication with appropriate library staff; provide improved search and retrieval tools; give the library's clients "intelligent" information services; and automate library and administrative services.

► *Enabling direct communication*

Users can submit inquiries to the library directly via Web forms that we have developed. Questions and service requests are automatically routed via electronic mail to the appropriate library staff person for response or action. Online forms are available or under development for such services as literature searches, patent searches, book purchases, journal subscriptions, user surveys, and general questions. Information submitted via the forms can be automatically stored in a database for analysis. This is useful for analyzing survey results, for example.

► *Improving search and retrieval tools*

The library has come a long way from the familiar card catalog. It is providing ever increasing access to its collections and electronic information services over the Internet. The library's collections are cataloged on Sage, our local implementation of Unicorn from Sirsi. In addition, the library has developed a tool that allows users to search technical journals and worldwide patent information, and then examine the full-text image of the document.

146

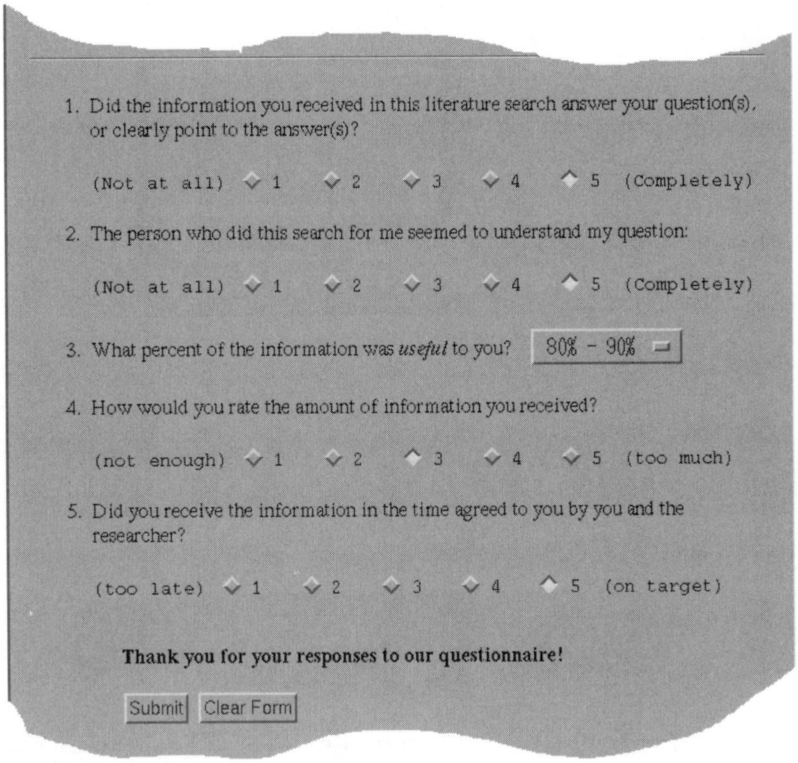

Figure 4: Online forms can be found on the library home page which patrons can complete and submit from their desktops.

1. Did the information you received in this literature search answer your question(s), or clearly point to the answer(s)?

   (Not at all) ◇ 1 ◇ 2 ◇ 3 ◇ 4 ◆ 5 (Completely)

2. The person who did this search for me seemed to understand my question:

   (Not at all) ◇ 1 ◇ 2 ◇ 3 ◇ 4 ◆ 5 (Completely)

3. What percent of the information was *useful* to you? [80% – 90% ⊟]

4. How would you rate the amount of information you received?

   (not enough) ◇ 1 ◇ 2 ◆ 3 ◇ 4 ◇ 5 (too much)

5. Did you receive the information in the time agreed to you by you and the researcher?

   (too late) ◇ 1 ◇ 2 ◇ 3 ◇ 4 ◆ 5 (on target)

Thank you for your responses to our questionnaire!

[Submit] [Clear Form]

We are also developing a new version of the home page that uses graphical buttons to help users quickly find the information they want (see Figure 1). New features will also be added, such as answers to frequently asked questions and direct library feedback forms.

The library staff has also worked to identify good sources of information for the kinds of inquiries we get. The library's Information Jetport is a launch pad to credible, library-validated information sources on the Web. Supplementing the Jetport are tools based on WAIS that are being developed to help users quickly find information in the library's Web pages.

An Experts Resource Directory will provide a database of information on resident experts. HP employees will be easily able to find in-house help in areas such as object-oriented design, software reuse, ISDN, and VLSI circuit design. In the future, we hope to offer patrons the ability to search for desired information simultaneously across several databases of different types from a single user screen.

▶ *Providing intelligent information services*

The amount of information available via the Internet can be overwhelming, and we want to help our users avoid information overload. We are now working

147

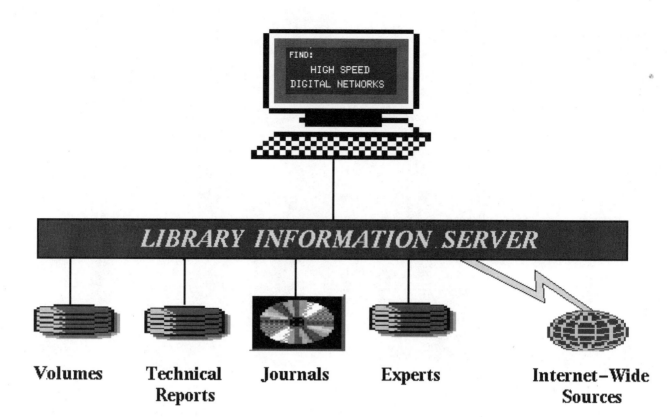

FIND:
HIGH SPEED
DIGITAL NETWORKS

LIBRARY INFORMATION SERVER

Volumes   **Technical
Reports**   **Journals**   **Experts**   **Internet–Wide
Sources**

Figure 5: A single user interface shields users from the complexity of searching across multiple databases/systems.

on tools that let subscribers to any of our electronic information services create their own profiles to filter information for them. Information fitting their profiles can then be delivered to them in the form they request (electronic mail, fax, hard copy). In essence, users will be able to create a customized journal of information that is matched to their needs and interests.

▶ *Automating services*

The Internet has also provided the means for the library to automate certain processes. When patrons use library services from their work areas (such as subscribing to electronic information services), applications extract information from the company personnel database and send it to the library's billing system. Automated routines then feed monthly billing information to the finance department for charging the costs of these services back to the subscriber. These processes remove a great deal of paperwork from the library staff and let us concentrate on our real job: getting patrons the information they need.

148

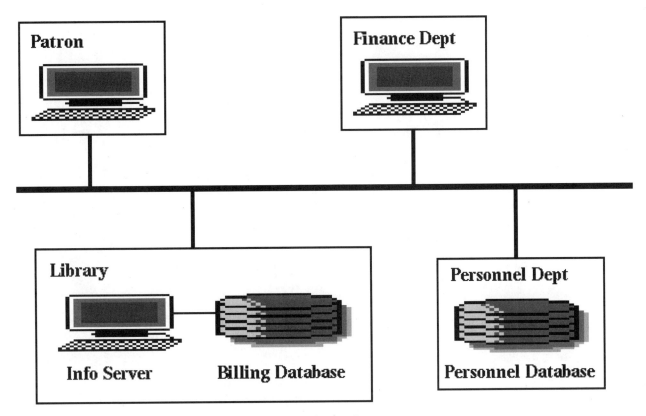

Figure 6: The Net provides the means to automate processes that require communication between various Hewlett-Packard departments and systems.

Conclusion

The use of the Internet via Mosaic has been overwhelmingly positive for the library. It has allowed the library to expand both the amount of information offered to patrons and the ways in which patrons can access that information. The learning curve has not been too steep. We have discovered new information sources and new ways of streamlining our users' access to information that could not have been achieved in any other way. We expect the future to provide more of this two-pronged growth: new sources of information, and new ways of searching and filtering that information so that patrons can get exactly what they want. Since that's our mission, we are truly excited and gratified at how use of the Internet has enriched our role.

section five

connection

linking to school and community education

Sharyl G. Smith

UtahLINK
A Model for Statewide Educational Use of the Internet

*tahLINK, one of the largest Frame-Relay wide area networks in the
United States, brings together students and teachers in Utah's public
schools and applied technology centers. It is an evolving electronic
service, providing users with a menu of electronic educational materials
and information resources, including the Internet. Part of the Utah
Education Network (UEN), UtahLINK was invented in cooperation with
USWEST — a major telephone and telecommunications service in the
intermountain West, independent carrier companies, a number of business
partners, public schools, higher education, and state government agencies. This
chapter describes Utah's educational use of the Internet through UtahLINK,
examining why UtahLINK was created and which problems it addresses. Key
players are introduced, from governing and advisory bodies to those who benefit
and those who support the Internet and UtahLINK. A brief history and the plan
for implementation are included for those who embark on similar projects.*

Sharyl Smith serves as the state specialist for library media at the Utah State Office of Education. Her
library media training includes a master's degree from the University of Washington and a doctorate
from Columbia University. Twenty-five years of experience in school library media programs and
school administration have taught her the traditional way of doing things; technology and the
Internet are rushing her headlong into the future. Mail will reach her at the Utah State Office of
Education, 250 East 500 South, Salt Lake City, UT 84111. Phone (801) 538-7789, fax (801) 538-7769,
e-mail sgsmith@usoe.k12.ut.us and URL: *http://www.uen.org*

The big pipeline

In Utah, the Internet serves public education, higher education, and government agencies though various networks. These organizations and institutions all use the same pipeline, making it one of the country's largest Frame-Relay wide area networks. UtahLINK, the education component, is made possible by several organizations including the Utah Education Network (UEN), an organization of public and higher education that began in 1978. UEN represents public, higher, and vocational education as well as business and industry. It coordinates the Governor's educational technology initiatives. Why do UEN and UtahLINK exist?

Utah's need for the Internet

Why is the Internet and a medium for delivering educational resources on it so important to Utah education? Distance and topography comprise one large part of the answer. The state encompasses 84,916 square miles. Within its borders lie such diverse topographic features as mountains, desert, red rock canyonlands, and the Great Salt Lake. The four larger metropolitan areas — in Salt Lake, Utah, Davis, and Weber Counties — are home to 1,335,817. The rural population numbers only 387,033. Long distances and geographic barriers often make the physical exchange of educational resources impossible. With UtahLINK and the Internet, these distances and barriers become meaningless.

A second part of the answer relates to the state's tax base and the number of taxpayers supporting education. In Utah, there is a lopsided ratio of children to taxpayers. Utah has the most children between the ages of four and eighteen and the fewest number of people between ages eighteen and sixty-five. Even with 48 percent of the state budget going toward public education, Utah carries the doubtful distinction of allocating the lowest educational expenditure per pupil of all states and the District of Columbia. As elsewhere, the tax base varies widely from school district to school district. A statewide distribution system based on a weighted pupil unit, purchasing services and resources remains a problem, especially in sparsely populated areas.

UtahLINK comes in response to these problems and from a widely shared desire to bring technology to the aid of education. The Internet has been viewed as a source of new and additional resources and a major means of restructuring education in the state.

Vision

As a part of the Utah Education Network (UEN), the Internet, through UtahLINK, will reach every student in every school in the state. Primary

154

among the electronic offerings will be much of Utah's high school and college curricula. Governor Mike Leavitt, who has taken a highly visible role in promoting education reform in general and reform through technology in particular, clearly defines his vision for the Internet:

> The Internet is an international computer network that our teachers, parents and students could use today — right now — if we provide relatively inexpensive modem hookups across the state. Much interaction between schools and homes could occur on the Internet and lessons and curriculum could be downloaded by anyone with a computer and a modem. And by the end of our Centennial year [1996], it will be possible to transmit not just words and data over the Internet, but video and graphics. What does this mean? It means a student could use an ordinary computer with a telephone and extract at any time or any place a lecture, complete with graphics and video and interactive exercise…We must get used to the idea of students learning at home, in dorms, at libraries, other community centers, and at work, not just in college or school classrooms. The learning experience must be extended to any location where a student can access teachers, lessons, tests, and other educational activities. To do this, we must make a major shift, a historic shift, in our basic strategy. We must invest less in bricks and mortar, and more in technology.

Mission

UEN, the organization that facilitates UtahLINK, has made Internet access an integral part of its mission. UEN sees UtahLINK as a means to provide

Figure 1: On September 14, 1994, Governor Mike Leavitt of Utah held a video teleconference, highlighting the electronic highway's influence in education. On stage with the Governor were Mark Stromberg, Utah Vice President for USWEST Communications; Jerry Peterson, Associate Superintendent of the Utah State Office of Education; and, Cecelia H. Foxley, Commissioner of the Utah System of Higher Education.

155

education opportunities, regardless of student or teacher location. UtahLINK brings to the learner the best of curriculum, programming, instruction, and materials when and wherever they might be needed.

The fledgling UtahLINK takes its place beside three other established UEN educational technology services: KUED, KULC, and EDNET. KUED is the University of Utah's licensed public television broadcasting station. It has delivered, since 1958, daytime programming to classrooms for teachers to use in conjunction with public education curriculum. KULC, The Utah Learning Channel, began broadcasting for-credit college telecourses in January 1987. It also supplements KUED with alternative instructional television programming. KULC operates on behalf of Utah's Systems for Higher and Public Education and state government.

Since 1986, EDNET, the state's interactive, closed-circuit, microwave and telephone based television system, has distributed post secondary and public education course work and vocational education to communities, faculties and students, both rural and urban, where these services and resources are not otherwise available. Besides providing a forum for distance learning, EDNET serves administrative communication, training, teleconferencing, and satellite needs of both public and higher education.

EDNET includes specially equipped studios and classrooms in communities throughout Utah. These rooms are electronically connected to form a network of interactive audio and video sites. For example, a math teacher at Grantsville High School can simultaneously teach her students as well as two other classes situated in the far reaches of the same school district. Using interactive audio and video communication, students and their teacher tackle the conundrums of trigonometry as though the miles were nonexistent.

Distribution is far reaching. Ninety-nine percent of the Utah schools and homes can access KUED. KULC reaches 85 percent of the state. As of March 1995, EDNET linked 56 schools, colleges, applied technology centers, and universities. With an education network so well established, the possibilities for coordinating UtahLINK with those already in place are strong and make good sense.

Services for teachers

Teachers use UtahLINK to search and retrieve information on the Internet and to publish their own or their students' work on the Internet. They also use it personally to interact and exchange ideas with experts, fellow teachers, and other classrooms around the world.

156

UtahLINK is not just access to the Internet. Among the resources and services offered, teachers can find core curriculum guides, reach the state curriculum server, examine electronic resources for K-12 teachers, download EDNET information, retrieve schedules for KUED and KULC, reach Utah's academic libraries, and send and receive electronic mail. UtahLINK also includes job opportunities, career guidance, and calendars of educational events. As an integral part of UEN's educational technology services, UtahLINK represents a coordinated effort to implement the electronic highway through data network services.

The key players

Participation in the vision, planning, and implementation of UtahLINK has been broadly based. There are three organizational levels associated with UEN and UtahLINK: governing, advisory, and staff. As a component of the Utah Education Network, UtahLINK is governed by the State Board of Education and the Board of Regents, with the governor and the legislature also holding policy-making functions. All four governing entities are represented on three advisory committees, the Utah Education Network Steering Committee, the Instructional Television and Video Services Committee, and the UtahLINK/LibNet/EDNET Coordinating Committee. LibNet links Utah's college and university libraries and selected public libraries to the Internet and UtahLINK.

The committees act as an information clearinghouse and plan for the continuing growth of the technological infrastructure of the network. They coordinate the development of UEN policies and procedures with those initiated at participating institutions. The committees support the implementation of education and training programs for network technical support staff and for end-users of network services. They also explore and promote innovative applications of data communications and evaluate network operations and services. Finally, these groups identify funding needs and review public and higher education and public library funding proposals that go to the legislature.

A brief history and plan

In his State-of-the-State address on January 19, 1994, Governor Mike Leavitt announced the building of a wide area network to revolutionize education. Prior to this announcement, a successful technology proposal from the state's academic librarians to the 1990 state legislature, provided a library systems and data communications network that linked the libraries from Utah's nine colleges and universities with the state library. The network, named LibNet, received technical support from the University of Utah Computer

157

Center. In 1992, LibNet expanded to include public libraries at model sites. The Governor's plan to involve education was based on this successful effort.

His plan also was influenced by the 1990 Educational Technology Initiative (ETI), a $60 million allocation to public education over four years to improve quality and productivity through the placement of microcomputers in classrooms. Front-runner schools who benefited from ETI early on, already had experimented with the higher education/state library network and showed the way for other schools who would join through a more formal entry, UEN

Once UEN became involved, plans developed for connecting 126 secondary schools to UtahLINK in the 1994-95 school year and 80 to 100 schools per year in the following two years. These activities would bring the total number of sites to approximately 300 secondary schools by the end of the 1996-97 school year. Each of the 40 school districts would be responsible for connecting their elementary schools to their secondary schools.

The architecture of this plan employs a hub strategy that includes the various school district offices and academic institutions. It encourages closer working relationships between public and higher education in creating an uninterrupted educational environment. Using cost-effective point-to-point connections at these hubs, the network supports mail gateways and other Internet application services. Plans also provide for dial-in services through these hubs.

UtahLINK, and other components of UEN, are accessed currently through a variety of delivery systems that gradually will give way to newer technologies. Frame-Relay and point-to-point technology of the first phase, operating at speeds of 56 kbps or 1.544 MB (T1), will be replaced by Asynchronous Transfer Mode (ATM) and other advanced technologies in later phases. These more advanced technologies will allow for the integration of video and data services into a single high-speed backbone. On-demand video library services and other traffic-intensive applications, such as multimedia data services, will be facilitated in this later phase.

In 1994, the fiber-optic backbone reached nearly border to border, extending along the main axis of the state, south to St. George by autumn and north to Logan by winter.

Once the telecommunication carriers have completed cable and fiber installation, implementation of the plan involves school application, hardware installation, and training. The UEN evaluates the needs, resources and level of preparation of sites. It provides guidelines to ensure that requirements for eligibility for connection and service are understood. Local site responsibilities include configuration of the local area networks. Wide area network router

158

Figure 2: In November 1994, fiber optic cable was being installed to link Richfield High School and other schools in the area. With the cable, connections, and equipment in place, students and instructors can take advantage of interactive classes and other digital resources.
Photo ©*The Richfield Reaper*, and reprinted with permission from the November 30, 1994, issue, p. 1.

configuration is coordinated with major network providers such as WestNet, UEN, and the state agency, Information Technology Services.

UEN specifies the wide area network hardware, including routers, Channel Service Units/Digital Service Units (CSU/DSUs), monitoring equipment, and software. Data routers are of major importance. For the smaller networks, the selection of data routers can determine the quality of performance and reliability of the overall network. Such broadcast routing protocols as Routing Information Protocol (RIP) prove satisfactory in use, without real negative impact on the network. Open Shortest Path First (OSPF) and other newer networking protocols offer a reasonable standard of quality for smaller networks. Given the projected number of users at educational sites in Utah, the reliability of using proven technology increases in importance. Growth cannot be allowed at the expense of reliability.

As the implementation and installation of UtahLINK begins to accelerate, there is a need for intermediate hub sites to provide localized services to schools and district offices. These sites will deal with programming, intrahub scheduling, training, and meetings; and will assist with local area network interconnections and operational support.

Training

Training is essential to the successful implementation of UtahLINK. As a policy, training was mandated for the teachers who would teach on the system,

159

Figure 3: The installation of fiber cable was page one news in some communities, such as the local newspaper, *The Richfeld Reaper.*
Photo ©*The Richfield Reaper,* and reprinted with permission from the November 30, 1994, issue, p. 1.

for technical staff who would operate the system, and for other support personnel who would assist in these efforts. Of primary importance is the training of classroom teachers. To this end, UEN has implemented a "trainer of trainers" component in which every person who receives training is obliged to train ten others for ten hours.

UtahLINK technical training for site coordinators began in 1994. This training was developed and sponsored by UEN in cooperation with the University of Utah Computer Center, the Utah State Office of Education, the Educational Network Consortium, and other education organizations throughout the state. Initial training took the form of two workshops: a one-day workshop, "Introduction to the Internet for Site Coordinators," followed later by a two-day workshop, "Configuring and Installing the Internet Protocol (IP) Client Software for Site Coordinators."

Classroom teachers, from kindergarten through high school, receive training through a series of twelve regional three-day workshops. This training is offered

160

by UEN and supported with a grant from the USWEST Foundation. There is a focus on hands-on, cross-curriculum use of UtahLINK and the Internet in teaching. A team of four master teachers is found in kindergarten, high school, or staff development classrooms, when they are not conducting UtahLINK workshops. Class size, limited to 26 or less, allows for a good deal of individual help.

As a special incentive, laptop computers go home with participants when they complete workshop training. These computers remain with the participants as long as they stay in their school districts. USWEST estimates that 60 teachers will be trained by the end of the 1994-95 school year. An additional 150 teachers will be trained over the summer, during the first year of the two-year operation.

Teacher trainees are chosen through an application process which does not always correspond to UEN site selections. However, the training schedule is contingent on installation, since it is considered highly undesirable to train teachers in advance of UtahLINK and Internet access.

Library media specialists will receive Internet training that focuses on library applications. Regional training workshops, sponsored by the Utah State Office of Education, are coordinated by the state specialist for library media and conducted by a training team composed of the State Office Internet specialist, two master secondary library media specialists, and a local technical specialist.

Funding

The legislature has sustained support for UtahLINK and other UEN activities throughout all phases of planning and implementation. It is anticipated that UtahLINK will cost the state $5 million per year. During the first four years, this allocation of $20 million funds the infrastructure and the ongoing costs for these years. In 1994, 130 sites were connected to UtahLINK. Once the infrastructure is complete, it is estimated that $5 million will support on-going costs. This budget pays for routers, CSUs/DSUs, hub infrastructure hardware, software, and training. It also includes line charges, Internet access fees, and administrative costs.

Concurrently, over the same four years, EDNET will be installed in 160 sites. Wherever EDNET is installed, UtahLINK comes along. The budget for EDNET installation totals $7,640,960 and covers T1 or fiber-based installation, hub sites, and on-going communication charges.

Federal funding also assists the project. A grant from the Rural Electrification Agency (REA) will fund additional facilities and enhancements to the southeast portion of the network. In addition, independent carrier companies have worked with the state to support UtahLINK. USWEST chose Utah

161

from the fourteen states in its service region to create a pilot site for involvement in the Internet. To that end, USWEST's $600,000 grant to UEN and the Utah State Office of Education will be used over two years to purchase laptop computers with modems for over 300 teachers to use as they complete training. Finally, local school districts are expected to pay the charges for access connections for their elementary schools. State funds cover the installation and ongoing costs only for secondary schools.

Cooperation

Sometimes hard-won, cooperation proved to be a key to initial and on-going successes. The level of cooperation between public education and higher education is without parallel in the state. USWEST and independent carriers are installing fiber in their service areas as quickly as possible. As they work, they must resolve environmental, financial, and regulatory issues before installation can be completed. However, to help meet deadlines, in an unprec-

Figure 4: The logo for UtahLINK, the symbol of friendship in American Sign Language, appears on a background in the shape of Utah.

edented level of cooperation, these carriers are working together to facilitate the interconnection of the various fiber networks as they are installed.

Marketing

The marketing program is a special strength of UtahLINK. Personnel, experienced in the effective promotion of KUED, KULC, and EDNET, are applying their efforts to UtahLINK. A distinctive and attractive logo is drawing very positive attention to the network.

162

The icon is an abstraction of linkages and chain links. In American Sign Language it is a symbol of friendship. The block that forms the background is the shape of Utah. Training participants carry away the requisite cloth bag, mug, and tee-shirt, all bearing the UtahLINK logo. *NetNews*, a monthly newsletter from UEN, reports the various activities of the network and is distributed to Utah teachers, principals, media, committees, and the legislature. UEN's home page is **http://www.uen.org**

Getting the water to the end of the road

Looking ahead, Utah plans to investigate and incorporate new technologies and applications to meet the changing needs of every site. They are committed to implementing such technologies as ATM that will merge video, voice, and data services into one electronic highway. They plan to extend interactive video and data services to homes and to develop and implement a near-on-demand video library service.

Eventually all video services will migrate from scheduled, linear services to an on-demand basis. The feasibility of distributing one-way, high-speed data services through broadcast television is slated for study. Implementation plans also include CD-ROM library access through the use of data and video services. And there are plans for the future integration of these services into a single high-speed network supporting education entities throughout the state.

"Getting the water all the way down to the end of the road." This is a familiar phrase in the dry climate of Utah, where irrigation is practiced, even alongside some of the manicured lawns and rock gardens of residential Salt Lake City. With UtahLINK and the Internet, the phrase takes on new meaning — getting information down to the end of the road, or passed along the information highway to the end user, at school or at home — all the way out to Trout Creek in the West Desert or down to Monument Valley High School on the Navajo Indian Reservation.

The challenges are great, but vision, planning, support, and cooperation are moving the water along.

connection

Thomas Eland

Literacy on the Internet

The National Institute for Literacy and State Literacy Resource Centers World Wide Web Information Network

his chapter reports on the development of the National Institute for *Literacy/State Literacy Resource Centers'* information dissemination *network on the World Wide Web. It also discusses the Internet search tools developed by the Minnesota/South Dakota Regional Adult Literacy Resource Center and points the way for librarians to develop similar tools to better enable citizens to more easily navigate the Internet.*

Thomas Eland is currently the coordinator of the Minnesota/South Dakota Regional Adult Literacy Resource Center. He has worked in academic and special libraries for the past six years. He can be reached at the Minnesota/South Dakota Regional Adult Literacy Resource Center, University of St. Thomas, Mail #5019, 2115 Summit Avenue, St. Paul, MN 55105. Phone (612) 962-5570, fax (612) 962-5406, e-mail tweland@stthomas.edu

Rethinking the librarian's role

"May you live in interesting times" is an old Chinese curse — or blessing — depending on how you wish to interpret it. An interesting aspect of our times, as far as librarians are concerned, is the amazing speed at which information is being produced and distributed in electronic format. The Internet, a concept known to few outside of academic and government circles only a few years ago, is now a household word. And though many in North America still don't understand how it works, they are about to be provided with access to this complex network for the price of a cable TV connection. A transition is in the making. We are moving into a new era where our modernist philosophical assumptions about the individual, society, and relationships no longer hold true. This new environment challenges librarians to rethink the ways in which we organize and provide access to information. Indeed, it is this new environment that challenges us to rethink the very concept of librarianship.

One way to rethink the library profession is to question the definition of a library. With the passage of the 1991 National Literacy Act, Congress created the National Institute for Literacy (NIFL) and the State Literacy Resource Centers (SLRCs). The NIFL and SLRCs were given a number of responsibilities. However, at the heart of their mission lies the mandate to develop an information dissemination system that will advance the knowledge available to literacy and adult educators.

NIFL and the Net

To meet this mandate, the National Institute for Literacy called on the expertise of librarians and literacy educators to develop record structures and cataloging guidelines that would enable the SLRCs to organize information in a uniform format. The NIFL's committees developed record structures for unpublished materials and literacy organizations. These record structures are based on the USMARC format and the cataloging guidelines are based on AACR2 and LC rule interpretations. Another committee developed a literacy thesaurus to provide controlled subject access to information. It is the intention of the NIFL and SLRCs to have the thesaurus adopted by the Education Resources and Information Clearinghouse (ERIC). Adding the NIFL/SLRC literacy thesaurus's terms to the *Thesaurus of ERIC Descriptors* will increase the depth of ERIC descriptors in the areas of adult literacy and basic skills education.

The NIFL must be commended for its leadership in developing these structures and guidelines. But as valuable as the structures, guidelines, and thesaurus would be to the SLRCs, these tools would not be of much use if the SLRCs were unable to make their information available to the public online.

165

The reason that most SLRCs are unable to provide their holdings online in a uniform and systematic way is because they are not part of traditional library networks. Most SLRCs do not have trained catalogers on their staffs and therefore do not qualify for membership in OCLC. Knowing that this situation would not change drastically in the next few years, the NIFL decided to mount its information network on the Internet. The NIFL realized that the Internet provided the SLRCs with a vehicle whereby they could catalog their materials and make them available to educators in the field, using the record structures and cataloging guidelines that the NIFL developed. Rather than centralize the information at the NIFL, it was decided to decentralize the network, allowing the information to reside at each of the SLRCs. Each SLRC would have access to the other SLRCs and to the NIFL.

The next decision concerned the type of server on which to mount the network. In 1992, when the decision was made, Gopher was far easier to access and was used by more organizations than the World Wide Web. However, the NIFL realized that the limitation of Gophers, the ability to display only ASCII text, would not serve the long-term interests of the system. Therefore it was decided to use the World Wide Web. Those who did not have access to the Web via a graphical browser like NCSA Mosaic could still access the system using the Lynx text-based browser. The World Wide Web also offers the potential to store and transmit audio and video materials, thereby allowing the SLRCs eventually to mount government and locally produced video and audio recordings.

As of February 1995, the NIFL was in the process of providing funding for the SLRCs to bring up their own servers on the World Wide Web. By the end of 1995, each of the four SLRC regions will have at least one Web site up and running. Each lead site will be responsible for providing support and training to the other SLRCs in its region. In the Midwest, the lead site will be in Ohio with Minnesota as the secondary site. The Ohio Literacy Resource Center will be responsible for loading and managing the information of the smaller Midwest SLRCs, which are unable to manage a site of their own. Those SLRCs that can manage a site will be linked to the regional site's home page in Ohio. The actual processing of information will take place at the local site's Web server. Using the record structures and cataloging guidelines provided by the NIFL, each SLRC will catalog information and add it to a WAIS database which can be searched from its home page.

The NIFL/SLRC system

With this background of the NIFL/SLRC network, let's take a look at the system. Examine the following screen prints taken with Spry's AIR Mosaic

166

software (see Figures 1-4). These screen prints give an idea of how the system is designed. The system is still under construction and will no doubt evolve greatly in the next few years. To search the system, point a World Wide Web browser at the NIFL's home page located at **http://novel.nifl.gov**

Figure 1: The National Institute for Literacy's home page.

The Institute's home page is divided into six major headings which contain lots of information. Web pages are easy to produce using HTML (HyperText Markup Language) authoring software. Two such products that can be downloaded from the Internet are HoTMetaL and HTML Assistant. To retrieve a shareware version of HoTMetaL, FTP to **ftp.ncsa.uiuc.edu**, and look under the **/Web/html/hotmetal** directories. For HTML Assistant, FTP to **ftp.cs.dal.ca**, look under the **/htmlasst/htmlazip.exe** directories, and read the *readme.1st* text. I prefer HTML Assistant as a more intuitive and easy-to-use package.

Forums are available by clicking on the link or by sending e-mail to **listproc@novel.nifl.gov** Discussion forums could also be sponsored by public libraries on a variety of topics. A library would not have to moderate the forum. Like the National Institute for Literacy, it could sponsor the forums and find organizations in the community willing to cooperate in

167

Figure 2: Each forum is moderated by a separate organization that has expertise in the given subject area.

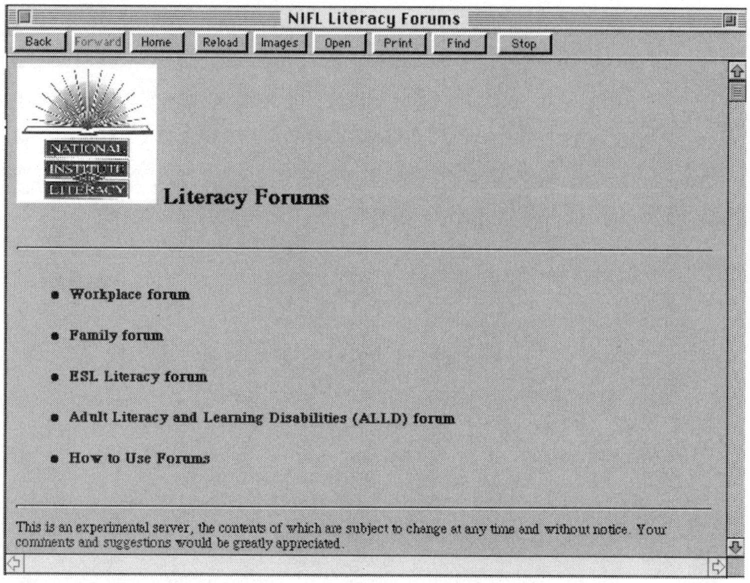

Figure 3: As more of the State Literacy Resource Centers are added to the network they will appear on this menu.

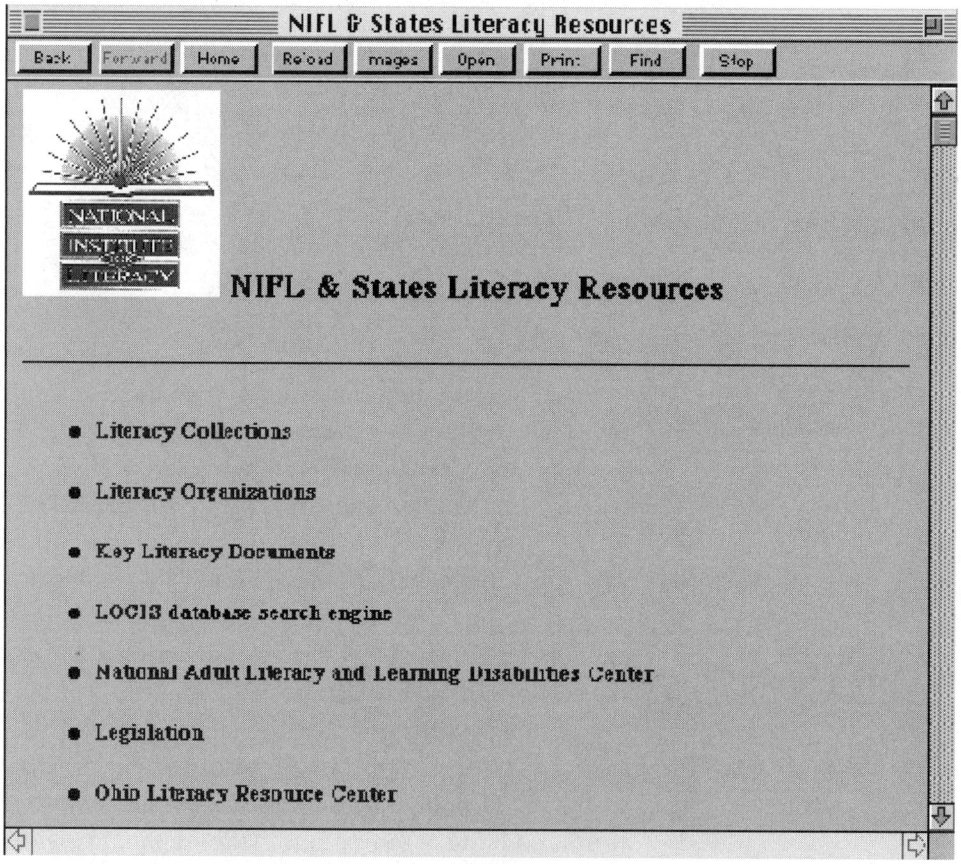

moderating the forums. Patrons access the discussion groups from the library or from their home computers.

The Ohio Literacy Resource Center heading will be changed to the Midwest Literacy Resource Center System. Clicking on the heading will bring users to the next level of the system, where they choose between the eleven SLRCs in the Midwest region. The top three choices on the page allow the user to search the NIFL databases (see Figure 4 for an example of the search screen).

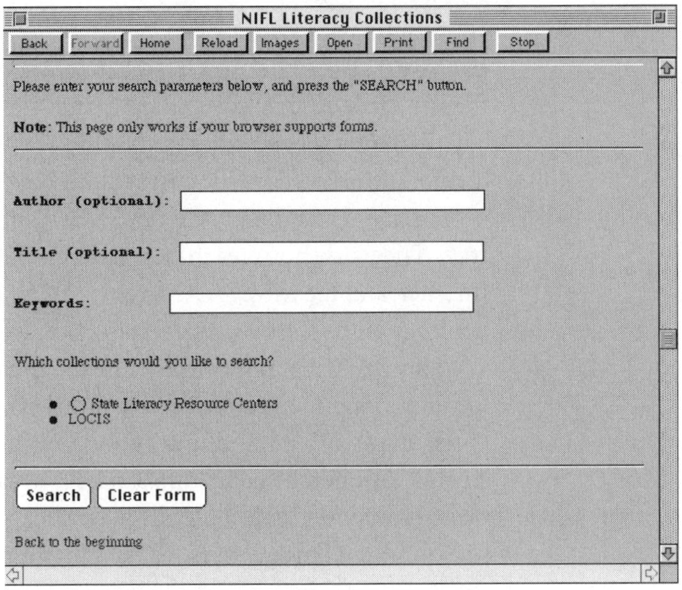

Figure 4: Search screen used by the National Institute for Literacy.

Keyword searches are done by using the terms from the NIFL/SLRC Literacy Thesaurus. The Thesaurus will be mounted on the system so that searchers can easily retrieve terms for keyword searches. Clicking on the "State Literacy Resource Centers" button will direct the search to all SLRC databases. This allows the searcher to conduct systemwide searches from one site.

Simply making information available on the Internet is not enough. The major problem with the Internet for literacy educators is that the information is not organized in an easy-to-search fashion. And even though there are tools to help organize and navigate the Internet, most educators do not have the time to browse multiple sites to determine if any are worthwhile. To ease this situation I created the *Internet Directory of Literacy and Adult Education Resources* which is available in both SGML and HTML editions (URL: **http://www.cybernetics .net/users/sagrelto/elandh/home.htm**). The *Directory* catalogs literacy-related LISTSERVs, Gophers, and Web sites on the Internet. It also includes a subject index using ERIC and NIFL/SLRC Literacy Thesaurus terms. The *Directory* goes beyond most Internet subject guides in that it includes a scope note, listing what will be found at a site as well as a subject index. The first edition contained 97 sites, the second edition scheduled for June 1995 will contain over 200 sites. The *Directory* and subject index were created using Inmagic Plus database software.

The *Internet Directory of Literacy and Adult Education Resources* is currently being developed into a hypertext edition using both SGML and HTML, and will be mounted on the National Institute for Literacy's and the Minnesota/South Dakota Regional Adult Literacy Resource Center's home pages. This will allow those with World Wide Web access to use the **Directory** in a truly interactive way. The searcher will be able to search the **Directory**, read the note about the site, click on the link, and go to the site.

Currently, a print copy of the *Directory* is available free of charge to educators in Minnesota and for cost recovery to those outside the state. It is also used in training workshops at the Resource Center and at workshops throughout the state. The workshops teach educators how to search the ERIC database, the Internet, and the MSUS/PALS regional library database which contains the holdings of the Resource Center.

Literacy skills must include the intellectual processes involved in searching for information, therefore those processes must be integrated into literacy curriculums. Literacy educators and librarians need to work together to teach such skills. Literacy educators can help librarians develop a curriculum that will provide students with the skills necessary to become literate information searchers and library users. To encourage this cooperation, Virginia Heinrich, the Resource Center's library services specialist, is contacting Minnesota libraries that currently offer literacy programs. She will encourage these programs to add information-searching skills to their curriculum, and she will encourage librarians to teach the courses.

Future

By autumn 1995, the Minnesota/South Dakota Regional Adult Literacy Resource Center will have a fully operational home page on the World Wide Web. This home page will contain information and resources available at the Resource Center (see Figures 5 and 6). It will also contain information from other literacy service providers in Minnesota. The Resource Center has entered into cooperative agreements with other agencies and will mount their information on its home page. This information will be invaluable to literacy providers and will help the agencies connect their services to potential clients. The Resource Center is also writing grants with other state agencies. The goal of the grants is to raise enough money to provide every adult basic education and literacy program in the state with the hardware, software, and training needed to access the Internet. For as helpful as all this online information can be, what good is it if those who need it most have no access?

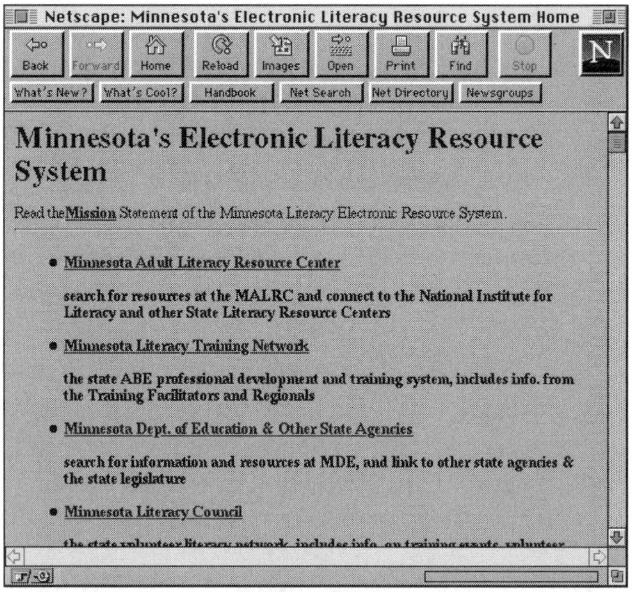

Figure 5: Prototype of Minnesota's Electronic Literacy Resource System, the eventual entry site to all literacy provider information in Minnesota. With links to the other SLRCs, the NIFL literacy educators can have access to information and resources throughout the country.

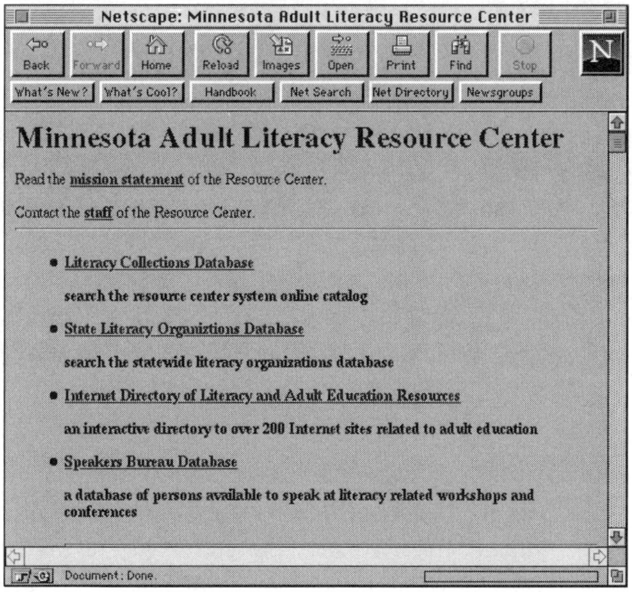

Netscape: Minnesota's Electronic Literacy Resource System Home

Minnesota's Electronic Literacy Resource System

Read the **Mission** Statement of the Minnesota Literacy Electronic Resource System.

- **Minnesota Adult Literacy Resource Center**

  search for resources at the MALRC and connect to the National Institute for Literacy and other State Literacy Resource Centers

- **Minnesota Literacy Training Network**

  the state ABE professional development and training system, includes info. from the Training Facilitators and Regionals

- **Minnesota Dept. of Education & Other State Agencies**

  search for information and resources at MDE, and link to other state agencies & the state legislature

- **Minnesota Literacy Council**

  the state volunteer literacy network, includes info. on training events, volunteer

Figure 6: The Web page for the Minnesota Adult Literacy Resource Center (MALRC) allows searchers to search the collections and databases of the MALRC as well as those of the NIFL/SLRC system. A reference form allows online patrons to initiate reference requests. If a reference question is incomplete or unclear, Resource Center staff contacts the patron and conducts a reference interview.

Netscape: Minnesota Adult Literacy Resource Center

Minnesota Adult Literacy Resource Center

Read the **mission statement** of the Resource Center.

Contact the **staff** of the Resource Center.

- **Literacy Collections Database**

  search the resource center system online catalog

- **State Literacy Organiztions Database**

  search the statewide literacy organizations database

- **Internet Directory of Literacy and Adult Education Resources**

  an interactive directory to over 200 Internet sites related to adult education

- **Speakers Bureau Database**

  a database of persons available to speak at literacy related workshops and conferences

Document: Done.

171

connection

Judy Hallman

A Regional Free-Net and Internet Access

ill the National Information Infrastructure be available to all? If so, how? Access to the Internet by libraries provides one model for universal access. Free-Nets such as the Triangle Free-Net, dial-in access, and other methods demonstrate the role of librarians as intermediaries in providing digital resources for the public.

Judy Hallman is Campus-Wide Information Systems Manager in the Office of Information Technology (OIT) at the University of North Carolina at Chapel Hill. She is also WebMaster of the University's home page. Judy has been at the University since January, 1967. She has also worked with other volunteers for more than five years to create the local community information system called Triangle Free-Net. She is Executive Director and Vice President of Public Information Network, Inc. (the parent organization of Triangle Free-Net) and she chairs its publicity committee. Mail to Office of Information Technology, CB3460 Wilson Library, University of North Carolina, Chapel Hill, NC 27599. Phone (919) 962-5277, e-mail judy_hallman@unc.edu

What is Triangle Free-Net?

The purpose of Triangle Free-Net, a nonprofit organization, is to promote the electronic communication of information of public interest to and among the general public and governmental entities. The organization consists entirely of volunteers and serves the communities of the Research Triangle area in North Carolina, including Raleigh, Durham, Cary, and Chapel Hill. Available 24 hours a day, it provides one-stop shopping for information on community activities, educational resources, job openings, health care information, social service information, environmental issues, local government, and many other subjects. While the emphasis is on local information, there are links to state and global information as well.

Triangle Free-Net allows people to get involved with their community, chat with friends about hobbies, swap recipes — just about anything imaginable. It opens a door to immense educational opportunities for the whole family. Triangle Free-Net also presents information on the Triangle area for people around the world via the Internet. In this way, it promotes the Research Triangle region. To visit, set your World Wide Web browser to the URL: **http://tfnet.ils.unc.edu** or **telnet://tfnet.ils.unc.edu** (login as "freenet").

From BBS to WWW

Triangle Free-Net began with supporters of bulletin board systems meeting in Chapel Hill, North Carolina, in 1989 to discuss the possibility of a service to disseminate information and discuss items of local interest. The group was incorporated as the Public Information Network, Inc., in 1990. By 1992 the local effort had expanded to include Raleigh, Durham, and Cary. Concurrently, thanks to the work of Tom Grundner, the originator of Cleveland Free-Net, free-nets were becoming more common and nationally known. The National Public Telecomputing Network (NPTN), URL: **http://www.nptn.org/**, was providing assistance at this time to new free-nets. As a result, the Public Information Network became an official organizing committee of NPTN and began doing business under the name of Triangle Free-Net.

During 1993 and 1994, a prototype service using Gopher was developed by the volunteers on a University of North Carolina – Chapel Hill computer. When a Hewlett-Packard 9000/360 computer was donated to Triangle Free-Net, the Gopher server was moved to this machine. It was temporarily housed at the University's School of Information and Library Science (ILS) for the convenience of its students. In turn, several ILS students have worked on Triangle Free-Net's software and menu design as class projects.

173

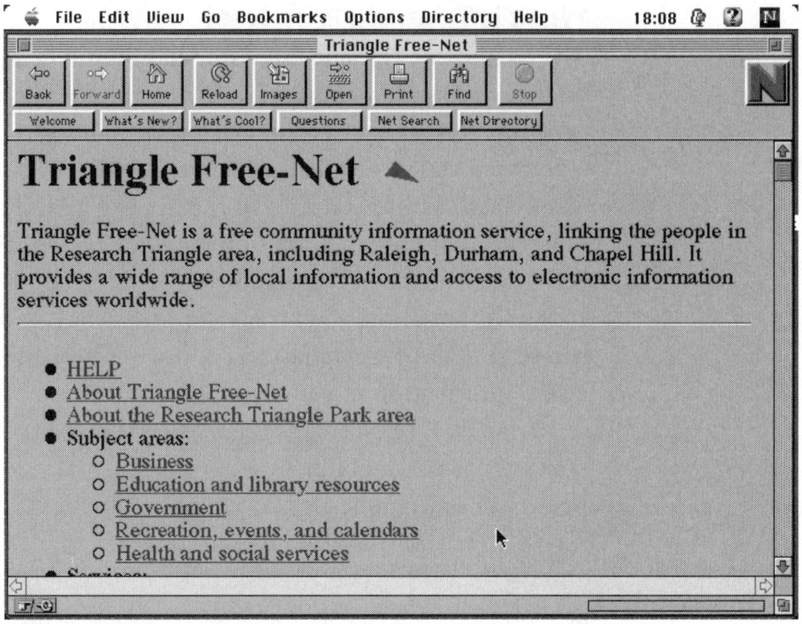

Figure 1: The Triangle Free-Net home page (**http://tfnet.ils.unc .edu**) provides information about the communities in the Research Triangle area of North Carolina, including Raleigh, Durham, Cary, and Chapel Hill. Details on community activities, educational resources, job openings, health care, social services, environmental issues, and local government can be found at this site.

File Edit View Go Bookmarks Options Directory Help   18:08

Triangle Free-Net

Back Forward Home Reload Images Open Print Find Stop

Welcome | What's New? | What's Cool? | Questions | Net Search | Net Directory

Triangle Free-Net ▲

Triangle Free-Net is a free community information service, linking the people in the Research Triangle area, including Raleigh, Durham, and Chapel Hill. It provides a wide range of local information and access to electronic information services worldwide.

- HELP
- About Triangle Free-Net
- About the Research Triangle Park area
- Subject areas:
  - Business
  - Education and library resources
  - Government
  - Recreation, events, and calendars
  - Health and social services

The Triangle Free-Net Gopher proved to be an excellent way to distribute information. In 1993-94, modifications were made to the client to allow electronic mail services from the Gopher menu. However, no interface was available to newsgroups and this was a serious problem. During spring 1995, the service was converted to the World Wide Web (WWW). It includes all the functions of the original Gopher plus access to selected newsgroups and a means to view and post messages using Web browsers.

Gearing up

Triangle Free-Net is in the process of moving its machine to a new location, where it will rely on three local businesses — one for the physical site, one for an Integrated Services Digital Network or ISDN line, and one for Internet access. The current service is a shell that can be demonstrated to show the potential of Triangle Free-Net. Planning is focused on the development of policies and procedures and the establishment of the first public access facility, in a local library.

In the near future, Triangle Free-Net will expand its community involvement by publicizing its efforts through presentations and newspaper coverage. It will recruit content managers, to be responsible for the development of specific sections of the database. Many of these will be librarians. Potential information providers, such as local governments, visitor and convention bureaus, libraries, schools, churches, nonprofit organizations, merchants, and industries will also be recruited. University expertise will be added from the faculty, staff, and students of the four universities in the Research Triangle area: Duke University, North Carolina Central University, North Carolina State University, and University of North Carolina – Chapel Hill. They will work on ask-an-expert bulletin boards, a particularly valuable service of other free-nets. Triangle Free-Net currently has one such service, called "ask an astronomer." It uses the contents of newsgroup **nc.ask-an-astronomer** and is moderated by Tom Hocking, Education Coordinator at the UNC Morehead Planetarium.

In addition, funds will be secured for phone lines into public facilities, and for computers, where needed. Training and assistance will be offered to those who want to use electronic information services, especially to novices in computers or the Internet.

Shifts in support

Who has access to the Internet now? Where does it come from? Only a few years ago, it was rare for the average person to have an Internet account. Major universities — but not all institutions of higher education — and some major corporations were connected to the Internet. Internet fees for educational institutions were often supplemented by government funds and grants. With the completion of much of the developmental work on the Internet, the federal role is lessening with a greater emphasis on commercial enterprises to provide the basic services. Now telephone and cable companies and entertainment giants vie for the opportunity to provide the transport medium for information services.

Many local commercial Internet service providers have emerged in the past couple of years. In some areas of the country, several companies sell Internet accounts at rates that vary with service, from just providing electronic mail to a full array of options. The price for a personal Internet account is similar to the cost of cable television connection, as little as $20 per month. In addition, commercial online services, such as America Online, CompuServe, and Prodigy make the Internet available through their systems. A variety of bulletin board systems (BBS) exist, some of which provide a connection to the Internet or at least act as gateways for electronic mail. While some BBS systems charge for their services, many are free.

So far it appears that most Internet users have above-average education and income. They've been taught or heard about the value of the Internet. They are willing to track down a service provider and pay for service if necessary. These Internet users will deal with the problems and frustrations involved in making the connection. Many have personal computers at home or, at a minimum, in their offices at work.

Issues of access via free-nets

Why is universal access essential? Children in affluent homes often have access to a wealth of information resources and to interactive person-to-person communication provided via computer, modem, and CD-ROM. How will children from low-income households compete with the Internet-haves? The inequity extends across all ages. Since the Internet provides information on health, social services, job and educational opportunities, it is critical that the Internet be available to all.

How will universal access be provided? Some government agencies envision a road to the information highway through the schools, libraries, hospitals, and prisons, bringing physical connections into local communities. In many cases, these efforts are centered on interactive video. However, video is slow in arriving and its costs will be high, both for the medium itself and the monthly fees. While the telephone or cable companies may be willing to bear the initial costs for this sort of service, funding for normal usage will be scarce. Some assume that the federal government will play a larger role. Given the concerns over budget reduction and the emphasis on local and state solutions, this is probably unlikely in the near future.

The originators of these early community services understood the value of electronic communication and the utility of the Cleveland Free-Net model: Universities pay the commercial service providers for Internet access. Personal accounts are provided for the faculty, staff, and students of the university as well as personal accounts for area residents as part of the university's public service.

Not surprisingly, some commercial Internet service providers frown on this union of academic institutions and community systems. If a free-net provides Internet access for free, why would a person need a commercial account? However, for the public who lack a computer and modem and cannot afford $20 a month for a personal Internet account, a local service such as a free-net provides the only means to acquire digital information.

Triangle Free-Net offers a compromise. Access to Triangle Free-Net's phone lines will be restricted to calls coming from public facilities. These facilities include restaurants, hotels, and other local businesses, as well as schools, churches, libraries, government offices, recreational facilities, and senior citizen centers. Those who have computers and modems at home will be encouraged to use commercial accounts and access Triangle Free-Net's services via the Internet.

Community services benefit commerce

Where does a community service go for sponsorship and Internet connectivity? Sponsorship through universities remains an option, but today other options exist. Given Triangle Free-Net's policy, commercial services need not be threatened by community services. In fact, they realize that these services are beneficial. Many commercial service providers do not provide their own databases, they provide access to the databases of others. Since community services provide community information, commercial service providers gain content by merely supporting the efforts of a local free-net.

Community information services have a mission of outreach, to help people understand the relevance and harness the power of information and electronic communications. To this end, volunteers work in the community and explain how to use a community information service, describe the kinds of information available, and help others understand electronic mail and bulletin boards. Clearly this activity expands the potential market for commercial providers.

Volunteers play other important roles in outreach. They may train trainers and provide advice and assistance to others on hardware and software. For example, suppose the members of a church decide they want to get on the information highway. Community service volunteers will meet with church leaders, help them select and install hardware and software, and identify possible funding sources. They will teach members of the congregation how to use the equipment and software. In turn, this newly earned expertise would be passed on to children after school and to adults in the evenings.

Thinking creatively

To make the Internet more accessible, we need to think creatively. Where can computers and training be provided? What are the roles for libraries and librarians?

People take their requests for information to libraries, so these are logical places to house community networking services. Librarians can play a major role in ensuring that community services are easy to use, that the information is well organized and clearly presented, and that the services provide useful search tools. They can help identify resources most needed in community services and potential information providers. They can also help define procedures to ensure that information is accurate and reliable.

Beyond libraries, where do people spend time? Imagine computers connected to the Internet in laundromats. Trainers would have a potential captive audience for about an hour. Fast food restaurants are ubiquitous and accessible. They tend to be clean, open all the time, and usually supervised. Some restaurant managers might be encouraged to try out a computer with Internet access.

What is the role for universities? Even if a university chooses not to provide the physical site and Internet connectivity for a local community service, it can play a major role in it. Most universities have a mission of public service, so faculty, staff, and students could help the community operate a local service. This staff would provide pointers to valuable collections elsewhere, moderate bulletin boards, and make expertise available online.

No single approach

One of the most important Internet issues today is access. How will people obtain access to the resources available on the Internet? Will the Internet expand the gap between the haves and the have-nots? There probably is no one solution. Several approaches, with provisions made available by state and federal agencies as well as commercial and community services, may work together to provide access to all.

Those familiar with the benefits of Internet connectivity cannot always wait for an agency or bureaucracy to give direction. We must use our talents and imaginations to provide access in every way we can.

section six

opportunity

a postscript

internet as
opportunity

he Internet. It's the cover story on countless magazines. It's the subject of any number of stories in newspapers. Authorities filling the highest political offices in our cities, states, and country are Internet aware. What has this thing called the Internet become and how should libraries approach it as a service?[1]

The Internet is a highly decentralized global phenomenon, more human than computer in its chaos. Trying to describe it is like trying to nail jelly to the wall. It is a computer amoeba composed of over 38 thousand computer networks, 3 million individual computers, miles of cable, hundreds of telephone lines, and dozens of satellites above. You could encircle the Earth 43 times with all of the cable in computer networks in the United States alone. The Internet knows no central command, yet hundreds act as technical angels, well-versed lobbyists, and bureaucrats for it. No one knows how many people really use the Internet; some say that there are at least 20 million users, others argue that there are only a million hardcore Internet junkies. Whatever the population, the Internet itself can be defined as a connection that allows people around the world to communicate, to exchange ideas, and to solve problems.

What are the library opportunities? Staggering! First the public needs navigators of the Internet. Second, the Internet is creating a surge of interest in information in all forms. It is causing a revitalized interest in reading. Librarians will have new roles as intelligent agents for readers. This interest in reading digital and paperbound information will highlight librarians' roles as promoters and marketers for the publishing industry. Our relationships with the

---

1. A portion of this postscript appeared in *Minnesota Libraries* 30, nos. 9–10, (Autumn–Winter 1993/94):166–74 and was heard as the keynote presentation at the annual meeting of the Minnesota Library Association in Duluth on October 6, 1994.

owners of intellectual property are changing. These changes create yet another set of opportunities for us as policy makers, involved in new rules that govern the use of property on the Internet. In turn, this policymaking means that we will be asked to govern the use of the Internet. Our positions may be as trainers, "netiquette" advisors, or even traffic officers. Finally, the Internet will give us the opportunity to be the architects of new libraries, libraries that are filled with books and journals and connected to networks around the world.

Let's look at these opportunities. First as navigators. One of my favorite descriptions of the Internet comes from Mike Royko, the syndicated columnist for the *Chicago Tribune.* Royko described his attempt at using the Internet as "driving a car down a narrow road in a snow storm, a car in which the windshield wipers and headlights don't work. All of the signs along the highway are backwards and upside down and of no help at all. Finally when you see someone along the side of the road and stop for directions, they can only speak to you stuttering in Albanian."[2] Given that some 40 million people may be using the Internet by the end of 1995 and 100 million by the end of 1998, there certainly will be a need for Internet navigators who speak Internetan *lingua franca.*

Part of Royko's dilemma is that most of the information on the Internet — at least 90 percent of it — is unstructured. It is not embedded in databases or spreadsheets or other organizational schemes. Every month at least 1,600,000 pages of information are used on the Internet, and probably more would be used if searchers could find what they want. There is already a huge demand for intrepid Lewises and Clarks, exploring the electronic wilderness, finding the best and quickest ways to documents, letters, and reports.

Librarians are well equipped to deal with the Internet because, beyond the computers and the protocols and the cables and the disarray of files and documents and images, the Internet is about information, communication, and connectivity. In this book, the chapters by Doreen Hansen, Robert E. Mayer and Suzanne Sweeney, and David R. Clark among others, bring the point home. Librarians have been in the business of information, communication, and connectivity for decades.

The information overload on the Internet is nothing new for our library profession. Over a century ago, the earliest modern catalogers at the British Museum were dealing with a flood of printing born of new mechanical technologies. New printing devices — such as rotary presses — and inexpensive wood pulp–based paper made books available at low cost and in incredible quantities. Traditional repositories, like the British Museum, were overwhelmed by the products of a new publishing industry taking advantage of lower production costs. Librarians dealt with this flood of information at the

2. Mike Royko, "$126 Million Ranks as Expensive Date," *Chicago Tribune* (Feb. 10, 1994), sec. 1, p. 3.

time by reengineering access to information, by reexamining the performance of the library catalog and cataloging rules. In the waning years of this century, Internet tools will take the organizing concepts of the library catalog and reapply them to the disorganization that is known as the Internet.

What will librarians become? Navigators and intelligent agents

Librarians are building organizational structures imposed on the Internet that will enhance our roles as navigators and intelligent agents. Some argue that software will replace us. There are applications out there already that search for information on the Internet, and do so with questions based in ordinary English and not Albanian. They perform their work and bring back results ranked according to relevancy and even do this work on schedule to deal with ever changing Internet resources. Programs such as Apple Computer's AppleSearch may look like digital replacements for librarians as navigators, but that's not the case. Instead, software like AppleSearch actually will make our roles as navigators even more important.

The work of Bonnie Nardi, an anthropologist working at Apple Computer in the Advanced Technology Group, supports this notion. Nardi helps programmers remember that they're not coding away just for each other or for machines, but for real people.[3] In the tradition of anthropology, Bonnie's studies take her into the field, where she studies the natives at their computers. She's observed how people really use programs, and more importantly how they do *not* use them. Bonnie discovered that we humans use software in very human ways. We develop our expertise in a given application as we need to, and become quite skilled in certain components, but cheerfully enjoy our ignorance in other parts of the same program. Carefully written manuals are only used when we have to try to learn some new procedure.

Nardi discovered that most successful organizations that use computers are saved by a small group of experts. These experts don't think of themselves as having any special skill, but when ordinary users are faced with a deadline and an unfamiliar program, these experts are begged for help. When the computer freezes up and nothing will stop it from acting as if possessed, ordinary computer users dial the extensions of these fearless friends. Their job descriptions rarely label them as programming wizards or computing saviors, but every organization that uses computers productively has a number of these intelligent agents awaiting those emergency calls.

These rescuers are called upon not only for their expertise, but their ability to treat you with care when you feel most frazzled. These folks do not use

---

3. For more information, read Bonnie A. Nardi, *A Small Matter of Programming: Perspectives on End User Computing* (Cambridge, Mass.: MIT Press, 1993).

Geekspeak. They do not treat you like a moron even when you feel like one. And they have a sense of humor. Many organizations identify librarians as these personable agents, just because many librarians have been working with computers longer than almost anyone else; are rarely intimidated by any computer weirdness; and for the most part can socially interact with nearly anyone. Nardi also noticed that librarians are for the most part faster than any program in finding information on demand. Librarians, too, understand the idiosyncrasies of clients better than any server especially when given very little information to go on. Finally, librarians can adjust more quickly to the changing landscape of Internet resources.

Nardi has been telling programmers that it's essentially impossible to create an artificial librarian. The best written software agent on the Internet can only do a small portion of the navigational work of an experienced librarian. The chapters by Monica Ertel on the role of librarians at Apple Computer, Mary Pettengill at the University of Texas at Austin, and Thomas Eland on the Minnesota/South Dakota Adult Literacy Resource Center support the notion of librarians as important intermediaries to information on the Internet.

Rebirth of reading

In turn, our navigational skills on the Internet will point Internet users to all sorts of information, much of which is not digitized. Already, in a subtle way, the Internet has become a catalyst for reading. In spite of the average household watching 49 hours of television a week, we are living in a time when there is a resurgence in reading. The net sales of books over the past few years have increased markedly by over seven percent annually; the sales of juvenile books have risen by at least thirteen percent. Over a hundred book superstores, each carrying more than 75,000 titles, have opened around the country in the last 24 months. In a suburb of Chicago, three book superstores opened within twelve months of each other at a single intersection. Reading has become desirable in this express-delivered and faxed world as an escape, reading that's based on paper, not on computers. In fact, nearly half of all readers claim that they read to relax, something that's hard to do in front of a computer monitor blinking away. Computers are actually driving readers back to paper.

It will be some time before a computer will be as physiologically and aesthetically pleasing as paper. We may never hear of someone curling up with a good monitor to read in bed, or learn of an electronic book that's a real "window turner." The color, texture, smell, and even flavor of paper cannot be duplicated digitally, yet. Paper-based text and computer-based text are used

184

differently. Electronic text stimulates the use of paper, especially for documents amounting to more than a few pages.

A study at the Livermore National Laboratory in California examined the uses of 19,000 pages of online text.[4] The study found that readers search documents online only for specific information. They have no intention of digesting hundreds of pages at a terminal. These readers — because of the intolerance of their eyes to computer monitors — can tolerate text on a screen only when it satisfies a focused demand. When they need a document longer than a few pages, they print it out or search for it in a library, or buy a copy from a bookstore.

Opportunity: Promoters and marketers

These findings suggest another Internet-related opportunity. Librarians have long been pointers to printed matter and copyrighted information. That means we have been advancing the economic gains of the owners of intellectual property such as publishers and authors. We should see this opportunity as a means to prove the value of libraries as marketing agents. Librarians have been derelict in pointing out that our institutions have economically benefited publishers for years.

How do libraries stimulate sales of commercial products? Let us offer just one example. A public library in upstate New York circulates hundreds of software packages to its community. Software stores and computer retailers in this metropolis are not complaining at all about lost sales or dwindling revenues. In fact, they strongly support the library and its software circulation collection. They refer potential customers to the library to test software from the library's collection at home or on their office computers. Patrons return the software to the library and go to the store to make an educated purchase of the right word processor, spreadsheet, or game. Sales of software in this community have actually increased thanks to the public library providing a way for the public to test programs intelligently before they purchase them.

The owners of intellectual property — the traditional publishers, software developers, the music and movie industries — must see libraries as special kinds of agents, because access to their products in libraries will open up even more possibilities for sales. Libraries provide a means for publishers to exploit markets in the most targeted kind of way. The kinds of customers who use libraries also use bookstores and magazine racks. The kinds of clients who use software in libraries have computers in their businesses and homes. The kinds of patrons who check out movies and compact discs from library racks also purchase movies and music in retail outlets. Libraries indeed are catalysts for

---

4. T. R. Girill, Clement H. Luk, and Sally Norton, "The Impact of Usage Monitoring on the Evolution of an Online-Documentation System: A Case Study," *IEEE Transactions on Systems, Man, and Cybernetics* 18, no. 2 (March/April 1988):327.

sales, and we need to emphasize this as we work as policy makers. Yet another opportunity: We need to ensure that new policies, governingse of intellectual property, do not strand libraries and their patrons. Why?

Not all patrons of libraries have the surplus income to purchase information. Libraries are a haven for the information poor, especially those who cannot afford digital data. See the chapter by Judy Hallman for an explanation of the importance of free-nets. The information poor are not just adults and children with barely the funds to put food on the table and clothes on their backs. They are scholars without a pot of research funds or affiliations with properly endowed institutions. They are undergraduate and graduate students scratching every penny from odd jobs and accumulating huge loans, with not a cent for an electronic surf ride in Dialog or Nexis. They are writers who lose themselves in institutions like the Boston or New York Public Libraries to do their research, because they can afford to pay with their time what they cannot afford to pay with their wallets. Libraries for these users are the last great bargain in the world. Even in high-tech organizations, like Hewlett-Packard (H-P) and Syntex, libraries play a vital role as an information resource. The chapters by Eugenie Prime and Pamela Jajko explain this role of libraries as information factories and distilleries.

Our work in creating policy may lead us into new roles as digital Ann Landers, electronic Miss Manners, or even cyberpolice. There are also few clues in electronic mail to identity. An address that reads U25112@UICVM provides no clue to the sex, age, occupation, location, or mood of its owner. There is more to the ambiguity of electronic communications than might first meet the eye. Those who work and play on networks, actively reading and sending and lurking, know of a certain electronic schizophrenia that exists in this world where physical appearance is meaningless. Without an identity to your address you can be whoever you would like to be. Anyone who participates in the Internet can create their own artificial realities with their computers.

Is it possible to provide social parameters for Internet interactions? Will we act as censors of mail, randomly checking discussion lists, to see if subscribers are naughty or nice? Probably not. Instead, librarians will find an expanded role as educators on using the Internet well intellectually and socially. There are some librarians that are already working in this role, training others as electronic assistants. The chapter by Terry Metz on the use of students as Internet intermediaries is just one example. One institution trains students in the use of the Internet, explaining resources and accepted behavior. After a number of sessions, students are tested on their knowledge of resources and on their ability to communicate on the Internet. If they pass the exam, they're granted a license to

186

use Internet-hooked computers. The license and their right to use these computers can be revoked if they use the Internet in unacceptable ways. This sort of education indicates one way in which librarians are acting not only as intelligent agents but as social troubleshooters, preventing problems before they occur.

In spite of the programs in Utah (as described in this book by Sharyl Smith), Alaska (in the chapter by Susan Elliott and Steve Smith), Maryland (Rivkah Sass' chapter), and Texas (in Mike Clark and Lisa deGruyter's chapter), many libraries are not yet connected to the Internet. Charles R. McClure's survey of public libraries found only 20.9 percent connected in the United States. Public libraries serving small communities with less than 10,000 citizens were the least connected, yet are these are the very libraries needing connections the most.[5] Another recent survey, by the U.S. Government Printing Office, found only 30 percent of depository libraries connected to the Internet, yet there is great enthusiasm in some quarters of Washington for more digital government information.[6] In spite of the success stories in this book from Billings, Montana (in the chapter by Bill Cochran), Colorado Springs (David R. Clark's chapter), Michigan (Gerald Furi, Christine Hage, and Stephen Kershner's chapter), and Virginia Beach, Virginia (in the chapter by Carolyn Caywood), many libraries are without Internet access. Whole communities lack the Internet experience.

Programs like the Clinton administration's Get Connected Campaign, a public education effort to link citizens into the Information Age, are a start. But there are economic and educational biases in making the Internet understandable and useful that only libraries and librarians can handle. Denise A. Garofalo's chapter on the role of the Internet in rural libraries in New York State certainly makes this clear. Statistics from the U.S. Census Bureau prove that economics and education play a major role. Households with incomes greater than $75,000 per year are three times more likely to own a computer than households with a third of that annual income. Families headed by a person with a college degree are eleven times more likely to own a computer than those families led by someone without a high school diploma.[7] The examples in this book will lead many librarians to work even harder to find ways to connect to the Internet; and perhaps influence policy makers in Washington, in state capitals, and in corporations to recognize the significant role of libraries and librarians as catalysts for change as the Global Information Infrastructure becomes a reality.

Edward J. Valauskas

5. Charles R. McClure, John Carlo Bertot, and Douglas L. Zweizig, *Public Libraries and the Internet: Study Results, Policy Issues, and Recommendations* (Washington, D.C.: National Commission on Libraries and Information Science, 1994), 17.

6. U.S. Government Printing Office. *Electronic Capabilities of Federal Depository Libraries, Summer 1994* (Washington, D.C.: 1995), 28–30.

7. U.S. Department of Commerce, "Get Connected Campaign Press Release" (Washington, D.C., March 9, 1995), 1.

internet sites mentioned in this book

Apple Computer, Inc.
http://www.apple.com

Carleton College, Minnesota. Library. Student Jobs
http://www.carleton.edu/campus/library/studentworkers/jobs.html

Carnegie Mellon University. Lycos
http://lycos.cs.cmu.edu/

Carroll County, Maryland Gopher
gopher://sailor.biap.lib.md.us:70/11/CommInfo/Carroll

Code of Federal Regulations (CFR)
http://www.pls.com:8001/his/cfr.html

Federal Bulletin Board (FBB)
telnet://federal.bbs.gpo.gov:3001

Federal Web Locator
http://www.law.vill.edu/Fed-Agency/fedwebloc.html

GPO Access
http://www.access.gpo.gov (free through depository libraries)
http://thorplus.lib.purdue.edu/bpo. (free Web version through Purdue University)
telnet://bigcat.missouri.edu (login as "guest")

Hampton Roads Internet Association
http://www.hria.org/hria/

Harford County, Maryland Gopher
gopher://sailor.biap.lib.md.us:70/11/CommInfo/Harford

Hewlett-Packard Laboratories
http://www.hpl.hp.com/

HoTMetaL
http://gatekeeper.dec.com/pub/net/infosys/NCSA/Web/html/hotmetal
ftp://ftp.ncsa.uiuc.edu/Web/html/hotmetal
ftp://ftp.cs.concordia.ca/pub/www/Tools/Editors/SoftQuad

HTML Assistant
ftp://ftp.cs.dal.ca/htmlasst/htmlazip.exe

Internet Directory of Literacy and Adult Educational Resources
http://www.cybernetics.net/users/sagrelto/elandh/home.htm

Brendan P. Kehoe. Zen and the Art of the Internet
ftp://ftp.cs.widener.edu/pub/zen/zen-1.0.ps (Postscript file)
ftp://ftp.cs.widener.edu/pub/zen/zen-1.0.dvi (DeVice Independent file)
ftp://ftp.cs.widener.edu/pub/zen/zen-1.0.tar.z (compressed tar file)

Library of Congress
http://lcweb.loc.gov/

MacHTTP, BIAP Systems, Inc.
http://www.biap.com/

MAGGnet – Pikes Peak, Colorado Library District
gopher://peak.ppld.org

Maryland Sailor Gopher
gopher://sailor.biap.lib.md.us

Metro Net Library Consortium, Inc.
http://198.111.64.10/
gopher://metronet.lib.mi.us
telnet://metronet.lib.mi.us (login as "public" with password "library")

Terry Metz
http://www.carleton.edu/campus/library/staff/terry/terry.html

National Institute for Literacy
http://novel.nifl.gov

National Public Telecomputing Network
http://www.nptn.org/

National Technical Information Service's (NTIS) Fedworld
http://www.fedworld.gov/

North Star (State of Minnesota)
http://www.state.micro.umn.edu/state/index.html

Oberlin Group Library Directors
http://www.carleton.edu/campus/library/obegroup.html

SLED – Alaska's Statewide Electronic Doorway
http://sled.alaska.edu/

Stanford University. Graduate School of Business
http://gsb-www.stanford.edu/home.html

Stat-USA
http://www.stat-usa.gov/stat-usa.html (free through depository libraries)
gopher://stat-usa.gov
ftp://stat-usa.gov

Texas State Electronic Library (TSEL)
http://link.tsl.texas.gov/

Triangle Free-Net
http://tfnet.ils.unc.edu
telnet://tfnet.ils.unc.edu (login as "freenet")

U.S. Department of State
gopher://dosfan.lib.uic.edu

U.S. Securities and Exchange Commission
http://town.hall.org/edgar/edgar.html

U.S. Supreme Court
http://www.law.cornell.edu/supct/supct.table.html

University of Illinois at Urbana-Champaign. National Center for
Supercomputing Applications
http://www.ncsa.uiuc.edu/

University of Minnesota Internet Gopher
gopher://gopher.tc.umn.edu/

University of Texas at Austin. Department of Petroleum and Geosystems
Engineering. Carter Reading Room
http://www.pe.utexas.edu/Departmental_Information/Reading/

Utah Education Network (UEN)
http://www.uen.org

Webstar, StarNine Techologies
http://www.starnine.com/webstar/webstar/html

Wendy's Connection
telnet://billings.lib.mt.us (login as "library")

Yahoo
http://www.yahoo.com/

glossary

Archie

Developed at McGill University in Montreal, Archie records the names of files available at File Transfer Protocol (FTP) sites around the world. You search Archie's records stored at various servers around the world for files and directories on specific subjects. Bunyip Information Systems in Montreal (phone (514) 875-8611, fax (514) 875-8134, e-mail bajan@bunyip.com or **http://services.bunyip.com/**) can provide further information on the availability of Archie.

ARPAnet

The Advanced Research Projects Agency Network, ARPAnet started in 1969 as a means to connect the military and U.S. Department of Defense with researchers in academic and private institutions. As the precursor of the Internet, ARPAnet operated on a completely different scale than the current Internet. By December 1969, there were just four nodes on ARPAnet and only ten some six months later. There are at least four million nodes on the Internet right now. ARPAnet officially ended in 1990.

ASCII format

American Standard Code for Information Interchange, or ASCII, is a means for different computers using different systems to exchange letters, numbers, punctuation, and other characters. Text files are frequently sent from one computer to another as ASCII format, allowing different users to open and read the contents of the files. Each letter or number in ASCII is symbolized by a number that any computer can read and understand. Commonly used to mean plain text without formatting.

Asynchronous Transfer Mode (ATM)

In telecommunications, a fast (as much as hundreds of millions of bits per second) connection-based network capable of sending rich and large files, such as audio and video, quickly. ATM requires special hardware and software, including special switches and optical fiber.

bulletin boards or bulletin board systems (BBS)

Based simply on a personal computer, a telephone line, a modem, sufficient hard disk storage, and special software, a bulletin board provides access to hundreds of programs and files, a means to communicate by electronic mail, and in some cases connections to the Internet. Sponsored by organizations or individuals, bulletin board operators usually charge modest fees for access to their systems and ask users to follow a limited set of rules. There are at least 60,000 public and 180,000 private bulletin boards serving more than 20 million users.

Channel Service Unit/Digital Service Unit (CSU/DSU)

A special kind of modem that connects a dedicated telecommunications line to a group of computers like a local area network via a router.

CommerceNet

A nonprofit organization bringing businesses together on the Internet to experiment in a practical way with digital commerce. The concept was based on a $6 million grant from the U.S. government. Its membership includes many high-tech companies and its home page can be found at **http://www.commerce.net**

DAT cartridge

Digital Audio Tape, or DAT, used in drives to back up information on computers, especially servers. DAT drives operate at higher speeds than normal tape drives and the tapes have a greater capacity than average cartridges, up to eight gigabytes of information.

Domain Name Service (DNS)

A database operating on Internet servers or hosts that translates Internet protocol names of computers on the Internet, like UICVM.CC.UIC.EDU, into numeric Internet protocol addresses, such as 128.248.24.54. DNS also takes 128.248.24.54 and translates it back to UICVM.CC.UIC.EDU so Internet users do not have to remember long rows of numbers. It can allow online resources to change machines and keep the same Interent name to provide continuous service.

electronic mail or e-mail or email

A means to send text and other information to one or more recipients over a network. E-mail is specifically read when a recipient opens an electronic mail subsystem or software, and downloads or receives incoming mail. Mail then can be read, forwarded, discarded or replied to, depending on the reader. The ability to send, receive, and read electronic mail is considered one of the most important functions of the Internet. Electronic mail is considered more convenient and responsive than communicating by telephone or the postal service (frequently referred to as snailmail).

Ethernet

A way of connecting computers in a local area network to each other, Ethernet allows computers in a network to communicate with each other at speeds up to ten million bits per second. Ethernet-connected computers are often then linked to a router or server for a connection to the Internet.

Eudora

A program developed at the University of Illinois at Urbana-Champaign that gives Internet users an electronic mail client to handle their incoming mail and files. A Eudora client on a specific computer communicates with a mail server and downloads messages on demand. Eudora operates like many word processors and prints easily, an advantage over older mail subsystems. Eudora is commercially available from Qualcomm; phone (800) 2-EUDORA, fax (619) 587-8276, e-mail eudora-sales@qualcomm.com or **http://www.qualcomm.com/QualHome.html** for further information.

Fiber Distributed Data Interface or Interconnect (FDDI)

A standard used in fiber optic links for local area networks, FDDI allows large numbers of computers to communicate with each other at millions of bits per second over large distances. Operating at greater speeds than Ethernet, a FDDI network analyzes and corrects problems within the network.

56K or 56 kbps line

A line or circuit connecting networked computers to the Internet, a 56K line sends information at 64,000 bits per second, with 8,000 bits per second reserved for signals. A CSU/DSU takes this line and, through a router, makes it available to the network.

firewall

A computer set up between the Internet connection and a local area network, a firewall protects users and their files from unauthorized access. A firewall provides limited access to network information to the public, and full access to authorized users. In some cases it blocks certain kinds of files and waits for authorized users to retrieve them. In some cases, software has been developed to handle the exchange of files across the firewall to users.

Frame-Relay

A protocol for sending files at speeds over a million bits per second over digital and other kinds of lines, Frame-Relay is used extensively in wide area networks (WAN) and private networks. Increasingly it is being used to allow sites to connect multiple machines to a single incoming wideband Internet connection.

free-net or freenet

A network open and free to the public, providing local and Internet services. Free-nets are popular services created largely by volunteers and offered by libraries, universities, and other nonprofit organizations. More information on free-nets can be found at National Public Telecomputing Network **http://www.nptn.org/** The original free-net is the Cleveland Free-Net, which can be reached by Telnet to **freenet-in-a.cwru.edu**

FTP, Anonymous FTP

A way for users to send and receive files over the Internet. FTP consists of a client program that contacts a remote server for access. The server in turn lists directories found on a remote computer, identifies files for use, and handles the actual transfer of information. FTP requires a user to have formal access rights to a remote computer, including an account and password. One common flavor of FTP is known as Anonymous FTP, which permits users access to public directories and files on a remote computer.

GIF

A means to store and shrink (or compress) graphic files for their easy transfer electronically over the Internet. Files in GIF are operating-system independent but may require a program to open them for eventual manipulation in a graphics application. GIF was originally developed by CompuServe.

Gopher, TurboGopher

Invented at the University of Minnesota, Gopher allows an Internet user to connect to remote and local Gopher servers, in order to access text and other files. A Gopher server organizes information in a hierarchy, and requires little expertise on the part of the user in file transfer and server connectivity. Some 5,000 Gopher servers exist around the world, leading to the development of Jughead and Veronica to search for files and directories in Gopherspace. TurboGopher is the Macintosh-specific Gopher client; Gopher clients and servers operate on a wide range of computers from mainframes to laptops using a diverse lot of operating systems.

195

hacker

In popular usage, an individual with an obsessive interest in computing, in working with programs and improving their performance. It may also apply to anyone using computers with enthusiasm. The term has been misused to include anyone with a dedicated interest in anything, as in an "antique hacker." It also has been misapplied to those who break into secure networked computers, searching for files and passwords. According to some, the term cracker, not hacker, should be applied to anyone looking for security holes in a system.

home page

The opening screen or document that an Internet user with a World Wide Web browser connects to on a remote Web server. It contains text, graphics, and pointers to other files or Web servers. This interface is constructed with HyperText Markup Language (see entry) software, such as HoTMetaL (see entry), HTML Assistant (see entry), or HTML Editor.

HoTMetaL

Created by SoftQuad, Inc. in Toronto, Canada, HoTMetaL is a word processor that allows users to create HTML documents with tags and pointers for use with NCSA Mosaic, Netscape, and other World Wide Web browsers. A commercial version, HoTMetaL Pro, available for Apple Macintosh, Microsoft (MS) Windows and UNIX platforms, provides additional features. SoftQuad can be reached by phone (416) 239-4801, fax (416) 239-7105, e-mail mail@sq.com or **http://www.sq.com/** for more information.

HTML Assistant

Created by Howard Harawitz, HTML Assistant is an editor that allows users to create World Wide Web readable documents. Operating under Microsoft (MS) Windows, this software gives the user the capability to create HTML-sensitive files and the ability to examine those documents with any of the Web browsers. A free version of HTML Assistant is available as well as a commercial version, with added features, known HTML Assistant Pro. For more details contact Brooklyn North Software Works in Bedford, Nova Scotia, phone (902) 493-6080, fax (902) 835-2600, e-mail sales@brooknorth.bedford.ns.ca or **http://cs.dal.ca/ftp/htmlasst/htmlafaq.html**

httpd

HyperText Transfer Protocol (HTTP) Daemon, or httpd, is a Unix-based program to create a server for HTML documents and files on the World Wide Web. Several flavors of httpd exist including NCSA httpd from the National Center for Supercomputing Applications at the University of Illinois at Urbana-Champaign (**http://hoohoo.ncsa.uiuc .edu/ docs/Overview.html**) and CERN httpd from the European Center for Particle Physics in

Geneva, Switzerland (**http://info.cern.ch/hypertext/WWW/Daemon/Status.html**).
httpd improves access for Internet users.

hypertext
Credited to Ted Nelson, hypertext is a visual database featuring links built into text and
objects. These links connect users to other files and resources, so that a user uniquely
defines the meaning of a specific hypertext. Hypertext requires a creative approach to
resource sharing and construction; the architecture of hypertext will vary from one creator
to another depending on the kinds of information at hand, linking skills, and imagination.

HyperText Markup Language (HTML)
A variation of Standard Generalized Markup Language (SGML). HTML is used to create
documents for display with a World Wide Web browser. HTML contains specific tags and
markers to identify parts of a document as headers, text, and anchors or links to other
Internet resources. While any word processor or text editor can prepare HTML documents,
special software packages make it simpler to work with HTML. Among them are HoTMetaL
(see entry), HTML Assistant (see entry), and HTML Editor (**http://dragon.acadiau.ca:
1667/~giles/HTML_Editor/Documentation.html**). A document entitled *A Beginner's
Guide to HTML* can be found at **http://www.ncsa.uiuc.edu/General/Internet/WWW/
HTMLPrimer.html**. Other useful documents include *Introduction to HTML* at **http://
melmac.corp.harris.com/about _html .html** and *How to Write HTML Files* at **http://
www.ucc.ie/info/net/htmldoc.html**

Integrated Services Digital Network (ISDN)
A high speed (64,000 to 200,000 bits per second or bps) standard for communications over
existing telephone cables, ISDN is available in three flavors in the U.S. The Primary Rate
ISDN or PRI provides two 64 kilobits per second (kbps) channels and a 16 kbps for a
signal. A Primary Rate ISDN gives twenty-three 64 kbps channels and a Broadband ISDN
can deal with as much as 150 million bits per second.

Internet Relay Chat (IRC)
Invented by Jarkko Oikarinen, IRC allows individuals to converse with each other over the
Internet on a variety of topics. A number of sites are available by Telnet including **telnet
sci.dixie.edu 6677** or **telnet irc.nsysu.edu.tw** To learn more about IRC, examine the IRC
Frequently Asked Questions (FAQ) document by using Anonymous FTP to **rtfm.mit.edu**

IP addresses
An Internet Protocol (IP) address is specific and unique number assigned to a given
computer on a network. A Domain Name Service (see entry) translates this number into a

197

name which is more easily recognized by a user. If I telnet to Whole Earth 'Lectronic Link or the WELL, I probably will not remember the IP address **198.93.4.10** but I will remember **well.com** Computers are much better with series of numbers like **198.93.4.10** while users tend to be better with text strings like **well.com**

Jughead

A software agent to index a small part of Gopherspace, Jughead searches local directory titles and provides a listing of matches to a query. Jughead, created by Rhett Jones at the University of Utah, provides a search of a single Gopher server's menus compared to Veronica which searches all of the names of files in Gopherspace. Information on Jughead, including a list of servers, can be found at several sites including **http://www.yahoo.com/Computers/Internet/jughead/**

LAN or Local Area Network

A group of computers in close proximity within a given building, connected by cables and software. Groups of local area networks may be linked together by servers and software over a larger area to form a Wide Area Network or WAN.

LISTSERV

Subscribed to by thousands of Internet users, there are hundreds of discussion groups on the Internet, all operated by software known as LISTSERV. The LISTSERV software permits these lists to be moderated, and for postings to be sent to users in several modes. Electronic journals and newsletters are also distributed by this software. One collection of academic LISTSERVs and other digital conferences is Diane Kovacs' *Directory of Scholarly Electronic Conferences* which can be found at **http://www.mid.net/KOVACS/**

Lynx

Developed at the University of Kansas, Lynx is a text-based World Wide Web browser. Unlike NCSA Mosaic or Netscape, Lynx does not provide access to graphics, video, and other complex files on the Web. It allows Unix and VMS based systems to access World Wide Web resources easily. Lynx also permits computer terminals with VT100 emulation to view the Web as well. Lynx can be downloaded by anonymous FTP to **ftp2.cc.ukans.edu**

MacHTTP

BIAP Systems' MacHTTP allows an Apple Macintosh computer to act as a World Wide Web server. A commercial version, WebStar, runs in native mode on Power Macintoshes typically three times faster than its predecessor. More information on MacHTTP can be found at BIAP Systems' home page **http://www.biap.com/** and Frequently Asked Questions are at **http://arpp1.carleton.ca/machttp/doc/**

198

MacWeb

A product of the Microelectronics and Computer Technology Corp., MacWeb is a World Wide Web browser for the Apple Macintosh. MacWeb requires less memory and uses less space than other Macintosh-based Web browsers. Its interface is also simpler than other Web browsers. MacWeb can be found at **http://galaxy.einet.net/EINet/MacWeb/MacWebHome.html**

Mosaic

Like pieces of colored tile in mortar, Mosaic presents a multicolored view of the Internet and the World Wide Web, giving a user access to text, graphics, video, and audio. Several versions of the Mosaic client exist. The original version was developed at the National Center for Super Computing Applications (NCSA) at the University of Illinois at Urbana-Champaign, and is often referred to as NCSA Mosaic. Flavors of Mosaic operate on computers using MS Windows and Unix as well as the Apple Macintosh and Amiga. Information on Mosaic can be found at the NSCA home page **http://www.ncsa.uiuc.edu**

MUD

Multi-User Dungeons or in some circles Multi-User Dimensions, MUD is a role-playing game, played over the Internet by hundreds of virtual escapists. Originally designed to simulate the fantasy game Dungeons and Dragons, there are versions of MUD devoted to many serious and not-so-serious topics. MUD has evolved into MOO, or MUD Object-Oriented, a more challenging version of MUD, and MUSE, Multi-User Simulation Environment, which includes the features commonly found in MUD and Internet Relay Chat (see entry).

netiquette

On the Internet, as in any other gathering of social creatures, there are rules governing behavior and communication. These rules, called netiquette, have been informally codified by years of experience. Like any rules on the Internet, they are not written in stone but in the ether and so are frequently broken. Certain kinds of behavior are universally (if the Internet is a universe) considered in bad taste, such as *spamming*. Sending one long message to a number of discussion groups and other sites, especially to those with no interest in the topic, is considered a form of spamming.

Netscape Navigator

Marc Andreesen, one of the creators of NCSA Mosaic, and James Clark, founder of Silicon Graphics, Inc., formed in spring 1994 the Netscape Communications Corp. to further develop Mosaic as a World Wide Web browser. Their product, Netscape, is one of the most popular Web browsers on the Internet. Netscape Navigator claims to be faster and more fully featured than NCSA Mosaic; frequent new versions of both programs make qualitative comparisons obsolete. Learn more about Netscape Navigator by visiting **http:// home.mcom. com/**

newsgroups

A bulletin board or online discussion group dedicated to a specific topic, a newsgroup can create hundreds of messages or postings per day. These messages will be devoted to answering a single topic, or providing a vehicle for complaint or concern. Over 5,000 groups are available. They are broken down into specific groupings or hierarchies. A newsreader allows you to follow postings and to track certain themes over time.

NNTP

Network News Transport Protocol or NNTP is a standard that controls the distribution of newsgroup messages or postings. It provides rules for retaining messages and controlling the length of postings, among other guidelines.

NSFnet

The National Science Foundation Network, or NSFnet, connects computers throughout the United States, and in turn links these computers and networks to computers elsewhere in the world. This network transports the equivalent of millions of pages of information every month. The nature of this network is changing rapidly with diminishing government support as a greater portion of the financial burden for maintenance and operation is shifted to the private sector.

OCR

Optical Character Recognition or OCR is a combination of hardware, such as a scanner, and software allowing the transfer of print to bytes. The mechanics of OCR have vastly improved within the last five years, and the costs have dropped dramatically. OCR is far from perfect, and still requires the use of a spell checker for even the most efficient systems.

Open Shortest Path First (OSPF)

A protocol that manages the routing of information in a network, specific OSPF routers calculate the fastest and shortest routes for transmission. OSPF routers are often faster than other routers especially if specific problems arise on the network.

Perl

According to different sources, Perl is an acronym for a Unix scripting language, allegedly meaning Practical Extraction and Report Language. Perl is used for system administration, especially to develop reports and collect statistics on activities. Source code for Perl is free but a C compiler is required to put together a Perl script.

Point-to-Point Protocol (PPP)
A specific protocol that allows personal computers, equipped with high speed modems, to connect to the Internet over normal telephone lines. A modem connection is made to an Internet server, temporarily allowing the use of Internet tools such as Mosaic, Netscape, and Gopher. PPP is considered by some as superior to Single Line Internet Protocol (see entry) by virtue of its abilities to handle errors and to compress information.

RAM
Random Access Memory or RAM is memory on the motherboard of a computer that handles instructions and commands for specific tasks and assignments. Information in RAM changes, depending on software in use and work at hand. Some Internet applications are RAM hungry, requiring a lot of memory to store instructions for specific kinds of tasks.

Routing Information Protocol (RIP)
A protocol to handle information over networks, RIP analyzes a network or networks and finds the most efficient path to send packets of data. RIP routers are quite common but are being replaced by another protocol known as Open Shortest Path First or OSPF.

Serial Line Internet Protocol (SLIP)
A means to connect to the Internet with a high speed modem and a telephone line, SLIP allows a user to temporarily connect to the Internet via a server and a phone call. SLIP is a popular way to connect to the Internet, but it is being replaced by software taking advantage of the Point-to-Point Protocol (see entry).

SGML (Standard Generalized Markup Language)
A specific way to describe text with tags and markers, SGML is based on an international standard and allows for the creation of electronic documents that are accessible by a broad spectrum of computers and software. An implementation of SGML called HTML or the HyperText Markup Language (see entry) has become indispensable on the Internet as it forms the basis of the World Wide Web.

T-1
A physical connection to the Internet, a T-1 line handles information up to 1,544,000 bits per second. T-1 cables are composed of several copper lines. A T-1 line can handle over twenty times the amount of data that a 56K connection can.

T-3

A T-3 connection is well over twenty times as robust as a T-1 line, capable of handling 44,210,000 bits per second. NSFnet is built upon T-3 lines in the U.S.

TCP/IP

Transmission Control Protocol/Internet Protocol or TCP/IP is a collection of rules that govern the ways in which computers communicate and link together over networks and the Internet. Components within TCP/IP permit the transfer of files, electronic mail, and other activities between computers. Transmission Control Protocol governs how bytes are communicated and the Internet Protocol provides the roadmaps to route bytes from one place to another.

technostress

Stress brought on by the use of technology, specifically the immediate demands of computers and computer-mediated information, technostress is becoming a common complaint both in the workplace and at home. A number of specific remedies have been suggested, including digital abstinence.

Telnet

One of the oldest protocols on the Internet, Telnet allows a user to remotely access another computer over a network like the Internet. The connection is viable as long as the user has access privileges to a remote system.

Trojan horse

A program acting as a real application such as a game or database, a Trojan horse is actually a vehicle for code to invade system software and storage devices, eventually retarding the performance of an infected machine. Trojan horses are detectable with virus protection applications. Unlike computer viruses, Trojan horses do not reproduce once installed.

Unix

Created in 1969 as a means to efficiently play a game on a DEC PDP computer, Unix has evolved into a multitasking operating system common in several flavors on workstations, personal computers, and other computers. Unix is written in C and, thanks to its built-in networking capabilities, is a popular operating system on Internet servers.

URL

A Uniform Resource Locator or URL is a pointer to Internet-accessible information. A URL may point to a home page, a Gopher server, or a FTP server. Throughout this book, these pointers have appeared as guides to Internet resources, such as the Library of Congress which has the specific address or URL: **http://lcweb.loc.gov/**

Usenet (Usenet news)

A collection of some 5,000 newsgroups supported by Unix computers and workstations globally, Usenet was born in 1979 in Chapel Hill, North Carolina, as a means for students to manage messages. Usenet is based on the Unix-to-Unix Copy Program or UUCP. Usenet newsgroups cover a wide range of topics from arcane to tacky to offending.

Veronica

A means to search Gopherspace, Veronica examines the titles of all files on Gopher servers for a user. Veronica searches can be modified to reduce the number of returns but there are some who prefer Jughead as a search mechanism. Veronica cannot search the actual contents of text files on Gopher servers, so that a user still needs to download and examine a document to determine its utility.

VT100

Terminal emulation allows different kinds of computers with differing operating systems to display information on a monitor and understand keyboard commands. The most common form of emulation on the Internet is known as VT100.

WAIS

Wide Area Information Servers were developed by Thinking Machines, Apple Computer, Dow Jones, and KPMG Peat Marwick as a means to handle and retrieve text over a network. WAIS databases provide a means to search the contents of large text files and retrieve information over the Internet. Clients exist for Unix, Microsoft Windows, and X Windows computers as well as for the Apple Macintosh.

WebCrawler

Developed by Brian Pinkerton, WebCrawler searches the World Wide Web for words in Uniform Resource Locators and in documents, producing results in relevance order. WebCrawler's text searching is demanding and time consuming in comparison to other Internet agents. For further information visit **http://www.biotech.washington.edu/ WebCrawler/WebCrawler.html**

Winsock

Software that enables a computer using Microsoft (MS) Windows to understand TCP/IP.

World Wide Web

Invented at the Centre Europeen de Recherches Nucleaires (CERN) in Geneva, Switzerland, by Tim Berners-Lee, the World Wide Web is the most practical and used application of Ted Nelson's concept of hypertext (see entry). The original concept was born in 1989 in a proposal to create an interface that would provide hypertext capabilities, straddle a wide variety of computers and operating systems, and prove networkable. The success of the Web on the Internet and specific Web browsers have led to a broader acceptance of the Internet as a medium for communications and a reliable source of information.

X.25 network

The X.25 standard manages the transfer of digital data over telephone lines. A network that follows these standards is said to be a X.25 network. These networks are private with their own specific cables, connections, and relays.

Z39.50

A specific standard that allows different computers over a network to query databases such as online library catalogs, Z39.50 allows users to use a consistent access method to search information buried in different systems. For an excellent description of Z39.50 see Clifford Lynch's *The Z39.50 Protocol in Plain English* at **http:// www.research.att.com /~wald/pe-doc.txt**

204

b i b l i o g r a p h y

There are many hundreds of books about the Internet, and the number grows daily. This list does not pretend to be comprehensive. It merely points you to selected groups of recent printed resources.

Introductory

Badgett, Tom. *Welcome to...The Internet*. New York: MIS:Press, 1995. 2nd ed., 461p. paper (ISBN 1-558-28424-9).

Cady, Glee Harrah and Pat McGregor. *Mastering the Internet*. San Francisco: SYBEX, 1995. 1,258p. paper, with two diskettes containing NetCruiser and NetManage's Chameleon Sampler (ISBN 0-782-11645-0).

Comer, Douglas E. *The Internet Book*. Englewood Cliffs, N.J.: Prentice-Hall, 1995. 312p. paper (ISBN 0-131-51565-9).

Crumlish, Christian. *A Guided Tour of the Internet*. San Francisco: SYBEX, 1995. 276p. paper (ISBN 0-782-11619-1).

Eager, Bill. *The Information Superhighway Illustrated*. Indianapolis, Ind.: Que, 1994. 185p. paper (ISBN 1-565-29892-6).

Engst, Adam C. *Internet Starter Kit for Macintosh*. Indianapolis, Ind.: Hayden Books, 1994. 2nd ed., 990p. paper, with diskette containing Anarchie, Eudora, InterSLIP, MacPPP, MacTCP, MacWAIS, MacWeb, TurboGopher, and other applications (ISBN 1-568-30111-1).

Estrada, Susan. *Connecting to the Internet*. Sebastopol, Calif.: O'Reilly & Associates, 1993. 170p. paper (ISBN 1-565-92061-9).

Falk, Bennett. *The Internet Roadmap*. San Francisco: SYBEX, 1994. 263p. paper (ISBN 0-782-11365-6).

Fisher, Sharon, Steven Vaughan-Nichols, and Rob Tidrow. *Riding the Internet Highway*. Indianapolis, Ind.: New Riders Publishing, 1994. Deluxe ed., 381p. paper, with diskette containing WinNET Mail version 2.11 (ISBN 1-562-05315-9).

Fraase, Michael. *The Windows Internet Tour Guide*. Chapel Hill, N.C.: Ventana Press, 1994. 344p. paper, with diskette containing Chameleon Sampler (ISBN 1-566-04081-7).

Gaffin, Adam. *Everybody's Guide to the Internet*. Cambridge, Mass.: MIT Press, 1994. 211p. paper (ISBN 0-262-57105-6).

Godin, Seth. *Point & Click Internet*. Berkeley, Calif.: Peachpit Press, 1994. 103p. paper, with diskette providing access to America Online (ISBN 1-566-09161-6).

Grossbrenner, Alfred. *The Little Online Book*. Berkeley, Calif.: Peachpit Press, 1995. 426p. paper (ISBN 1-566-09130-6).

The Internet Unleashed. Indianapolis, Ind.: Sams, 1994. 1,387p. paper, with diskette containing Chameleon Sampler, HGopher, UUCode, and other applications (ISBN 0-672-30466-X).

John, Nancy R., and Edward J. Valauskas. *The Internet Troubleshooter: Help for the Logged-On and Lost*. Chicago: ALA Editions, 1994. 145p. paper (ISBN 0-838-90633-8).

Kane, Pamela. *The Hitchhiker's Guide to the Electronic Highway*. New York: MIS:Press, 1994. 366p. paper (ISBN 1-558-28352-8).

Kent, Peter. *The Complete Idiot's Guide to the Internet*. Indianapolis, Ind.: Alpha Books, 1994. 2nd ed., 367p. paper, with diskette containing SuperHighway Access Sampler (ISBN 1-567-61535-X).

Kent, Peter. *10 Minute Guide to the Internet*. Indianapolis, Ind.: Alpha Books, 1994. 162p. paper (ISBN 1-567-61428-0).

Krol, Ed. *The Whole Internet User's Guide & Catalog*. Sebastopol, Calif.: O'Reilly & Associates, 1994. 2nd ed., 544p. paper (ISBN 1-565-92063-5).

Lichty, Tom. *America Online's Internet*. Chapel Hill, N.C.: Ventana Press, 1994. 272p. paper, with diskette for Microsoft (MS) Windows-based computers to access America Online (ISBN 1-566-04176-7).

Magid, Lawrence J. *Cruising Online*. New York: Random House, 1994. 481p. paper (ISBN 0-679-75155-6).

Miller, Michael. *Easy Internet*. Indianapolis, Ind.: Que, 1994. 228p. paper, with diskette containing Chameleon, WinSocket Gopher, and Eudora (ISBN 0-789-70012-3).

Peal, David. *Access the Internet!* San Francisco: SYBEX, 1994. 235p. paper, with diskette containing NetCruiser (ISBN 0-782-11529-2).

Pfaffenberger, Bryan. *Internet in Plain English*. New York: MIS:Press, 1994. 463p. paper, with diskette containing NetManage Chameleon sampler (ISBN 1-558-28385-4).

Pike, Mary Ann and Tod G. Pike. *The Internet QuickStart*. Indianapolis, Ind.: Que, 1994. 387p. paper (ISBN 1-565-29658-3).

Randall, Neil. *Teach Yourself the Internet*. Indianapolis, Ind.: Sams, 1994. 676p. paper (ISBN 0-672-30519-4).

Randall, Neil and Celine Latulipe. *Plug-n-Play Internet for Windows*. Indianapolis, Ind.: Sams, 1995. 383p. paper, with three diskettes containing Internet Chameleon, WinSock TCP/IP software, WebSurfer, Archie, Gopher and other applications (ISBN 0-672-30669-7).

Rutten, Peter, Alfred F. Bayers III, and Kelly Maloni. *netguide: Your Map to the Services, Information and Entertainment on the Electronic Highway*. New York: Random House, 1994. 356p. paper (ISBN 0-679-75106-8).

Sachs, David and Henry Stair. *Instant Internet with WebSurfer*. Englewood Cliffs, N.J.: Prentice-Hall PTR, 1995. 217p. paper, with three diskettes containing Internet Chameleon, WinSock TCP/IP software, WebSurfer, Gopher and other applications (ISBN 0-132-10675-2).

Savetz, Kevin M. *Your Internet Consultant: The FAQs of Life Online*. Indianapolis, Ind.: Sams, 1994. 550p. paper (ISBN 0-672-30520-8).

Smith, Richard J. and Mark Gibbs. *Navigating the Internet*. Indianapolis, Ind.: Sams, 1994. Deluxe ed., 640p. paper, with diskette containing Chameleon Sampler, HGopher, UUCode, and other applications (ISBN 0-672-30485-6).

Stone-Martin, Martha, ed. 51 *Reasons: How We Use the Internet and What It Says about the Information Superhighway*. Lexington, Mass.: FARNET, Inc., 1994. 124p. paper.

Tolhurst, William A., Mary Ann Pike, and Keith A. Blanton. *Using the Internet*. Indianapolis, Ind.: Sams, 1994. Special ed., 1,188p. paper, with diskette containing WinNET Mail and other applications (ISBN 1-565-29353-3).

Wiggins, Richard W. T*he Internet for Everyone: A Guide for Users and Providers*. New York: McGraw-Hill, 1995. 655p. paper (ISBN 0-070-67019-6).

Wolf, Gary and Michael Stein. A*ether Madness: An Offbeat Guide to the Online World*. Berkeley, Calif.: Peachpit Press, 1995. 297p. paper (ISBN 1-566-09020-2).

Intermediate

Baczewski, Philip and many others. *Tricks of the Internet Gurus*. Indianapolis, Ind.: Sams, 1994. 809p. paper (ISBN 0-672-30599-2).

Gilster, Paul. *Finding It on the Internet*. New York: Wiley, 1994. 302p. paper (ISBN 0-471-053857-1).

Goldman, Neal. *The Complete Idiot's Pocket Reference to the Internet*. Indianapolis, Ind.: Alpha Books, 1994. 214p. paper (ISBN 1-567-61528-7).

Hoffman, Paul E. *Internet Instant Reference*. San Francisco: SYBEX, 1994. 317p. paper (ISBN 0-782-11512-8).

Kent, Peter. *The Complete Idiot's Next Step with the Internet*. Indianapolis, Ind.: Alpha Books, 1994. 373p. paper, with diskette containing Pipeline for Windows (ISBN 1-567-61524-4).

Maxwell, Christine and Czeslaw Jan Grycz. *New Riders' Official Internet Yellow Pages*. Indianapolis, Ind.: New Riders Publishing, 1994. 802p. paper (ISBN 1-562-05408-2).

NorthWestNet. *The Internet Passport*. Englewood Cliffs, N.J.: Prentice-Hall PTR, 1995. 5th ed., 667p. paper (ISBN 0-131-94200-X).

Otte, Peter. *The Information Superhighway: Beyond the Internet*. Indianapolis, Ind.: Que, 1994. 241p. paper (ISBN 1-565-29825-X).

Ross, John. *Internet Power Tools*. New York: Random House, 1995. 374p. paper, with diskette containing Trumpet Winsock, Cello, Eudora, Trumpet for Windows, Trumpet Telnet, BC Gopher, WS FTP, and QWS3270 Extra (ISBN 0-679-75815-1).

Tolhurst, William A. and Mary Ann Pike. *The Internet Resource Quick Reference*. Indianapolis, Ind.: Que, 1994. 492p. paper (ISBN 1-565-29748-2).

Advanced

Breeding, Marshall. *TCP/IP for the Internet: the Complete Buyer's Guide to Micro-Based TCP/IP Software*. Westport, Conn.: Mecklermedia, 1995. 304p. paper (ISBN 0-887-36980-4).

Comer, Douglas E. *Internetworking with TCP/IP*. Volume 1: *Principles, Protocols, and Architecture*. Englewood Cliffs, N.J.: Prentice-Hall, 1995. 3rd ed., 613p. cloth (ISBN 0-132-16987-8).

Dumas, Arthur. *Programming WinSock*. Indianapolis, Ind.: Sams, 1995. 358p. paper, with diskette containing source code for all programs in text (ISBN 0-672-30594-1).

Gilster, Paul. *The SLIP/PPP Connection: The Essential Guide to Graphical Internet Access*. New York: Wiley, 1995. 442p. paper (ISBN 0-471-11712-9).

Parker, Timothy. *Teach Yourself TCP/IP in 14 Days*. Indianapolis, Ind.: Sams, 1994. 438p. paper (ISBN 0-672-30549-6).

Specific issues

▶ *Bulletin Boards*

Hedtke, John. *Using Computer Bulletin Boards*. New York: MIS:Press, 1995. 3rd ed., 516p. paper, with diskette containing Qmodem (ISBN 1-558-28391-9).

Pope, Markus W. *Que's BBS Directory*. Indianapolis, Ind.: Que, 1994. 256p. paper (ISBN 0-789-70018-2).

Wolfe, David. *The BBS Construction Kit*. New York: Wiley, 1994. 373p. paper, with diskette containing GAP BBS software and other applications (ISBN 0-471-00797-8).

Wolfe, David. *Expanding Your BBS*. New York: Wiley, 1995. 371p. paper, with CD-ROM containing BBS utilities and other applications (ISBN 0-471-11566-5).

▶ *Business and Finance*

Ellsworth, Jill H. and Matthew V. Ellsworth. *The Internet Business Book*. New York: Wiley, 1994. 376p. paper (ISBN 0-471-05809-2).

Ellsworth, Jill H. and Matthew V. Ellsworth. *Marketing on the Internet: Multimedia Strategies for the World Wide Web*. New York: Wiley, 1995. 404p. paper (ISBN 0-471-11850-8).

Maloni, Kelly, Ben Greenman, and Kristin Miller. *netmoney: Your Personal Guide to the Personal Finance Revolution on the Information Highway*. New York: Random House, 1995. 288p. paper (ISBN 0-679-75808-9).

▶ *Education*

Ellsworth, Jill. *Education on the Internet*. Indianapolis, Ind.: Sams, 1995. 591p. paper (ISBN 0-672-30595-X).

Frazier, Deneen. *Internet for Kids*. San Francisco: SYBEX, 1995. 314p. paper, with diskette containing NetCruiser (ISBN 0-782-11741-4).

► Electronic Mail

Gibbons, Dave, David Fox, Alan Westenbroek, Dick Cravens, and Andrew B. Shafran. *Using E-Mail*. Indianapolis, Ind.: Que, 1994. 376p. paper (ISBN 0-789-70023-9).

► Ethics and the Law

Cavazos, Edward A. and Gavino Morin. *Cyberspace and the Law*. Cambridge, Mass.: MIT Press, 1994. 215p. paper (ISBN 0-262-53123-2).

Forester, Tom and Perry Morrison. *Computer Ethics: Cautionary Tales and Ethical Dilemmas in Computing*. Cambridge, Mass.: MIT Press, 1994. 2nd ed., 347p. paper (ISBN 0-262-56073-9).

Williams, Frederick and John V. Pavlik (eds.). *The People's Right to Know: Media, Democracy, and the Information Highway*. Hillsdale, N.J.: Lawrence Erlbaum Associates, 1994. 258p. paper (ISBN 0-805-81491-4).

► Graphics

Howard, Jim. *The Internet Voyeur: A Guide to Viewing Images on the Internet*. San Francisco: SYBEX, 1995. 388p. paper, with diskette containing WinZip, Wincode, WinJPEG, and WPLANY (ISBN 0-782-11655-8).

► HyperText Markup Language (HTML)

Aronson, Larry. *HTML Manual of Style*. Emeryville, Calif.: Ziff-Davis Press, 1994. 132p. paper (ISBN 1-562-76300-8).

Graham, Ian S. *HTML Sourcebook*. New York: Wiley, 1995. 416p. paper (ISBN 0-471-11849-4).

Herwijnen, Eric van. *Practical SGML*. Boston: Kluwer, 1994. 2nd ed., 288p. paper (ISBN 0-792-39434-8).

Morris, Mary E. S. *HTML for Fun and Profit*. Englewood Cliffs, N.J.: Prentice-Hall PTR, 1995. 264p. paper, with CD-ROM (ISBN 0-133-59290-1).

► Libraries

Kinder, Robin, ed. *Librarians on the Internet: Impact on Reference Services*. Binghamton, N.Y.: Haworth Press, 1994. 410p. cloth (ISBN 1-560-24672-3).

► *Modems*

Crawford, Sharon. *Your First Modem*. San Francisco: SYBEX, 1995. 2nd ed., 314p. paper, with diskette containing NetCruiser (ISBN 0-782-11683-3).

Gofton, Peter W. *Mastering Serial Communications*. San Francisco: SYBEX, 1994. 2nd ed., 352p. paper (ISBN 0-782-11202-1).

► *Mosaic*

Branwyn, Gareth. *Mosaic Quick Tour for Mac*. Chapel Hill, N.C.: Ventana Press, 1994. 185p. paper (ISBN 1-566-04195-3).

Gilster, Paul. *The Mosaic Navigator*. New York: Wiley, 1995. 243p. paper (ISBN 0-471-11336-0).

Gunn, Angela. *Plug-n-Play Mosaic for Windows*. Indianapolis, Ind.: Sams, 1994. 307p. paper, with two diskettes containing Enhanced NCSA Mosaic, TCP/IP software, Plug-n-Play Mosaic, and Microsoft Win32s extensions (ISBN 0-672-30627-1).

Kraynak, Joe. *The Complete Idiot's Guide to Mosaic*. Indianapolis, Ind.: Alpha Books, 1994. 278p. paper (ISBN 1-567-61588-0).

Pfaffenberger, Bryan. *Mosaic User's Guide*. New York: MIS:Press, 1994. 274p. paper, with diskette containing Chameleon Sampler, HOTURLS, and Maze (ISBN 1-558-28409-5).

Pike, Mary Ann, Peter Kent, Kamran Husain, Dave Kinnaman, and David C. Menges. *Using Mosaic*. Indianapolis, Ind.: Que, 1994. 390p. paper (ISBN 0-789-70021-2).

Tauber, Daniel A. and Brenda Kienan. *Mosaic Access to the Internet*. San Francisco: SYBEX, 1995. 257p. paper, with diskette containing Spry Mosaic (ISBN 0-782-11656-6).

► *Networks*

Bobola, Daniel T. *The Complete Idiot's Guide to Networking*. Indianapolis, Ind.: Alpha Books, 1995. 324p. paper (ISBN 1-567-61590-2).

Boisseau, M., M. Demange, and J.-M. Munier. *High-Speed Networks*. New York: Wiley, 1994. 192p. paper (ISBN 0-471-95109-9).

Eager, Bill. *Networking Illustrated*. Indianapolis, Ind.: Que, 1994. 213p. paper (ISBN 1-565-29893-4).

Feibel, Werner. *Novell's Complete Encyclopedia of Networking*. San Francisco: SYBEX, 1995. 1,216p. cloth, with CD-ROM containing complete digital copy of text (ISBN 0-782-11290-0).

Kosiur, David R. and Jonathan Angel. *How Local Area Networks Work*. Englewood Cliffs, N.J.: Prentice-Hall PTR, 1995. 282p. paper (ISBN 0-131-85489-5).

Madron, Thomas W. *Local Area Networks: New Technologies, Emerging Standards*. New York: Wiley, 1994. 3rd ed., 386p. paper (ISBN 0-471-00959-8).

Miller, Mark A. *Analyzing Broadband Networks: Frame Relay, SMDS, & ATM*. New York: M&T Books, 1994. 522p. paper(ISBN 1-558-51389-2).

Miller, Mark A. *Internetworking: A Guide to Network Communications LAN to LAN; LAN to WAN*. New York: M&T Books, 1995. 2nd ed., 530p. paper (ISBN 1-558-51436-8).

Saadawi, Tarek N. and Mostafa H. Ammar with Ahmed El Hakeem. *Fundamentals of Telecommunication Networks*. New York: Wiley, 1994. 485p. cloth (ISBN 0-471-51582-5).

Sasser, Susan B. and Robert McLaughlin. *Fix Your Own LAN*. New York: MIS:Press, 1994. 2nd ed., 326p. paper (ISBN 1-558-28354-4).

Steinke, Steve. *Guide to Managing PC Networks*. Englewood Cliffs, N.J.: Prentice-Hall PTR, 1995. 392p. paper (ISBN 0-131-85497-6).

▶ *Newsgroups*
Fristrup, Jenny A. *USENET: Netnews for Everyone*. Englewood Cliffs, N.J.: Prentice-Hall PTR, 1994. 396p. paper (ISBN 0-131-12367-7).

McFedries, Paul. *The Complete Idiot's Guide to USENET Newsgroups.* Indianapolis, Ind.: Alpha Books, 1995. 317p. paper (ISBN 1-567-61592-9).

► *Privacy and security*
Cohen, Frederick B. *Protection and Security on the Information Superhighway.* New York: Wiley, 1995. 301p. paper (ISBN 0-471-11389-1).

Kaufman, Charlie, Radia Perlman, and Mike Speciner. *Network Security: Private Communication in a Public World.* Englewood Cliffs, N.J.: Prentice-Hall PTR, 1995. 504p. cloth (ISBN 0-130-61466-1).

Schneier, Bruce. *E-Mail Security.* New York: Wiley, 1995. 365p. paper (ISBN 0-471-05318-X).

Siyan, Karanjit and Chris Hare. *Internet Firewalls and Network Security.* Indianapolis, Ind.: New Riders Publishing, 1995. 410p. paper (ISBN 1-562-05437-6).

Stallings, William. *Network and Internetwork Security.* Englewood Cliffs, N.J.: Prentice-Hall, 1995. 462p. cloth (ISBN 0-024-15483-0).

Stallings, William. *Protect Your Privacy: A Guide for PGP Users.* Englewood Cliffs, N.J.: Prentice-Hall PTR, 1995. 302p. paper (ISBN 0-131-85596-4).

► *Social aspects*
Goodman, Danny. *Living at Light Speed: Your Survival Guide to Life on the Information Superhighway.* New York: Random House, 1994. 244p. cloth (ISBN 0-679-43934-X).

Maloni, Kelly, Nathaniel Wice, and Ben Greenman. *netchat: Your Guide to the Debates, Parties, and Pick-up Places on the Electronic Highway.* New York: Random House, 1994. 281p. paper (ISBN 0-679-75814-3).

Maloni, Kelly, Ben Greenman, Kristin Miller, and Jeff Hearn. *nettrek: Your Guide to Life in Cyberspace.* New York: Random House, 1995. 387p. paper (ISBN 0-679-76186-1).

214

Mitchell, William J. *City of Bits: Space, Place, and the Infobahn*. Cambridge, Mass.: MIT Press, 1995. 217p. cloth (ISBN 0-262-13309-1).

Rose, Candi and Dirk Thomas. *net.sex*. Indianapolis, Ind.: Sams, 1995. 243p. paper (ISBN 0-672-30702-2).

Rose, Donald. *Minding Your CyberManners on the Internet*. Indianapolis, Ind.: Alpha Books, 1994. 194p. paper (ISBN 1-567-61521-X).

Wildhack, Billy. *Erotic Connections: Love and Lust on the Information Highway*. Corte Madera, Calif.: Waite Group Press, 1994. 258p. paper (ISBN 1-878-73978-6).

Wood, Lamont. *The Net After Dark*. New York: Wiley, 1994. 356p. paper (ISBN 0-471-10347-0).

► *World Wide Web*

December, John and Neil Randall. *The World Wide Web Unleashed*. Indianapolis, Ind.: Sams, 1995. 1,058p. paper (ISBN 0-672-30617-4).

Eager, Bill. *Using the World Wide Web*. Indianapolis, Ind.: Que, 1994. 648p. paper (ISBN 0-789-70016-6).

Pfaffenberger, Bryan. *World Wide Web Bible*. New York: MIS:Press, 1995. 584p. paper, with diskette containing Chameleon WebSurfer Sampler, SmartPages, a generic web site, and WinHTTPD (ISBN 1-558-28410-9).

Turlington, Shannon R. *Walking the World Wide Web*. Chapel Hill, N.C.: Ventana Press, 1995. 332p. paper, with CD-ROM providing access to the World Wide Web, Online Companion, and Mosaic (ISBN 1-566-04208-9).

index

217

218

about the editors

Edward J. Valauskas is Principal and founder of Internet Mechanics, consultants on the Internet to libraries, schools, companies, and other organizations. He is a frequent contributor to the magazines *Online, Database, Library Journal,* and other media. He co-edits *Macintoshed Libraries* with Bill Vaccaro, who designed the interior of this book. E-mail **g0094@applelink.apple.com**

Nancy R. John is assistant university librarian at the Library of the University of Illinois at Chicago (UIC). As manager of library systems at UIC, she oversees a range of Internet services for students and faculty. Active in the American Library Association, in national interest groups, and other organizations, she was recently anointed one of the nation's "digiterati" by *Computerworld.* E-mail **nrj@uic.edu**

The editors collaborated on the bestselling *Internet Troubleshooter: Help for the Logged-On and Lost* (Chicago: ALA Editions, 1994). Comments and suggestions for future editions are most welcome.